M000290524

Modernizing the Datacenter with Windows Server and Hybrid Cloud

John McCabe
Ward Ralston

Modernizing the Datacenter with Windows Server and Hybrid Cloud

Published with the authorization of Microsoft Corporation by:
Pearson Education, Inc.

Copyright © 2020 by Pearson Education, Inc.

All rights reserved. This publication is protected by copyright, and permission must be obtained from the publisher prior to any prohibited reproduction, storage in a retrieval system, or transmission in any form or by any means, electronic, mechanical, photocopying, recording, or likewise. For information regarding permissions, request forms, and the appropriate contacts within the Pearson Education Global Rights & Permissions Department, please visit www.pearsoned.com/permissions/. No patent liability is assumed with respect to the use of the information contained herein. Although every precaution has been taken in the preparation of this book, the publisher and author assume no responsibility for errors or omissions. Nor is any liability assumed for damages resulting from the use of the information contained herein.

ISBN-13: 978-1-5093-0802-6
ISBN-10: 1-5093-0802-4

Library of Congress Control Number: On file

1 2019

TRADEMARKS

Microsoft and the trademarks listed at http://www.microsoft.com on the "Trademarks" webpage are trademarks of the Microsoft group of companies. All other marks are property of their respective owners.

WARNING AND DISCLAIMER

Every effort has been made to make this book as complete and as accurate as possible, but no warranty or fitness is implied. The information provided is on an "as is" basis. The author(s), the publisher, and Microsoft Corporation shall have neither liability nor responsibility to any person or entity with respect to any loss or damages arising from the information contained in this.

SPECIAL SALES

For information about buying this title in bulk quantities, or for special sales opportunities (which may include electronic versions; custom cover designs; and content particular to your business, training goals, marketing focus, or branding interests), please contact our corporate sales department at corpsales@pearsoned.com or (800) 382-3419.

For government sales inquiries, please contact governmentsales@pearsoned.com.

For questions about sales outside the U.S., please contact intlcs@pearson.com.

EDITOR-IN-CHIEF
Brett Bartow

EXECUTIVE EDITOR
Loretta Yates

DEVELOPMENT EDITOR
Mark Renfrow

SPONSORING EDITOR
Charvi Arora

MANAGING EDITOR
Sandra Schroeder

SENIOR PROJECT EDITOR
Tracey Croom

COPY EDITOR
Charlotte Kughen

INDEXER
Erika Millen

PROOFREADER
Abigail Manheim

TECHNICAL EDITOR
Ed Fisher

EDITORIAL ASSISTANT
Cindy Teeters

COVER DESIGNER
Twist Creative, Seattle

COMPOSITOR
codeMantra

Contents

Introduction

Welcome to *Modernizing the Datacenter with Windows Server and Hybrid Cloud*. In this book, two consultants who have helped many organizations bring their environments to the cloud and modernize their approach to IT share their real-world experience to help you do the same.

This book examines the practices and technologies organizations can use in the Microsoft technology stack to upgrade their environments to support modern infrastructure, a secure-by-default environment, application modernization, and many other benefits.

Although we have taken every effort to ensure the technologies referenced in this book are the latest names and produce sets available and we have tried to include the latest screen shots where applicable, the nature of the cloud (and a core theme of this book) is change. Given the rapid pace of change in the cloud, it is impossible to keep certain items like product names and screenshots up to date! If you use the suggested URLs throughout the book, you will get to the latest information regarding the technology.

Who is this book for?

Modernizing the Datacenter with Windows Server and Hybrid Cloud is for every organization that wants to begin thinking about the cloud and expanding the company's approach to what change means for the organization. It is for the automation engineer who wants to make the operations of complex IT environments far easier to manage. It is for CIOs who want to read through how other organizations have taken steps. It is for IT managers who want to know how to grow their teams to support the cloud and their organizations more effectively on any modernization journey. In short, this book is for you no matter what your stage of modernization.

How is this book organized?

This book is organized into seven chapters

- Chapter 1: This book is for you
- Chapter 2: Modernizing IT
- Chapter 3: Azure and Azure Stack
- Chapter 4: Upping your security game
- Chapter 5: Application migration

- Chapter 6: Delivering datacenter efficiency
- Chapter 7: Supporting innovation

You can read each chapter independently of the others if you want, but we recommend that you walk through each chapter in consecutive order to build your knowledge as you go. We repeat certain concepts in each chapter to enforce those ideas and highlight how important they are to be delivering true modernization in a datacenter.

System requirements

This book uses a variety of different technologies. The following are required:

- Windows 10/Windows Server 2019

  You can find the latest system requirements for Windows 10 at www.microsoft.com/en-us/windows/windows-10-specifications

  You can find the latest system requirements for Windows 2019 at docs.microsoft.com/en-us/windows-server/get-started-19/sys-reqs-19

- Trial Azure subscription

  You can get 12 months of free Azure at azure.microsoft.com/free/

Errata, updates, & book support

We've made every effort to ensure the accuracy of this book and its companion content. You can access updates to this book—in the form of a list of submitted errata and their related corrections—at

   MicrosoftPressStore.com/ModernizingDatacenter/errata

If you discover an error that is not already listed, please submit it to us at the same page.

For additional book support and information, please visit https://MicrosoftPressStore.com/Support.

Please note that product support for Microsoft software and hardware is not offered through the previous addresses. For help with Microsoft software or hardware, go to *support.microsoft.com*.

Stay in touch

Let's keep the conversation going! We're on Twitter at *twitter.com/MicrosoftPress*.

Chapter 1

Introduction: This book is for you...

kigai. The Japanese culture is rich in descriptive words. For example, there are three words used to describe *love. Ikigai* is a Japanese reference for "a reason for being." As an IT professional or developer, it is important that you have your vocation centered on what you love to do and do it well because "change" in our world of technology is inevitable.

This "reason for being" can be found at the intersection of what you love and what you are good at, crossed with world needs and getting yourself paid. Anyone looking to get into a technology field should honestly answer the very basic question, "What do you really love?" If you're getting into the IT business just to make money, it will be a long road. You need to be able to take other value from your life in the IT world.

Let's take a few minutes to explore this concept of *Ikigai* and your role as an IT pro or developer.

Let's have some fun. Take out a piece of paper, draw a circle at the top of the page, and think critically about what it is you truly love to do. Write it in the circle. (See Figure 1-1.)

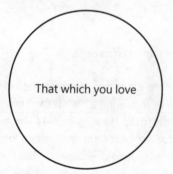

That which you love

FIGURE 1-1 Write somthing you love to do in the circle.

The next step in the *Ikigai* process is asking, "What do I do well?" On your paper, draw another circle lower and to the left of the first circle you drew, and write something you do well in. (See Figure 1-2.) For example, you may love to play football, but you may not have the athletic prowess to make your living at it. It's important to note that the things you do well do not have to align with what you love to do.

FIGURE 1-2   Write something you are good at doing in the circle.

To the lower right of the top circle and in line with the circle you drew on the left, draw another circle to continue with the process. In this circle, write something that answers the question "What does the world need?" which allows you a lot of subjective room. (See Figure 1-3.) We're sure if you lined up ten people and asked them what the world needs, by the time you got to the sixth person, the first person would have changed his or her mind. One opinion is that the world truly can use technology solutions to empower people. But, as we mentioned, that's just one subjective viewpoint. Take a shot and write your idea down.

FIGURE 1-3   Write something you think might improve the world in this circle.

Below the top circle but lower on the page than the other two circles on the left and right, draw another circle on the page. The question you're answering is, "what can I be paid for?" which is something that can be subjective and a little tricky. (See Figure 1-4.) This question more than any of the others can misguide one's true ability. It's not uncommon for students to latch on to a specific technology or programming language because of what they think their projected pay will be. Often, they can paint themselves into a corner where they have no broadly developed IT skills; instead, they become specialists that are highly resistant to any change. Luckily for IT professionals and developers there is (generally speaking) good opportunity and pay across the board.

FIGURE 1-4 Write something you think you can be paid to do.

Okay, here comes the fun part. Take the four circles and combine them into a Venn-style diagram of four overlapping circles (you can re-draw them as needed). You should have something that looks like Figure 1-5. The area where the four circles intersect is *Ikigai*.

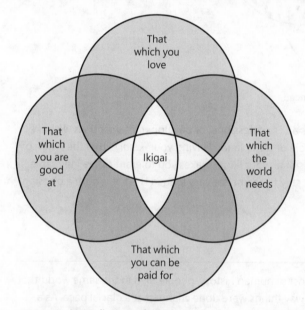

FIGURE 1-5 Venn diagram of *Ikigai*.

Another intersection of these circles reveals another layer of *Ikigai*. There is a reason why we addressed each of the questions in the order we did. In the Venn diagram, there are secondary intersections of the circles:

- **Your profession** is the overlap of "What I do well" and "What I get paid for."
- **Your vocation** is the overlap of "What I get paid for" and "What the world needs."
- **Your passion** is the overlap of "What I do well" and "What I love to do." Many people have trouble quantifying this.
- **Your mission** is the overlap of "That which the world needs." and "That which you love."

Pretty nifty? We think it is. At the end of this exercise you should have something that looks like Figure 1-6.

FIGURE 1-6   Venn diagram of Ikigai—enhanced.

How does *Ikigai* around your role as an IT professional or developer intersect? As we have explored, it gives you a base for your role on this planet. Having your *Ikigai* within the realm of technology as a developer or IT professional, your Ikigai makes you tolerant of the inevitable with technology: *change*. Things never stay the same for very long in IT. That is both a blessing and a curse.

Embracing change

Someone once pointed out that for most of human history, people died in the same world that they were born in. In other words, the way things were done changed at a glacial pace. As a child, a person learned how to get things done; that person taught his or her children the same skills, and that continued for generation after generation. If that sounds like a great world to you then you should not be in IT, and you should not be reading this book.

IT has always been about passionate people embracing and managing change. While it has long been true that the rate of change is accelerating, the increased speed at which the cloud moves makes it feel like someone has poured gasoline on a fire. When faced with this rapid change, you have two choices: shelter in place and hope the change won't affect you or put on your seatbelt and enjoy the ride. This book is for the latter audience—the adventurers, the heroes, and the brave of heart—the tribe of IT. Change is hard and requires effort and struggle, but the rewards and gratification are well worth it.

The first big change in the IT industry was the transition from mainframe computing to minicomputers. The business value of mainframes was clear and compelling, but they also were extraordinarily expensive, and the organizations running them were slow to keep up with growing demands. A new class of smaller machines from Digital, Prime, Wang, Data General, and other companies introduced the era of the minicomputer. These machines were dramatically cheaper, which enabled departments within companies to purchase and deploy them without the oversight and control of central IT. That is why we used to call these "departmental" computers. Departments eager to harness new technology to advance their business saw central IT as the problem. Departments' computers were too slow and unresponsive and were hurting the company's business. Freedom from central IT allowed departments to be agile and to adopt technology to drive their business forward.

The party was great at first, but then reality set in. Without financial oversight, departments' purchases were out of control. Some groups had too much capacity, whereas others didn't have enough and often failed to budget for ongoing support fees. Some groups purchased machines but then didn't have the skilled people to get them deployed or keep them running when a problem occurred. Newly empowered teams were painfully introduced to the concept of disk failures and gained an understanding of why IT had maintenance downtime to do backups. Company auditors discovered that business-critical data was unsecure and unprotected.

At many companies the music stopped, and central IT was called in to take control over departmental computers. The departments still benefited from the minicomputer revolution, but the company was able to get what it needed as well. The needs of the people advancing the business were coupled with the needs of the people preserving the business. However, the transition was a huge challenge for IT because all the skills they had learned were not applicable to the world of minicomputers. As they worked with the minicomputers, they quickly realized that their skills were not applicable. The languages they used and the techniques that they had mastered weren't useful in the world of minicomputers. Some people let their fears and insecurities get the better of them, thinking that they had nothing to offer in the world of minicomputers, and they retreated to the comfort of their mainframes (some of those people are still there). Others embraced the challenge and learned new tools; consequently they learned that what made them valuable in the world of mainframes made them even more valuable in the world of minicomputers. They needed to learn a new set of tools to express their skills, but once they mastered those tools, their skills in fiscal responsibility, ensuring data is safe and secure, and maintaining the availability of systems once again made them invaluable to the company.

And so, the die of IT transformation was cast. A similar pattern played out in the transition to the era of PCs and client-server computing, and it is being played out again as the industry transitions to cloud computing. Here are some points to think about:

- The interns of companies (for example) don't like the strict barriers enforced by central IT, and they desire and embrace radical new technology that they feel delivers compelling business value.
- A series of crises occur that require central IT to get involved.

- Some IT people retreat from the challenge and decide to ride out their careers with the skills they have.
- Other IT people embrace the challenge to retool and, after a period of discomfort, discover that the things that made them superstars in the old world also make them superstars in the new world. They become the new heroes of the company.

IT has been, is, and always will be the post-facto cleanup of the mess someone else made. It is the way of the world. That said, IT has been, is, and always will be the heroes of the company because they're able to adapt and partner with business teams to harness the power of new technology to deliver business results. Anyone can buy a wild horse and point out how powerful it is and the potential of that power. The real value comes when you can tame the horse and get it to wear a saddle, accept a bit, and go in the direction you need it to go in.

Radical change

It is important to get good at change. You've made the choice to get into one of the most dynamic, rapidly changing industries the world has ever seen. Of course, we've heard this all many times before. How many times have we heard talks start with a review of the incredible impact of Moore's Law?

In 1975, Gordon Moore predicted that the number of transistors in an integrated circuit would double every 24 months. This became known as Moore's Law. As impossible as it seems, this "law" has held true, and it's even been updated to state that the doubling would occur every 18 months. Apply that rate of growth for a few decades and incredible things happen. Combine that with the fact that a sufficient change in quantity produces a change in quality, and you have the magic that is Moore's Law.

In many respects, this stage of the industry is just like every other stage of the industry; Moore's Law is bringing us yet another wave of innovation. However, we believe that something very different is occurring that makes this period more important and, in many ways, less predictable than in the past.

After an initial period of figuring things out, the general model for computing has been worked out, and most of the industry has been implementing the model and filling out the details. In this world, it was pretty straightforward to predict the rate of progress and forecast what would happen in the next few years. Every now and again, a particular area of technology would experience radical change, and the industry would be less predictable for a while. Then the change would come into focus, and the model would be updated so people could go on with implementing and filling out the details. We believe this stage of the industry is different because almost every layer of the technology stack is undergoing a deep rethink and fundamental changes.

Digital transformation and the "other" Moore's Law

What really matters is IT's ability to focus on customer value delivery. Going faster at things that don't matter isn't a good strategy. If the thing you choose to do quickly doesn't have any impact to make things better, then why do that specific thing at all? Amdahl's Law addresses the maximal speedup you can achieve through parallelization. Consider a program that takes 100 hours to complete. If you can parallelize 80% of the application, the fastest the program can theoretically finish in is 20 hours. You need to focus on the goal rather than on the candy. In business, the goal is to create and retain customers by delivering something that the competition is not. The goal is to ensure the customers see value in consuming your business in a convenient and cost-efficient way that evolves with the changing needs of the marketplace.

How to use this book

This book talks about various concepts and ideologies, all of which are designed to help you build a toolkit of thought. This is a reference book to help you structure your approach by giving you scenarios to see where you can attach to and implement or iterate on what makes sense for the positions you are in.

We intend this to be a reference for you to go back to over the course of your transformation. Sometimes you will be ahead, sometimes you will behind. We describe some situations that don't apply and others that you will absolutely relate to.

No matter your situation, we hope that you adopt the concepts of change, monitoring, and feedback that underpins all the chapters. We know the journey is not easy, but we do know that the rewards far out weight the difficulty of the journey.

Throughout this book, we have references to specific technologies that are available now and screenshots of the current view of the technology. Although the software might change, the concepts surrounding why we use it don't change much. You might need to do some additional research to find what current technology is in place in Microsoft Azure. As we've said throughout this chapter, you're on a journey of change, and you need to be ready to embrace it!

Happy reading!

Chapter 2

Modern IT—the coming inflection point

In this chapter, we discuss what ultimately is the crux of the book, and we discuss the initial topics for beginning to understand the journey of Modernizing IT.

Modern IT is a new approach to information technology that enables companies to maximize their competitiveness by building things that differentiate them from their competitors while they minimize everything else. The term *digital transformation* is popular these days. That term concisely conveys how every business and endeavor (airlines, retail, manufacturing, and so on) is being transformed by putting the customer at the center of everything and using the power of software to compete. Companies that want to be successful at digital transformation need to adopt modern IT.

Modern IT consists of new

- Systems
- Roles
- Processes

In this chapter, we explore the traditional approach to IT and evaluate its strengths and shortcomings. Then we articulate modern IT's new approaches and suggest a path to get from traditional IT to modern IT. Finally, we share a set of value propositions for modern IT target audiences.

Traditional approach to IT

The current model for IT was largely established during the 1990s, during what has become known as the "disintegration of the computer industry." During this period, the computer industry shifted from vertical integration to horizontal integration. In the vertically integrated world, big companies like IBM, Burroughs, and Sperry would build and sell systems from the ground up. They would build chips, boards, operating systems, applications, and management software and sell them as a package to customers.

In the 1990s the industry shifted to a horizontal integration model in which companies specialized and optimized one layer—for example, Intel on chips, Microsoft on operating systems, Lotus on applications, and Tivoli on management. Horizontal integration allowed competition and choice at every layer of the computing stack but required someone to put together the components into a workable system. This is the task of systems integration, and it has been the central mission of traditional IT.

The traditional IT model is powerful and has served organizations around the world well. It includes

- **Hardware vendors** delivering components and systems: disks, NICs, motherboard, servers, and so on

- **OS vendors** delivering software platforms that provide functions and services that facilitate writing applications and allow multiple users to share common resources

- **Application vendors** delivering a domain-specific set of capabilities to accomplish tasks such as accounting, or manufacturing support

- **Management vendors** delivering functions to manage the life cycle of the hardware and software components, including provisioning, configuration, monitoring, diagnostics, and so on

- **IT** departments evaluating and selecting the vendors of each of these horizontal layers, and the IT professional integrating, operating, and maintaining all the components to serve the needs of the business.

Different markets and customers have unique requirements, so vendors produce components that are as general as possible so that they can be customized to meet the needs of most customers. IT departments must plan carefully to integrate all the components to meet their specific business purpose.

The traditional IT model's conceptual center is an individual server box whose parts are selected by one group of IT pros. Often, another group of IT pros provision and manage that server to deliver a function. That function is then used by yet another group of IT pros. Distributed systems are created using a bottom-up approach.

If you look at the systems created, the traditional IT model has worked incredibly well. If you look at the delivered business results, the model has severe problems that are realized every day. In the past, everyone had to deal with a common set of issues, so the problems of the model were generally hidden from view.

In recent years, technology changes—such high bandwidth/low latency networks, software-defined infrastructure, automation, cloud architectures, containers, and microservices—have allowed companies to take a different approach and achieve extraordinary results. This highlights both the problems of traditional IT and the need to adopt new approaches and architectures in a responsible and thoughtful manner.

Modern IT approach

For those working in Microsoft, a key concern to all roles is to make sure that we are building the right things for the future. Microsoft has more than 100,000 employees and a vast range of products, and it invests more than $10 billion per year in research and development. Imagine the complexity of the task and the importance of getting it right. If we take physics for example, you are always striving to look past the surface level facts and assumptions to understand the underlying principles or laws at play. Once you deduce those, you then can apply them to other circumstances to work out the right answer.

When we consider all the possibilities opened up by the recent technology changes, it doesn't take long to become overwhelmed or feel the need to retreat by hyper-focusing on one area. Instead, we need to step back, find the core principles, and then use them as the foundation of our new approach. You'll notice that most of the following principles are not about technology but rather about business.

- **The purpose of a business is to satisfy the need of a consumer, thereby creating a customer**   As Peter Drucker said, "Because the purpose of business is to create a customer, the business enterprise has two–and only these two–basic functions: marketing and innovation. Marketing and innovation produce results; all the rest are costs." Modern IT focuses on delivering customer value through innovation. It optimizes everything in that process and reduces the customer's involvement and the costs of everything else.

- **Just because it's hard doesn't mean it's valuable**   IT operations is hard. It can be incredibly hard. However, the difficulty of something doesn't automatically mean that it's delivering innovation or value to the company. Consider this: Email is critical to a modern company, and running it well is very hard. But does any business beat its competition because it runs its email servers better than the competition?

- **You must be effective; it's good to be efficient**   The most important factor in all IT decisions is whether something effectively delivers innovation that makes the company competitive. Once you are effective, it's good to be efficient to maximize profitability. If you're efficient but not effective, the company will die.

- **Customers' businesses depend upon trust. Trust depends upon security**   Modern IT prioritizes and delivers security. It takes a structured life cycle approach. It extends the traditional "hardening" model to embrace detection, and impact isolation. The approach also addresses the modern attack surface—admin identity.

- **The magic of software allows Platinum Service Level Agreements (SLAs) using affordable, high volume hardware**   Customer value requires systems have 5 9's SLAs. Modern IT recognizes that availability can be delivered more effectively and more efficiently by using modern software architecture instead of expensive hardware.

Building systems with a modern IT mindset

In the traditional IT approach to building systems, IT is responsible for understanding and forecasting the specific needs of the user community. IT then sizes, builds, and maintains systems to meet those needs in accordance with a budget. It specifies, procures, provisions, configures, and operates the following things:

- The components of servers and sets of servers
- The operating system
- The applications

- The management systems (monitoring, backup, security, configuration, desired state, patching, and so on)

The traditional IT approach to building systems expends much energy and effort addressing a set of issues that don't deliver customer value or move a company's business forward. After working closely to understand the user's needs, IT often creates "snowflake" servers that are finely tuned to address those needs but are fragile in the face of change. For IT, screwing up can lead to business failure, but getting things right doesn't lead to business success. Because reliability is critical, traditional IT often buys very expensive hardware to deliver reliability and avoids changes like patching or upgrading software. IT tightly controls systems to deliver reliability, which often requires users to go through lengthy change review processes.

Modern IT takes a different approach to building systems:

- **Robustness and reliability are delivered via software rather than by expensive hardware** The failure of components and systems is a core assumption and software systems are designed accordingly. Customers achieve greater robustness and reliability by adding more components. This is affordable because systems are built using high-volume, low-cost components.

- **Snowflake servers are shunned in favor of standardization** Individual components can be readily replaced without drama.

- **IT shifts from a mindset of control to a mindset of empowerment** IT delivers pools of capability and empowers teams to move quickly through self-service mechanisms.

A new approach to IT roles

The traditional approach to IT roles was centered in creating a predictable and stable environment that ran applications, controlled costs, and fixed things when they broke. Developers' responsibilities were to translate business requirements into code. They created business applications and "tossed them over the wall to IT" to be deployed and operated. The focus was on completing feature work on time with quality. Traditional IT was responsible for deploying and supporting those applications in production. The focus was on faults, uptime, compliance, and financial management.

Modern IT takes a different approach to IT roles. Roles are refactored to maximize innovation.

- **DevOps teams** are cross-functional teams comprised of developers and operations people. They have shared responsibility for creating, deploying, and operating customer-focused applications. These are engineering teams using engineering processes. Their work is grounded in code. Some of these engineers produce C# or JavaScript code while others produce PowerShell scripts and configuration documents (for example, ARM templates or DSC docs). All code is under source control so that changes are tracked, results can be reproduced, and mistakes can be reverted. The DevOps teams work in frequent small batches and move fast and safe by having quality controls designed into their processes.

- **Cloud architects** are trusted consultants that help teams understand their choices and produce designs that can scale out or in, are secure, can operate reliably in the face of failures, are optimized for cost, and provide agility. Cloud architects are cognizant of the benefits and drawbacks of using public clouds and on-premises computing. They guide teams in deciding which path to use for which workloads.

- **Infrastructure administrators** create and maintain pools of compute, storage, and networking resources to be used by cloud architects and DevOps teams. Some of these pools are local, on-premises resources, and others are based in public clouds.

Figure 2-1 shows the life cycle all teams will be integrated into in modern IT.

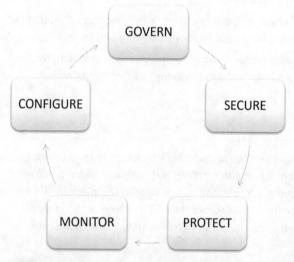

FIGURE 2-1 Modern IT life cycle.

Throughout the rest of this book, the diagram in Figure 2-1 will serve as the basis for our text, and we will discuss and relate all our topics to this life cycle.

New operation approach

The traditional IT approach to processes is grounded in failure avoidance. Because change is the root cause of most failures, traditional IT is wary of changes and focuses on controlling them. A typical strategy is to avoid change—to go for long periods between changes and combine lots of changes into a big change that can be thoroughly tested before it's deployed into production. Another strategy is to manage change through a formal change review process in which any change is fully documented and reviewed by a board of people who look for things that could go wrong.

Modern IT is grounded in change. Delivering innovation is all about listening to customers, gaining insight into what needs to change, and then delivering that change before the competition does—and then repeating that process over and over. Rapid change is the heart of modern IT. This brings about a new approach to processes:

- **Modern IT accepts that failures will occur**   It builds systems processes to minimize the impact. It has a well-defined deployment pipeline and quality controls to "move failures to the right" and catch them early in the process.

- **Automated testing allows modern IT to go fast with confidence**   The goal is to "push on green," which means that when a set of tests succeed, a change is automatically pushed to production. If something goes wrong in production, then it's a failure of the test rather than the change. Tests always improve because increases in speed translate to increases in the ability to compete.

- **Modern IT makes lots of small changes quickly**   When a failure occurs, the fact that the change was small means that the failure will be easy to identify and fix.

- **Modern IT automates as much as possible**   Automation allows reproducibility, recoverability, accountability, and speed, and it provides the basis for constant improvement.

Modern IT datacenters

Modern IT datacenters embrace and implement the principles of the cloud model of computing. Hyperstandardization on inexpensive components is combined with software-defined storage, networking, and compute to create a robust, scalable, and agile platform. This platform is then used to create pools of resources that are made available to teams. Sometimes a self-service portal is provided so that teams can get the resources they need when they need them without the intervention of IT.

In Figure 2-2, the two approaches are displayed. The left shows the old approach—with the sometimes-siloed infrastructure for specific tasks—and the right demonstrates the resource pools concept for modern IT.

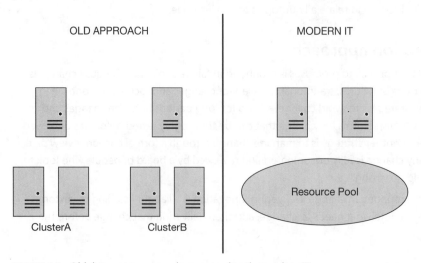

FIGURE 2-2   Old datacenter approach compared to the modern IT.

You have several different ways to use a datacenter built on the cloud model of computing. You can use a public cloud such as Azure, you can buy an on-premises cloud appliance running on integrated systems such as Azure Stack, or you can build your own components using operating systems that incorporate cloud technologies such as Windows Server 2016.

Modern IT security

Modern IT security starts with the understanding that the bad guys have gotten very capable very quickly and action is required. Modern IT security addresses modern threats using modern mechanisms. In the past, security was focused on controlling access to resources through system hardening: setting Access Control Lists (ACLs), firewall rules, minimal services, and so on. Today, the dominant attack vector is identity. A bad actor will use sophisticated phishing emails to steal the credentials of an IT admin and then exploit the enterprise using those admin privileges. Modern IT security also focuses on awareness of the organization and ensuring that employees are aware of all potential security violations. At the same time, it allows the IT organization to secure any device anywhere, greatly reducing attack surfaces and mitigation of a modern device strategy like Bring-Your-Own-Device (BYOD).

Protecting identity

Protecting identities and securing privileged access are core activities of modern IT. Simple things like account separation (giving an admin one account for privileged activities such as server management and a separate account for nonprivileged user activities such as web browsing and email), just-in-time administration, and Just-Enough Administration (JEA) with role-based access controls (RBAC) build the foundation of modern IT security.

However, today it's simply not enough; we need to employ additional layers for protecting our identities. Two-factor Authentications (2FA) is one of the most common ways to help protect identities and enforce access control. 2FA requires a user to *know* something (such as a password) and to *have* something (such as a registered phone). If a hacker steals an admin's password, he can't use it to access systems because he doesn't also have the admin's phone.

Central auditing and log collection with Big Data analytics to identify irregular patterns across entire IT estates further secure our identities and mitigate attacks. Automation attached to these systems allows responses to potential breaches to further protect a modern IT infrastructure. Figure 2-3 shows an example of using Azure Security Center to collect the logs from multiple sources and apply the necessary analytics to identify threats to an organization. The benefits of a cloud-based product such as Azure Security Center is that it combines a large set of customer signals, massive amounts of cloud computing, and machine learning to identify novel attack vectors. An attack on one is quickly transformed into a defense for all.

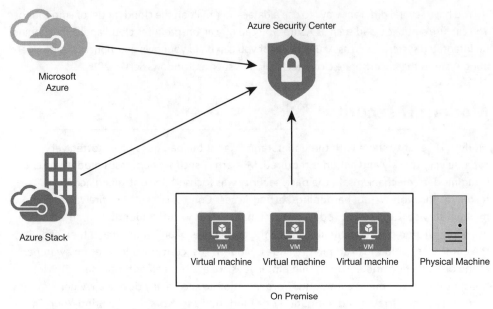

FIGURE 2-3 Example of central log collection and analytics using Azure Security Center.

In an attempt to protect against admins' passwords being stolen, people sometimes use privileged service accounts that are created and known by few but their details are written in a notebook and their passwords are set to not expire! This is a risky practice. To evolve away from potential exposures of this sort, we need to examine concepts like just-in-time administration/access in which a person obtains the privilege required to perform the operation she requires for a limited amount of time to help ensure systems stay protected by not exposing privileged accounts.

Furthermore, with Windows 10, Privileged Access Workstations (PAW)/Secure Access Workstation (SAW) (these terms can be used interchangeably) and/or conditional access reduce the entry points to privileged systems and restrict the types of machines that can access them. PAW's are machines that have been pre-hardened and have specific control software installed to ensure that no unauthorized software will run. PAW's also have additional layers of authentication required. Privileged systems can implement additional access control lists to prevent non-PAW machines from connecting. Figure 2-4 shows an example of a user trying to access from a generic laptop versus a PAW.

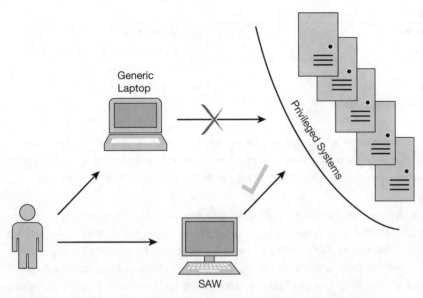

FIGURE 2-4 Privileged/Secure Access Workstation accessing Privileged Systems.

When starting to architect a modern IT system, enterprises should also consider creating a new privileged identity deployment. This hardened implementation would be built to be secure by default, and identities would only be used for privileged access (for example, no browsing or email access). This ensures no legacy service principals exist to potentially expose holes into an otherwise secure environment. Microsoft Privileged Access Management is an example of this approach in which we setup a bastion forest and create time-bound shadow principals when users want to do privileged tasks.

Protecting infrastructure

Designing and implementing controls to ensure that information is protected from unauthorized access or data loss is paramount in modern IT. Controls include disk encryption, transit encryption, and in-memory/process encryption. Modern IT also takes a more mature approach to security. Recognizing that something always can go wrong, modern IT adopts an "assume breach" mindset. In the past, a breach of any component often led to the breach of most components. With an assume breach mindset, IT redesigns systems to minimize the ramifications of a breached component. This is analogous to the design of a submarine where the breach of a compartment does not sink the ship. Table 2-1 highlights the differences in the traditional approach of preventing a breach versus assuming breach.

TABLE 2-1 Prevent breach versus assume breach

PREVENT BREACH	ASSUME BREACH
Threat model systems	Threat model components and war games
Code review	Centralized security monitor
Security testing	Live site penetration testing
Security development life cycle	

As highlighted in the table, while implementing a prevent breach model will provide many layers of security for an organization and keep developers and IT pros in a security-conscious mindset, modern IT goes one step further and takes an active approach, or assume breach, security model.

Beyond the traditional security models, especially when we're considering protecting infrastructure changes (that is, physical disk or server or network switch and so on), we now must think about public clouds. For example, physical access to these datacenters isn't possible. Knowing this implies that the processes for managing something like disk destruction also needs to evolve with the choices made regarding who, where, and how data is stored. We must spend time evaluating what we're going to store, and where it's going to be stored, and what technology exists to put adequate controls in place.

Even when an environment uses an appliance like Azure Stack or a standardized private cloud solution, a layer of understanding of what the vendor provides versus what is the responsibility domain of the IT organization needs to evolve. Organizations that deploy Microsoft Hyper-V Server 2016 can use features like Guarded Fabric Hosts to ensure that a deployed fabric can run only authorized virtual machines and protect those VMs even from compromised fabric admins.

Simply put, protecting infrastructure means IT pros should implement protections as a fundamental step when designing and implementing infrastructure services. For example, when implementing Storage Spaces Direct, we must enable encryption on the volumes for data at rest. If we're connecting to services in the public cloud, we must ensure encapsulation of all traffic and secure transport using something like TLS or enhanced multifactor/certificate-based authentication between endpoints.

Protecting the OS

We've talked about some infrastructure controls that we can put in place to ensure data leakage is kept to a minimum, but we also must consider the operating system. Modern IT doesn't just mean implementing new processes and assuming breach; it means stepping back and examining legacy systems and understanding that operating systems need to be updated to achieve this vision.

Take a public cloud, for example; it enforces a policy of running supported operating systems. Support in Azure essentially means an operating system has not been assigned to end of life and will receive no further active development. Even operating systems that have been paid under custom support agreements will not be accepted.

This introduces an obvious challenge for any enterprise because now you need to keep your operating system up to date. Line of business (LOB) applications—both third-party and homegrown—have contributed to many organizations having legacy operating systems in place and complicated the degree of difficulty required to upgrade to a modern operating system.

Windows Server 2016 took some big leaps toward providing safeguards against secret leakages—features like shielded virtual machines, Device Guard, control flow, and credential protection provide ways to mitigate leakages from the host hypervisor up.

Shielded virtual machines protect against a scenario where a corrupt administrator makes a copy of your virtual machines onto some external storage and bypasses all the encryption methods to run them at home at his leisure so he can extract the information he wants access to. Shielded virtual machines essentially won't boot outside of the hosts you have assigned. Figure 2-5 shows a sample shielded virtual machine infrastructure and highlights that shielded virtual machines will not boot on nonguarded fabric hosts.

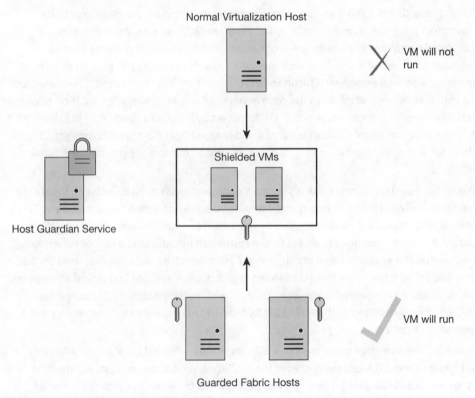

FIGURE 2-5 A shielded virtual machine deployment.

Device Guard in Windows provides a way to understand what software is deployed in your IT organization and essentially produce a trusted application list with signatures. Figure 2-6 shows that the feature allows you to monitor your environment, understand what applications are running, and then compare them to what you think the environment should be like.

You can disable applications that don't seem right by using a policy, which blocks them from executing on any system.

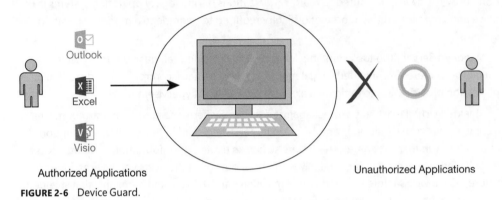

Authorized Applications

Unauthorized Applications

FIGURE 2-6 Device Guard.

Control Flow Guard (CFG) is an operating system security feature that developers can use to protect programs from Return Oriented Program (ROP) attacks. An ROP attack is a sophisticated technique that causes the program to call into a piece of malware that was dynamically constructed in the program's memory. These types of attacks have been difficult to protect against and extremely difficult to detect when they have been used. CFG is enabled with a compiler switch that modifies the code generation to enable runtime validation of call targets. The operating system supports CFG protection by building a fixed list of the valid call targets of a program (think subroutine names) and then, while the program is running, CFG ensures that every call target goes to a valid call site and terminates the program if an attack is detected.

Credential Guard protects credentials (user accounts and passwords) by isolating them with virtualization-based security, so only specific privileged system software can access them. This protects against one of the most damaging techniques in the malware toolkit: credential theft and lateral traversal. After gaining access to one system, an intruder uses a number of exploits and techniques (for example, mimikatz[1]) to harvest any credentials that were ever used on that system. The intruder then uses these credentials to attack other systems and repeat the process ("spidering their way through the network") until he reaches the systems and resources he's after. Credential Guard thwarts this technique by blocking the malware from harvesting the credentials on a system.

Figure 2-7 illustrates that while users can still access the traditional Local Security Author-ity Subsystem Service (LSASS) the hashes of the traditional passwords aren't stored there; in fact they're stored in an isolated part of the system backed by hypervisor technology, which provides a secure and guarded area that users can't access.

---

[1] I had heard about mimikatz for quite some time before I actually downloaded it and tried it out. It is one thing to hear about the tool, but it's not the same as the kick-in-the-stomach feeling you get when you actually run the tool and see your passwords in plain text. If you or one of your coworkers is not clear on the importance of this, download and run mimikatz for yourself.

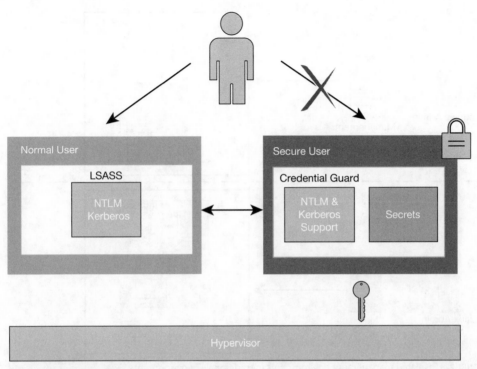

FIGURE 2-7 Credential Guard.

Windows Defender is enabled in Windows by default to protect you from potential zero second malware when the operating system is installed. Starting with Windows Server 2016, Windows Defender is also available and optimized for servers.

Detecting

Earlier in this section, we mentioned the need to assume breach. Assuming breach involves the proactive probing of your IT environment and trying to understand where you have potential exposure points. Modern IT drives the need to centrally collect environmental logs during these probes, as well as during normal operations. Collecting all this data drives a robust data set for which machine learning algorithms or event correlation techniques can be applied to detect anonymous events within a modern IT Infrastructure.

If we take a step back and take an environment that has a few hundred servers in a single datacenter, how do we collect the information regarding all these servers? It would be rare to have an environment like this that is totally Windows or totally Linux; usually it's a mixed environment. In traditional approaches, you'd have to deploy a mix of tools to monitor and detect events in this type of environment.

Figure 2-8 illustrates the isolation traditionally found in these environments.

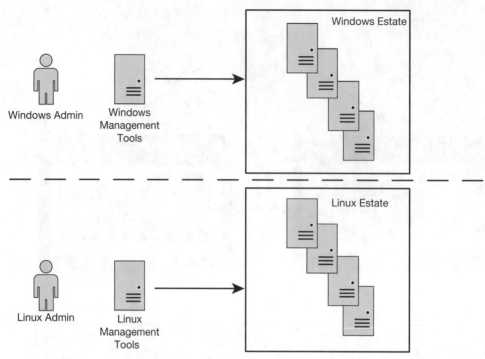

FIGURE 2-8 Isolated management environments in traditional IT environments.

Modern IT requires evolution. Mixed environments are the norm and have been for quite some time; the evolution happens around the management toolset that you use to understand how these environments are operating. Previously siloed Modern IT dictates that driving central simplified monitoring and management is essential. If we add public cloud environments and appliance environments into the overall technology mix, we produce additional challenges that legacy toolsets may not adapt to.

Although there are many toolsets that have multi–operating system management capability and provide a perceived central console for management and operations, the reality is that traditional IT environments still use a mix of tools to obtain the information they want, a separate set of tools to help them correlate events, and another set of tools to automate remediation events. These tools don't always have native integration and provide "loose" hooks between them.

Another aspect of management tools is the cadence at which they move. A simple example is System Center, which has its management pack technology to help discover and provide monitoring logic. While technology gets patched and potentially new features get included monthly, the management packs don't necessarily receive an update to adapt to these new features.

This stands true for many management tools available today but hinders the progress if your focus is adopting a modern IT strategy.

Given that threats are getting more complex on a daily/monthly/yearly basis, it's imperative that any toolset in a modern IT environment moves at similar speeds to the rate at which threats evolve. The tools should capable of detecting the anomalies happening in our environment across any cloud or datacenter you have deployed into.

Log Analytics is one of the tools that allow for the central log collection aspects from multiple environments. It's an agent-based collection mechanism that uses intelligence packs to collect information from the host machines and injections into a central log store. Data also can be injected from multiple non-agent-based sources, and data can be retrieved from native management tools already in place, such as System Center Operations Manager or Nagios.

Once the data is submitted to Log Analytics, you have a few different approaches. You can use inbuilt solution packs that get updated with cloud cadence. These solution packs can correlate data from different sources but which exist centrally in Log Analytics. The solution packs can help you identify problems with latency in your networks, expose ports communicating to unauthorized sources, or detect failed logons from public sources. Figure 2-9 shows a sample dashboard that uses the solution packs available in Azure.

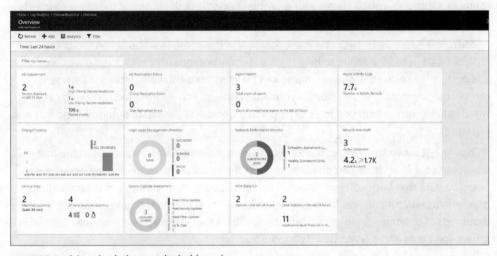

FIGURE 2-9 A Log Analytics sample dashboard.

Figure 2-10 shows a more detailed view of the Security and Audit Dashboard. It highlights threats, failed log-on attempts, and a variety information you can use to identify potential security breaches in your IT environment.

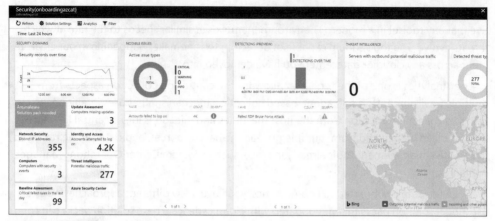

FIGURE 2-10 A Security and Auditing Log Analytics solution.

Microsoft uses its extensive experience in running hyperscale cloud environments and the data it collects from that to build comprehensive rules to detect potential threats in your environment. Of course, you can build your own intelligence, but this is one of the many elements in choosing the correct toolset for a modern IT environment you need to be aware of.

Microsoft Azure Security Center is another tool in the arsenal that builds on top of log analytics data. It has the ability to help IT pros identify potential threats in their environment and perform remediation activities. It also can be integrated into vulnerability assessment tools to quickly identify wider issues in your environment. This information and alerts can be wired natively into automation tools to help you automatically mitigate potential incidents and exposures.

Figure 2-11 shows the sample Azure Security Center events dashboard. You can see that it will scan your IT environment on premises or in the cloud and provide recommendations based on data that Microsoft has collected and analyzed from operating a hyperscale cloud. It will also use data it analyzes from support cases and best practice recommendations from thousands of customer deployments and the feedback that is shared to ensure that the tool is always up to date and alerting based on industry trends.

This dashboard allows IT pros to take rapid action to secure their environment and monitor it for changes or potential threats. For example, if a new administrator deploys a virtual machine to Azure ad hoc and forgets to secure it correctly, the machine can be auto monitored by Azure and will trigger an alert on this dashboard to highlight a potential exposure point.

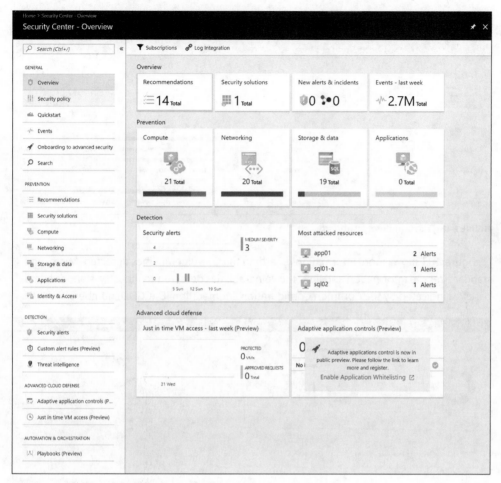

FIGURE 2-11 The Azure Security Center dashboard.

Figure 2-12 shows more data about virtual machines and the recommendations and issues that have been detected. The variety of different items it will alert you to are driven from the central log collection, which is performed and built on the rules that Microsoft has implemented from its experience. This information greatly reduces the amount of time it takes to identify systems that could be used to expose data or cause a security breach within an enterprise.

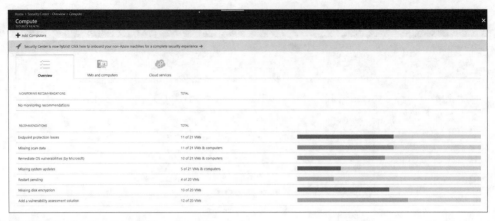

FIGURE 2-12 The Compute dashboard.

Figure 2-13 shows more information regarding the OS vulnerabilities detected. Microsoft standardizes the information and links the vulnerabilities detected to industry-standard databases, as indicated by the Common Configuration Enumeration ID (CCEID) numbers.

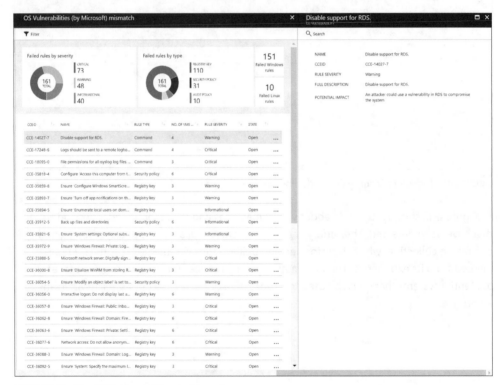

FIGURE 2-13 The OS Vulnerabilities dashboard.

Interestingly, with the rise of PowerShell as a modern management tool to rapidly administer large estates and drive automated tasks across them, the OS Vulnerabilities dashboard has become a tool of a hacker! Malicious IT users can create scripts that will probe IT systems for vulnerabilities. It is often a good idea to create systems in your environment that "look" exposed but have the necessary agents to collect data on malicious users attempting to breach the system. Using tools like Log Analytics and Azure Security Center can help you achieve this honeypot mecca!

Modern IT support for business innovation

Part of the evolution to modern IT is more than just the infrastructure. It also requires a business to look at its applications and the processes surrounding them.

Look at a traditional LOB app as illustrated in Figure 2-14; it has a three-tier architecture. There's a highly available web tier, app tier, and database tier. The database tier would be deployed with shared storage as an active-passive cluster, the web tier is based on IIS, and the app tier is custom processing logic built for the application.

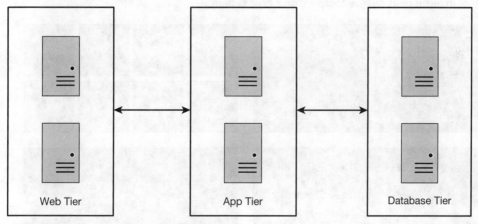

FIGURE 2-14 A traditional three-tier architecture.

When the application needs to be upgraded, it requires an outage no matter what we upgrade the web tier, app tier, or database tier to. This is an inherent flaw in the application because it cannot suffer version mismatches in the deployment. The upgrade process can be time consuming because it requires a complete uninstallation of the existing application and then redeployment of the new code provided by the development team. The development team package this as zip file, which requires several steps after it has been unzipped to register specific DLLs and update registry keys. The only part of the system that doesn't require code redeployment is the database itself; however, there is a service on the database tier that needs to be updated and the cluster failed over to repeat on the passive node.

Upgrades to the operating system are delayed as much as possible because it has caused significant problems in the past due to incompatibilities in modern operating systems.

Modern IT demands a different approach. Modern IT should allow not only the product to be upgraded for new features but require zero to no downtime unless the database itself must be upgraded. Modern IT also demands that applications be broken down into the smallest reusable parts, which can be then be deployed and managed independently. Eventually this will be integrated into an application development life cycle. This is to allow innovation in the technology that supports the app independently. It also will drive the LOB application to be deployable across IT environments no matter the location.

Containers

When approaching application modernization to drive business innovation, one of the first items we look at is containers. Containers allow the rapid deployment of applications across different IT estates and provide the simplest method to begin the modernization journey.

Take our three-tier app. Traditionally each tier would be deployed into a virtual machine, and each tier would be two virtual machines with two virtual CPUs and between 4 and 8 GB of RAM. They have an operating system disk of 60 GB fixed. For now, let's overlook the database tier and discuss it later. Figure 2-15 shows the difference between a virtual machine and a container in terms of its relative footprint on a host system.

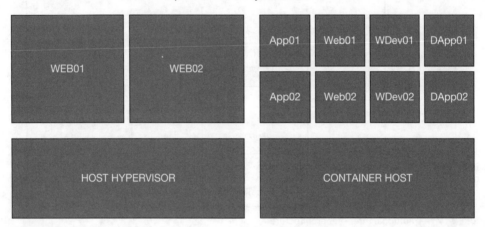

FIGURE 2-15 Traditional virtual machines versus containers footprint.

Given that the web tier is an IIS web app, we can deploy this into a container with relative ease. We obtain a base image of either Nano Server or Windows Server Core and deploy our web application into the container and store the changes into a registry.

The registry enables us to quickly download the image into different environments, which allows us to move rapidly from the on-premises datacenter to Azure. We can choose to use a managed service in Azure or build our own container host solution using technologies like Docker or Kubernetes.

When you examine the footprint of a container, you will notice it's considerably smaller than a virtual machine with a significantly smaller startup time. In our web tier example, we could run our container on one virtual CPU and a fragment of RAM around 150 MB per container. Using container orchestration, it will manage the container life cycle for us. For example, if the container stops responding, the orchestrator will destroy the container that has stopped responding and instantiate a new container to replace the destroyed version.

If the application needs to be patched, you can build out the new container image with no downtime and switch the traffic path to the new containers. This is considerably easier than building new virtual machines. Later in this chapter when we discuss DevOps and Continuous Integration/Continuous Delivery, we dive into this a little deeper.

The application tier can be treated in the same manner with minor exceptions, depending on different aspects of the application. This is beyond the context of this book, but a headless application with externalized state are key markers for an application that can be containerized.

Microservices

When moving toward modern IT, especially relating to modern applications, we begin to try to decouple the application from a single server to reusable components. Microservices allows you to break down an application into micro applications (or, as the name suggests, microservices) that have dedicated functions. These functions will have an interface so other microservices can interact with them and obtain the information that the microservice is designed to do.

Traditionally, if we look at our web application for our LOB application, it might have several sub websites. If we say this LOB application is our stock entry system, then we can clearly identify web apps for inventory, orders, and customers. Each web app has broken-down functions integrated into them; for example, in inventory we have three specific functions: get stock item, assign stock item, and delete stock item. Each of these could represent a microservice and essentially will be a completely independent application.

Figure 2-16 illustrates this concept further. We can see that the inventory and customer web apps are broken down into further components. For example, say we want to allocate stock to a customer. The process would essentially call the Get Stock microservice, which would collect the stock information required. Next it would obtain the customer information by calling the Get Customer microservice. The customer information would be returned and then call the Updated Stock microservice. This in turn would call into the ordering system. That's not illustrated in Figure 2-16, but it would be the Create Order microservice.

If we want to innovate or modify, the customer must get the Orders microservice to provide more data or be more efficient in its operation. It can be upgraded independently of the entire application. In the traditional IT approach, however, we needed to remove the entire application and reinstall.

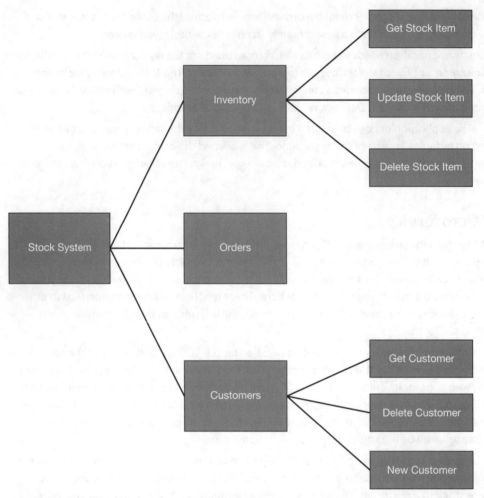

FIGURE 2-16 Breaking down a web app into microservices.

This approach can either be combined with containers where each microservice can be its own container, or we can deploy the code to a platform like Service Fabric. Both manage the life cycle of the microservices and scale up or down as required as well as monitoring its health state and recovering from any potential problems.

Microservices also can be written in the best "code" for the job, allowing you to achieve the goals the microservice is designed to do efficiently versus coding to what the language allows you to do.

DevOps

Rarely do people walk away from discussions about DevOps satisfied. We like to joke that at the heart of DevOps there are really just two concepts:

- Do work in frequent small batches.[2]
- Stop being jerks to one another.

While not entirely accurate, that joke is apropos, and it's easy to remember. When you put the customer at the center of everything, one thing becomes super clear: Development and operations need to work together much better. These traditionally siloed teams need to begin to understand what is important to each other to make them succeed in a modern IT environment.

Consider the differences in what is important between IT pros and developers in the rollout of an LOB application. IT pros want the application to be stable; they need to ensure the business can operate and process the transactions required. IT pros also want to ensure they can recover quickly if a failure does occur. Development teams want to ensure the code they write meets the business requirements. We can see that the needs of the two groups are different. Modern IT allows us to start to blur the boundaries through a set of practices and culture that has become known as DevOps. The DevOps community likes to spend a lot of time discussing what is and is not DevOps. We encourage you to take a look at some of those discussions, but don't fall down that rabbit hole.

DevOps also pushes for shorter development cycles with increased deployment frequency while targeting more stable releases that align to the business objectives.

There are multiple phases to DevOps that also can be used as a foundation to help blur the boundaries and establish trust between these siloes to achieve the rapid development and release of stable software.

Plan

Planning is different in DevOps; it is collaborative and continuous. Product owners start by defining what customer scenarios need to be enabled during the next product cycle (typically three- to six-month cycles). The best practice is to define these in terms of a set of customer-focused "I can" statements and avoid any discussions of technology or implementation. This grounds planning in customer value, and it gives the development and operations teams maximal flexibility and freedom in achieving those objectives. Whenever possible those "I can" statements are tied to specific measurable items known as key performance indicators (KPIs). Development and operations teams work together to determine what is feasible in this cycle, and everyone agrees upon a common set of prioritized objectives. Because the customer experience is the highest priority, a very large percentage of time is allocated to work on "Livesite"

---

[2] One of the milestones of the DevOps movement was John Allspaw's 2009 talk at the Velocity conference, "10 Deploys per day, Dev and Ops Cooperation at Flickr." The slides are available at https://www.slideshare.net/jallspaw/10-deploys-per-day-dev-and-ops-cooperation-at-flickr.

(addressing issues with the production service) and fundamentals (bug fixing, performance, security, and so on).

Perhaps the most important difference between this and traditional planning is that the software is released on a different cadence than the planning. In the DevOps model, software is released in small batches on a continuous basis. Some teams release dozens or hundreds of changes a day, whereas other teams release once a day or once a week. As new code is released, new insights are gained, and plans are adjusted.

Develop

Like the planning phase, both teams will interoperate and ensure the right code for the business is being written in the most efficient style. Furthermore, if the organization adopts something like containers, the development team will build the container image and fully test out the software in a development environment before deploying into production. The microservice approach allows the development team to evolve into an agile development framework and rapidly meet every changing need of their organization.

Test

Testing is paramount to ensure stable builds—more so building an automated test framework so that people are freed up and you cover all aspects of the software being built is paramount. Testing itself will evolve from the monitoring and planning phase. Whatever bug was identified in the monitoring phase should have an automated test built for identifying that scenario. Testing is an evolving process. Once the tests complete successfully, you can move to packaging.

Package

Packaging of the software involves putting the software in a state and place where it's possible for other automated tools to pick it up and deploy it. This package contains all the dependencies that are required to install the software. The package should also be in the format necessary for the ecosystems it will be deployed into. Standardization is core here because it will ultimately lead to simplified deployments from this package.

Release

In the release stage, the deployment items have been built and tested by the development team and the automated process has packaged up the release that's ready for deployment. IT operations have been involved at every stage to ensure a smooth transition from development environments to the production environments. Microservices and containers greatly contribute to this ease of transition.

Configure

When the package gets released, there may be minor configuration items (such as app settings, connection strings, and so on). This again should be automated based on the environment it is being deployed in to.

Monitor

Finally, in this stage, IT operations plays the bigger role by ensuring the software is performing as expected. Where there are issues, the correct feedback is submitted to the development team with all relevant information to help them understand what the problem is and correlating data to help them isolate the problem and rectify the issue.

DevOps is a culture change for an IT organization to adopt. It brings teams together, and building a complete end-to-end process takes time and requires cooperation on every level.

AGILE ADOPTION

One component of modern IT and a DevOps culture is the push to Agile development. Agile development has many different techniques, but when an organization decides to adopt a modern IT culture, Agile development will help it achieve the new culture at a rapid pace. Agile develop aligned with microservices examples allows innovation to happen in software in six-week sprints, for example. The development will be focused on individual microservices, and multiple parallel streams can occur. This leads to fast development time and rapid innovation to meet the demands of both the business and customer.

Agile is mainly a development culture concept, but it could be adopted by IT pros. Doing that would require building in similar automated processes as a DevOps strategy to manage large aspects of their environment. Release cycles for newer innovations in terms of IT infrastructure would shrink from months to weeks to days in most cases. IT pros must also think in terms of the public cloud; although on-premises IT infrastructures will be around for quite some time, public cloud adoption is happening at an accelerated pace. IT pros must have the automated tooling and monitoring systems in place to use the rapid cadence of technology change in public cloud systems.

One example involves virtual machine sizes. Public clouds have fixed configurations of virtual machines at a per-month cost. In month 4 of using a public cloud service, the public cloud vendor may release a new virtual machine size at a lower cost than the original size chosen. The IT pro should have invested in the tooling to allow this change to happen automatically, or maybe it would be triggered manually but the actual steps happen automatically so that they leverage this cost saving.

CI/CD PIPELINE

DevOps wants to reduce the time to innovation, and it wants to empower an IT organization and business to meet the needs of the customers in a rapid fashion while maintaining a stable production environment. A key feature to doing this is the development of a Continuous Integration/Continuous Development (CI/CD) pipeline. This essentially ensures that when new features are to be released, it happens automatically in a consistent and efficient manner.

The process revolves around the development team writing the new code. The code is checked into a source control system, where it undergoes an automated testing process. After its testing, the code gets packaged and deployed to artifact stores ready for deployment.

The software is then deployed into the production environment, where it takes over the load from the old code. CI/CD requires modern IT, a culture change, and trust.

Another interesting aspect of CI/CD is that when IT organizations are initially learning about the concepts, they think there will be expensive investment to buy many tools to build a CI/CD pipeline system. Figure 2-17 shows a sample of tools used in a CI /CD pipeline. We can see the process and tools defined as follows:

1. We begin coding in Visual Studio code.

2. We use GitHub as a source control system to store our code.

3. We use Visual Studio Team Services to perform the testing of the code.

4. We also use Visual Studio Team Services to perform the automated build or packaging of our software.

5. We can still use Visual Studio Team Services to deploy to our container registry as an artifact store or use the release manager, which could generate some executables or deploy it directly to a container service.

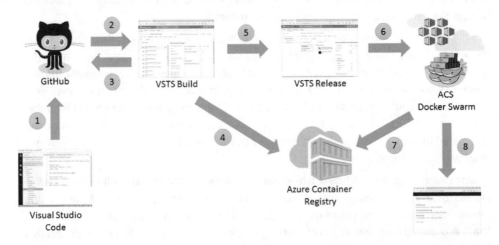

FIGURE 2-17 The CI/CD pipeline.

IT organizations likely already own the tools but aren't using them correctly today. There are hundreds of tools—both open source and full-blown commercial tools—to meet your organization's needs. The important thing is to standardize the tooling across the entire organization and not allow different branches of development or operations to use different tools. When different branches use different tools, it essentially defeats DevOps, Agile, and CI/CD Pipeline structures.

DevOps is an achievable goal for any IT organization, and those who choose to undertake this journey will benefit from implementing it, and in almost every scenario they'll be successful. Why? Because they can meet their customer needs rapidly.

However, don't be mistaken that the transition is an easy or smooth journey. There are several hurdles that span people, process, and technology. All hurdles can be overcome with the right approach and buy-in from all involved teams. Feedback is core, so it's important to build robust feedback processes so that the correct information is fed to the right teams to help them focus on the right improvement to make or the right feature to implement.

Remember—this is a process, and sometimes it's a lengthy one!

EATING THE ELEPHANT—ONE BITE AT A TIME

Over the last few sections we talked about many approaches and items related to evolving to a modern IT environment. Even as we write this book, we can hear the tension building and the points you'd like to make: "We don't have the time," "Holy cow; the learning involved in achieving that will take years," or "There is no way we will get buy-in for this."

Let us stop all these thoughts by stating that anyone who has gone through the journey to a modern IT environment has had the same ideas and has felt like they had come to the dining table with a small plate, a small knife and fork, and a small appetite to eat a huge elephant. Figure 2-18 shows us an elephant with a small piece—one bite, in fact—missing.

FIGURE 2-18   Eating an elephant one bite at a time.

One bite at a time—this is how we approach modern IT. What does this look like in practice? Let's use a simple example: How much time in a day do you or your team spend doing repetitive tasks? Could you script those tasks and share it with your team so the tasks happen more quickly and in a standardized way?

Many years ago, we automated a task of syncing information between two systems. Three people a day performed this job, and each usually took between 10 and 15 minutes per item they needed to duplicate. If there were 20 items per person per day, the total is 10 labor-hours a day duplicating information. Figure 2-19 shows the structure: In IT Silo A, the team managed their records; however, in IT Silo B, the users had to consume the records.

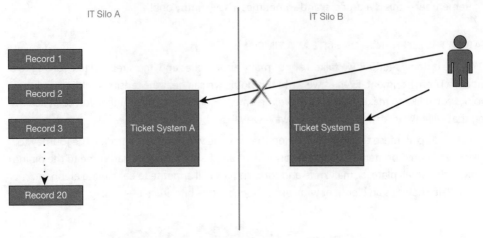

FIGURE 2-19 Silo IT, requiring duplication of ticket information.

The users in IT Silo B didn't have access to the ticket system in IT Silo A (the ticket system was proprietary for IT Silo A). The ticket system in IT Silo B was more generic and used by various different teams. The ultimate goal was to either merge the ticket systems or replace them with a central ticket system; however, this would take some time and a large investment.

We implemented a solution with automation using PowerShell. We were able to reduce the time required to scan for new entries, duplicate them, and inject them from ticket system A to ticket system B to roughly 2 seconds per item working on a frequency of every 5 minutes. Furthermore, we added functionality that if a ticket that had been duplicated in ticket system B had been modified, it would update the ticket in ticket system A, giving us bidirectional integration that had not been in place before.

What did this mean for this company? Ultimately this allowed 10 labor-hours to be given back to people to take the next time-consuming task and automate it. A few years later, they had more time to replace the IT systems to more centrally focused IT, and today all tasks undergo an automation process review, instead of someone building a manual task initially.

Eating the elephant is an ever-evolving journey. Through each iteration, each task we automate, and each system we monitor, we take another small bite of the elephant and keeping repeating until it's all gone!

Proposition on value

So, what is in it for you? Understanding the value of evolving to modern IT is extremely important: Without it, *any* IT is already a failed projected. Getting teams on board to buy into modern IT, the changes it requires, the culture shock that can come as part of it, and the adoption of a more open organization is difficult. Detailing the value proposition for them is important. It gives teams a chance to understand the goals and the benefits of buying in to modern IT, and it reduces the teams' resistance to change.

If resistance continues to occur, you need to reflect on the value proposition. Are you articulating the message correctly? Do the benefits of modern IT reflect to the teams the advantages of adopting it? Or are they afraid of a simple fact of losing their employment during this evolution? You must consider all this for everyone in the organization to feel comfortable about moving to modern IT.

To help in highlighting the value propositions, in this section we give detail of some of them to help you make the case for your organization to begin the journey toward modern IT:

- For **businesses**, modern IT maximizes the resources focused on delivering innovation.
    - Unlike traditional IT, modern IT aggressively outsources everything that doesn't drive competition. It uses Software as a Service (SaaS) for as many elements as it can.
    - Unlike Information Technology Infrastructure Library (ITIL), modern IT has a model of shared responsibility and ownership between developers and operators for creating, deploying, and operating business applications.
- For **businesses**, modern IT provides a cost-effective agile platform to grow your business. Unlike traditional IT, modern IT uses the magic of software to deliver great performance and reliability using inexpensive unreliable components.
- For **infrastructure admins**, modern IT minimizes stress and drama. Unlike traditional IT, modern IT allows infrastructure admins.
- For **developers**, modern IT provides an environment where you can do your best work with the lowest amount of friction and the maximal amount of impact.
    - Unlike traditional IT, modern IT maximizes the speed of changes from customer input to production systems.
    - Unlike traditional IT, modern IT leverages automation and testing to minimize the risk and impact of failure.

Although this is not a definitive list and, in most cases, you will need to adapt the individual message to your organization, these ideas are a basis for starting a conversation.

The Fourth Coffee case study

As we move throughout this book we want to focus on a set of challenges and opportunities that we consider to be typical of today's datacenter environments and IT organizations. We lay out our case study here, and throughout the book we refer to our fictitious company and its journey in adopting modern IT.

Consider the case of the mythical Fourth Coffee Corporation and their journey toward modern IT. Fourth Coffee is a trusted coffee company that has a strong and competent IT organization. They have a modest footprint with a few hundred stores scattered throughout the mainland United States and pop up locations in several international countries. However, the company aspires to be bigger! Unfortunately, it has recently seen its customer demand decline after its competitors rolled out a new set of loyalty reward programs and customer agility programs (such as mobile ordering).

Until now, Fourth Coffee ran quite a traditional IT model that was focused on operations. They have core datacenters running large virtualization clusters, and each coffee shop connects back to them via a VPN or leased circuit. The company has a duplicate datacenter for disaster recovery, but it's aging and becoming very costly to maintain. Figure 2-20 shows a layout of how the coffee shops connect back into Fourth Coffee's datacenters to the main application.

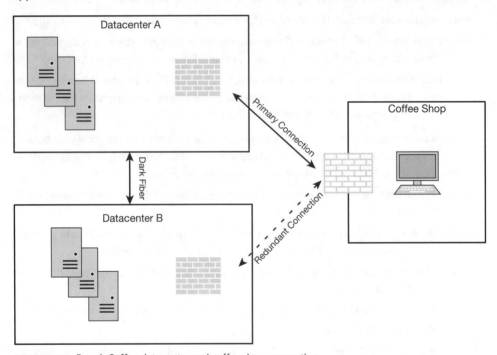

FIGURE 2-20   Fourth Coffee datacenter and coffee shop connection.

Fourth Coffee management feels that the company is being left behind in comparison to its competitors. Although the company has been focused on "doing more with less" (which often turned into "doing less with less"), its competitors focused on increasing customer satisfaction through innovation. For example, most of their competitors now have mobile apps that are delivering great functions and stealing customers. The mobile applications allow the competitors to understand their customers' buying behaviors, which enables those companies to offer incentives to them regarding time and product to make the customers more inclined to buy at the competitors' stores.

Fourth Coffee needs to switch gears and get into the modern world quickly. They have been focusing on efficiency while their competitors have been focusing on effectiveness. The CEO of Fourth Coffee understands that the company is facing an existential crisis. A change is needed;

Fourth Coffee needs to put maximizing customer value at the center of everything it does and have the courage to refactor everything to achieve it. The company needs to digitally transform. The existing CIO is close to retirement and didn't want to rock the ship. He ensures the low cost of running and keeps it as stable as an uninvested IT infrastructure could be.

With the retirement of the CIO, the CEO knows that his new CIO has to drive digital transformation and the adoption of modern IT so that Fourth Coffee can cover its position and start to grow again. He takes a risk and hires Charlotte. A few years ago, Charlotte was a first-level IT manager of an old-school brick-and-mortar retailer with a lackluster web presence. Charlotte led a grassroots effort within that company to adopt DevOps. She started small, but as her track record of success grew, so did her responsibilities and organization, and she became a well-known name in the DevOps community. The CEO knows that this will be a stretch job for Charlotte, but he's impressed by her initiative, courage, and grit and knows that these will be far more critical for Fourth Coffee's success than domain knowledge or a long track record of doing things the old way.

Charlotte is thrilled at the opportunity to try out her new ideas with a larger scope, but there's a snag. She has no new budget to do the transformation. In fact, given Fourth Coffee's recent decline in share, she has to reduce the existing budget. She hadn't planned on this.

To pursue digital transformation, Charlotte realizes that she needs to create bandwidth from what the company has been doing. She needs to find additional money in a failing system as is. First, she does a value inventory of the IT budget. She examines everything that money is spent on. She wants to know how each item contributes to the overall customer value and how it helps Fourth Coffee compete with its competitors and become a global business.

Charlotte also begins brainstorming with her teams about what digital transformation and modern IT means for Fourth Coffee. Her teams were not familiar with this line of thinking and immediately want to jump to technical issues, like moving to public cloud, replatforming the application, implementing an Internet of Things (IoT) solution, and retrieving telemetry data.

She likes those ideas but insists that they focus every conversation around delighting the customers. She tells her teams to think of it this way:

> Let's start with the cash register ringing at Fourth Coffee. What caused the customer to make that choice verses buying from our competitors? Let's figure that out and then work our way backward by asking "Why did that happen?" For every step in that chain, let's put together a plan to do it, and for everything that we are doing today that's not in that chain, let's figure out how to stop doing it or minimize our investment in it.

In her brainstorming sessions, Charlotte also discovers some culture and morale problems she needs to address. The recent hires have bought into the goals, are active in the discussion, and are eager to get started. They are hungry for change and innovation and for bringing their environments up to modern IT standards and new technology. However, that enthusiasm isn't evident among the senior IT staff. They're comfortable with the status quo. They're the experts at doing things the way they have been done. Many of them got their senior jobs because they invented the things that Charlotte seems to say aren't mission critical to the company anymore.

In one of the brainstorming sessions Eddie, the Exchange expert, opines, "A customer may not buy our coffee because of our Exchange system, but you just try to get anything done around here without it running 24-7." While the new hires want to automate everything with Power-Shell and use public cloud to drive innovation, the tenured staff are more interested in refining the systems that they have with enhancements like checking the backup every morning manually and creating administrative checklists.

Charlotte has seen this before. In her previous job, people initially were reticent to automate tasks because they didn't have the time to learn how to script and because they were concerned that they would automate themselves out of a job. She knows that she would have to make time for people to learn how to use PowerShell; after they learn, they will realize that scripting automates tasks, not people, and they'll enjoy their jobs more. Charlotte also knows that she will get higher quality IT operations and that it will free up her people so that they can work on digital transformation and become critical to the company's business.

During the inventory, the CIO identifies a large number of issues that impact customer value and/or are legacy and require large amounts of capital to replace, including the following:

- Eight percent of the IT budget was spent on keeping existing systems running.
- A combination of old hardware whose failures lead to service outages and gold-plated purpose-built servers that were reliable but cost them a large portion of their hardware budget.
- Multiple legacy hardware and software management tools.
- Unreliable and drama-filled operations. Ad hoc operations via Graphical User Interfaces (GUIs) meant that changes to the environment were unreviewed, unaudited, and unrecorded, so no one could determine who did what and when they did it. A "hero" culture in which heroic firefighting was valued without any attention being paid to the fact that the people fighting those fires were also the people who started them.
- Infrastructure teams that were unresponsive to the needs and requests of the developers.
- Outdated procurement processes leading to excessively long ordering times.
- Manual, error-prone provisioning processes for hardware and virtual machines.
- No clean hand-over from deployment teams to applications teams.
- Too many tightly coupled systems that required exceptional low latency between them.
- Virtualization spend that had tripled due to virtual machines sizes that were requested still have been growing.
- Waterfall-based development processes with long cycles and a poor track record of actually being deployed into production.
- Siloed IT – The Wall: Developers were responsible for creating the code. Operators were responsible for running the code. Developers tossed code over the wall, and operators deployed it and/or threw it back over the wall.
- Large datacenter connectivity required to handle all remote shops.

- Performance issues on branches furthest away from the datacenter.

- Legacy firewalls in place which are costly to maintain.

- Disaster recovery had never been fully proven.

One interesting scenario was discovered during the value inventory that highlights all the listed problems and that the preface text in this case study focuses around Exchange. Eddie was an Exchange MVP (Microsoft Most-Valuable Professional). Fourth Coffee was well known in the Exchange community as being particularly well run because of Eddie's skill and expertise and his willingness to share with the community.

During the value inventory, the department argued that although email wasn't in the "money path" of the business, it was absolutely mission critical, and they had one of the world's best Exchange admins in Eddie. The Exchange department's position was this:

> This place would grind to a halt if we couldn't do email." Charlotte acknowl-edged the team's argument but challenged their thinking by stating, "Although email is mission critical, and it has to work, Microsoft offers this and the other Office products as a very reliable service. So let me asks some questions:
>
> - How much time do we spend running Exchange?
> - Are we up to date on version and patching?
> - Where do we rate on securing our Exchange systems and how frequently do we perform penetration tests?
> - How does having a much better email system than our competitors get us more customers or make our customers more loyal?

The last question is the one that got everyone to understand that they need to change, but everyone is concerned about Eddie. He's a valued member of the team and a mentor to many, and they fear that using Office 365 instead of running their own Exchange servers might mean losing Eddie.

However, Eddie is ready for the change. He understands that reducing the physical infra-structure he has to maintain means freeing up time for him to focus on broadening his skills and building more integrated experiences from his messaging background.

In this case, the change is a win, but in a lot of other scenarios the challenges grow and require complex plans to solve and move forward.

Before we move forward, we're going to describe the team in a bit more detail to give context to any further conversations and help shape the issues you may come across on your journey to modern IT.

The Fourth Coffee IT team is probably one you are familiar with. They're best of breed, fully certified, and love their jobs! There are work horses who spend hours managing and maintaining the system and superstars who can fix any problem they're given. One such superstar is Eddie, who's an MVP on Exchange and literally one of the best administrators and troubleshooters in the world with regard to Exchange. As we previously mentioned, he's considered an asset to the team. There are other superstars on the team as well, but Eddie's MVP helps him stand out.

There are separate teams responsible for development and IT pro/operations. Little to no interaction happens between the teams except in the CIO meetings between the team managers.

Figure 2-21 shows the current IT structure for Fourth Coffee. Help desk roles, system administrator roles, infrastructure engineers, and architects are on the IT ops side, and software architects and application-specific development teams on the development side. The application development teams tend to focus on one major project in a year, release it, and move on to the next one.

Updating or patching previous applications happens, but it can take nearly two years before the resources are assigned to do work on the patches, which slows down how quickly Fourth Coffee can innovate with its customers.

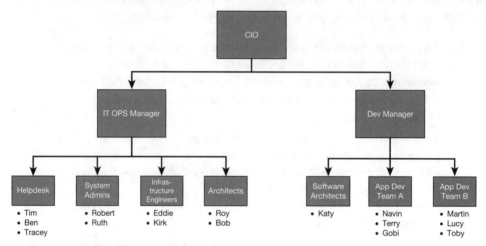

FIGURE 2-21   Fourth Coffee IT organization.

The IT operations have similar problems. When new resources are needed, it takes time to get them. Team members have official titles, but many of the roles overlap and have unclear responsibilities. However, in a crisis the team pulls together and keeps the systems and the business running.

While this is good, and it seems like the IT environment is stable and robust, this strong team has put in a lot of unnecessary effort to keep it running; in many respects, the IT system is being held together with tape. This leads to a lot of dangerous practices, like uncontrolled and unrecorded changes in the environment, to keep a system running. These practices mask true problems, which become difficult to identify and remediate.

Charlotte has made an active choice to evolve this structure into a more modern, DevOps-focused team while implementing a strong IT Service Management (ITSM) practice. In a modern IT environment and team, we introduce some new roles which have some of the responsibility of the previous roles with the addition of responsibility to start working with cloud technologies.

For example, the traditional model includes systems administrators; the modern IT model might map this role to a cloud administrator role. The role still requires system administrator tasks, but the breadth of the role expands to include something like Linux or a public cloud environment, whereas it might have originally focused on just Windows or VMware.

The role changes are made to invoke a culture change in the organization. These changes encourage teams to work together closely and strive for the DevOps culture of modern IT while giving the business the agility required to innovate rapidly to meet the customers' needs.

Figure 2-22 shows how the IT organization will evolve to meet the needs of Fourth Coffee and allow the company to innovate at a rapid pace to compete with its competitors.

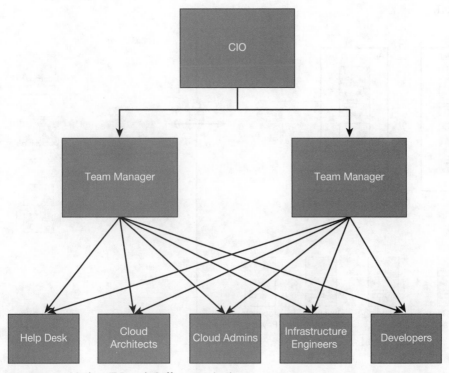

FIGURE 2-22 Modern IT Fourth Coffee organization.

In Figure 2-22, you can see we still have our help desk roles, which can manage end-user IT problems. The cloud admins replace the system administrators. The software and infrastructure architects collapse into cloud architects. The infrastructure engineers take on a wider breadth of responsibilities, but we have a central draw toward automation and self-service. Finally, our developers are pooled together; we will assign them to smaller pods with shorter cycles based on needs so they can innovate at cloud cadence.

Regarding the cloud architects role, we choose to merge two previous disparate roles to focus on the journey that organizations take when moving to modern IT. Initially the journey will begin with Infrastructure as a Service (IaaS), but eventually it will move toward Platform as a Service (PaaS) or SaaS depending on the software. If an infrastructure architect or a software architect cannot view the journey in terms of the agility of cloud, then they will not allow the organization to meet the goal of modern IT.

The CIO has a difficult choice when evolving to this type of structure. Sometimes the CIO has to make difficult decisions about people in a role. However, this change often gives stagnant employees a new lease on life and an incredible opportunity to grow.

Sample architecture of their point-of-sale (POS) application

Figure 2-23 shows a sample IT system architecture from Fourth Coffee to provide context for our discussion in terms on what we can do with people, process, and technology to evolve to modern IT.

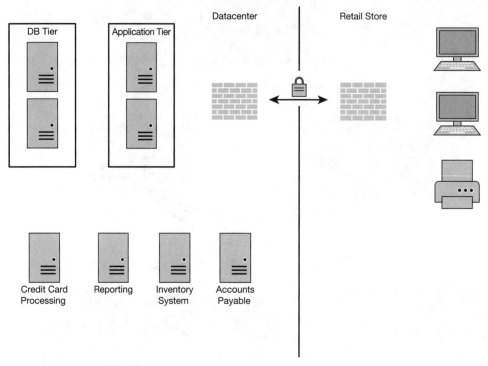

FIGURE 2-23   Point-of-sale system architecture.

This architecture is a typical two-tier, highly available monolithic architecture. The application tier performs multiple functions, including hosting a file share where clients connect into and run the POS application. The database is a Windows 2008 R2 Cluster with shared Fiber Channel Storage. The database software runs Microsoft SQL Server 2008 R2. The application tier and database tier are tightly coupled and require less than 2 milliseconds of latency between each other. The database system also requires direct database access into other systems like the Inventory System or the Accounts Payable application.

Credit card processing is done centrally via a dedicated Windows NT 4.0 credit card processing server. This has never been upgraded due to the absolute requirement of being available for stores that have 24-7 opening hours. The reporting system is a single server and is very slow. During month-end reports, it can take up to an hour to run a simple batch of reports to understand the coffee sales in a single state. The application makes calls into the inventory system and accounts payable to help ensure stock is replenished into the stores; however, orders often are wrong, and amounts charged to the stores vary greatly. This leads to a lot of manual verification and modifications.

The application itself is written in .NET 2.0 and has evolved over time to require a significant footprint to meet its ever-increasing demand for resources. The system currently requires the application tier servers to have 64 GB of random-access memory (RAM) and 8 x central processing units (CPUs), whereas the database tier requires 128 GB RAM and 12 CPUs.

These requirements are expected to grow further as new stores are added. All stores connect into the main datacenter via a dedicated line (Multi Protocol Label Switching [MPLS]) or via a VPN tunnel. The firewalls terminating the tunnels have not been upgraded in four years and currently peak at 75% throughput capacity.

The application itself was not designed to be active-active; the architecture is active-passive. Connections from POS systems have to always be directed to the active node. The POS systems themselves are locked down versions of Windows XP. They're generally stable, but Fourth Coffee has realized they're becoming a major security risk. As newer retail technologies and innovations are released, Fourth Coffee is unable to adopt them because the newer technologies can't be plugged into these POS platforms.

The system has no data warehouse for long-term storage, which means that the fiber channel storage area network (SAN) that stores the database is reaching capacity and requires replacement because of its age. This leads to regular performance problems on the database to which additional memory and CPU have been added to "fix" the problem.

Backup and disaster recovery exist, but the IT team is reluctant to test; the team members keep their fingers crossed that a true disaster never happens. They are fairly sure they cannot meet their stated recovery point objective (RPO) and recovery time objective (RTO), but they haven't been able to address it because the previous CIO felt that they could rebuild from scratch very quickly, which would be sufficient because the company can always make coffee and take cash in their stores.

As previously mentioned, the development teams work on a waterfall development model, which tends to lead to a new release of software per year with features and functionality that are often outdated by the time they are rolled in.

Fourth Coffee has a lot of problems, which many IT organizations would consider to be "normal problems." But if Fourth Coffee, or any other organization, wants to evolve to a modern IT organization and keep pace with its competitors, many things will need to change.

Various chapters within this book deal with the how of evolving to modern IT. We've talked through the why in this chapter. The what of modernizing begins here, but we touch on it throughout the entire book as we approach different subjects and work from real-world examples.

For now, let's examine how we might evolve Fourth Coffee to a modern IT organization first and then how that evolution can lead to greater innovation in the company's technology to provide a valuable customer experience which in turn will help it better tailor its business to the customers' needs.

How can Fourth Coffee evolve to modern IT?

Charlotte has recognized that Fourth Coffee has a willing and capable staff but antiquated processes and technology. The company has multiple challenges to overcome to get to its goal. One of the first things she will bring is an ITSM process with a focus on achieving a robust change-control system. The primary reason for this is to begin to understand the changes that happen in an environment and give everyone (from the executives all the way down to the IT admins) the ability to question and ask why, what customer value does this change bring for our customer.

This change takes time because trust has to be built with the team. The team members haven't been used to explaining their actions for a long time, and now they feel that doing so is an intrusion and an implication that they're not capable of making decisions. That transparency will help ensure adoption and success.

Once the team can begin to understand why the changes are being made, they can begin to plan on what areas need to be addressed first. In some cases, they will do multiple streams of work and begin to solve the problems in parallel. For example, while backing up the environment is important, the team needs to focus energy on improving backups so that Fourth Coffee can recover if a problem occurs. While not ideal, backup can also help them with the disaster recovery strategy until the IT modernization journey is farther along.

Another task we mentioned quite early was automating the tasks for the IT administrators. This will give back time so that they can tackle the problems moving forward. We also mentioned the challenge with the Exchange mail system; Fourth Coffee chose to adopt Office 365 (O365). This allowed them to save money by not having to invest in more physical infrastructure and freed up time for Eddie the infrastructure engineer to tackle more complex problems.

We previously mentioned that the Fourth Coffee development teams were on waterfall release schedules. Charlotte creates a shared development team and introduces an Agile development process with DevOps at its core. This is an iterative process designed to improve with every iteration. The first three tasks they will focus on are the following:

- Enabling interfaces for the application to avoid the necessity of requiring 1 to 2ms of latency

- Ensuring the POS system can support modern operating systems like Windows Server 2016 and SQL 2016 for the database

- Enabling the application active-active and scaling horizontally versus scaling vertically, allowing one node to be upgraded without impacting the entire system and to meet the growing demand of their newly opening stores

The Cloud Architects should begin to understand what a new architecture should look like when moving to a public cloud. They have various choices in terms of patterns they might achieve, some which can begin on premises and move to a public cloud, whereas others require working very closely with the development teams to build a PaaS solution.

For an IaaS solution, the team can begin to modernize the design by introducing technologies like SQL Server 2016 and Always-On Availability Groups for the database. Windows Server 2016 Storage Spaces Direct will replace the fiber-channel SAN and containerize the application tier and scale horizontally. The team also provides application programming interface (API) servers, so that instead of direct database reads in each system, they connect to these servers to retrieve the data that they need in a loosely coupled fashion. They also upgrade the reporting server to utilize PowerBI and introduce a data warehouse system.

Fourth Coffee is not quite ready to move all its systems to public cloud. While the cloud architects work to build a cloud architecture, the team can utilize some of the services available in public cloud to help them achieve a more modern architecture. Figure 2-24 shows a sample modern IT architecture for a POS system that could be hosted in a public cloud or on premises.

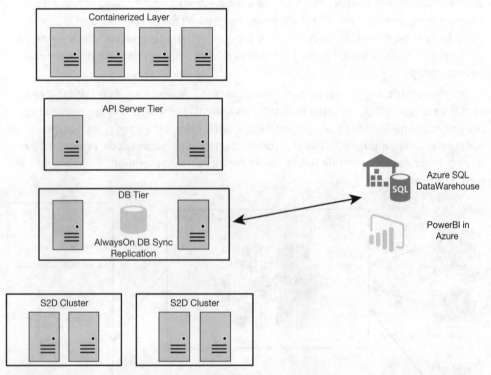

FIGURE 2-24   Point-of-sale system architecture for modern IT.

As you can see from Figure 2-24, the architecture "looks" more complicated, potentially more difficult to manage, and more expensive! The containerized layer is a fraction of the footprint of the original application tiers. Because of horizontal scaling, it can scale on demand to meet the load needs.

The API tier is introduced to decouple the application logic from the data stores. Latency between them shouldn't be an issue because the API tier will handle the communications and the software updated to support asynchronous transactions.

The database tier is upgraded to use SQL always on and use commodity systems that use storage spaces direct to meet its storage needs. The cost of upgrading the SAN in the old architecture was close to $1 million USD in this architecture. Even with a seemingly increased footprint, the team is still saving several hundred of thousands of dollars.

Finally, the team introduces the first cloud-based services: PowerBI for reporting and a SQL Data Warehouse to store the legacy data and allow the main database system to have a small footprint and stay performant. PowerBI can connect into the data warehouse and generate the reports required. Because PowerBI is a cloud service, it can scale to meet the demands of the end-of-month report runs. Instead of needing 1 hour, it runs the reports in minutes.

This architecture also contributes to ensure the application is highly available, can be integrated into a disaster recovery process seamlessly, and can reside on many public cloud platforms with little or no changes. This is one interpretation of modern IT architecture, but there are many others. Evolving the containerization tier and the API tier to a pure PaaS and using Azure SQL DB would be an evolution on the current design and would further simplify the infrastructure needs of the application and reduce the physical footprint Fourth Coffee would have to manage.

When Fourth Coffee evolves to more PaaS-based services (and even if they don't), it can start leveraging more cloud-based tools to begin analytics of the data and begin predicting the patterns of buying from the collected data. Fourth Coffee has a lot of plans that provide for further discussions around datacenter modernization throughout this book. Figure 2-25 shows a cloud-based PaaS architecture Fourth Coffee should evolve to over time—including IoT for their barista machines!

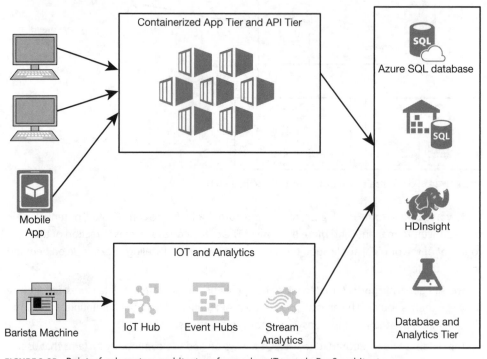

FIGURE 2-25 Point-of-sale system architecture for modern IT sample PaaS architecture.

This is a sample. Business decisions may change the direction and influence the choices made by the CIO, and architects may choose different elements based on their experience with platforms.

This is the challenge and success the path to modern IT will bring!

Where does Fourth Coffee want to go?

Fourth Coffee wants to become the leading coffee shop with the best customer offers and value for money globally, and it wants to best its competitors. That is the company's mission, and the teams are extremely focused on getting there.

Fourth Coffee has many lofty but achievable goals. We have discussed that a lot of items need to change from a technology standpoint, but the following list details some of the business asks:

- **Fourth Coffee wants to implement a customer loyalty program** Customers should have a digital card or physical card which enables them to get rewards points for the amount of purchases they make. Loyalty customers will get a small discount on every refill of their drinks.

- **Fourth Coffee want to predict customer patterns to influence shop locations and staffing needs** When a shop gets busy between 7:00 a.m. to 8:00 a.m. Monday through Friday, Fourth Coffee wants to have extra staff on hand to ensure they can meet their target of getting a customer in and out of the store in less than three minutes. Using data about how many transactions and a location services from their mobile app, the company can utilize machine learning to potentially achieve this.

- **Fourth Coffee wants to predict stock order based on customer patterns** Similar to staffing, the goal is just-in-time order so that a shop never runs out of the necessary stock. The company wants to be able to ship an order to a shop a day before it needs supplies based on the real-time data collected from the POS.

- **Fourth Coffee wants to provide custom experiences for their customers** When a customer walks into a Fourth Coffee store, Fourth Coffee would like the mobile app to notify the customers to a welcome message and offer them a small discount on a combination coffee product and food items. Additionally, if a customer has neither been in store in some time nor has placed online orders, the company wants to issue a "We miss you at Fourth Coffee" message with a small incentive to come back soon.

- **Fourth Coffee wants a mobile ordering experience** Fourth Coffee wants to give customers the option to be able to order a coffee from their office desks and walk to the nearest store at the time they've designated for picking up their coffees. The coffee and items will be prepaid via the application.

- **Fourth Coffee wants to predict machine maintenance of the barista machines** Fourth coffee wants to predict when barista machines need service and organize the necessary items that are failing due to wear and tear. They also want to

ensure the machines are being operated properly and will examine the collected data to
ensure the baristas are receiving the proper training.

- **Fourth Coffee wants to reduce the time and cost to set up a new store** Fourth
  Coffee wants standardized shop setups from a simple tablet-based POS system with
  Radio Frequency Identification (RFID) readers and a standard internet connection to run
  their shops. Equipment for all the shops—from the barista machine to the refrigerator—
  will be standardized and require data collection via their future IoT platform.

Summary

In this chapter we discussed the theory behind modernizing IT and in some cases gave potential examples of how we might solve the traditional challenges and evolve them to a modern IT
structure. In the rest of this book we also explore the how and the what of modern IT in more
detail.

The key points covered in this chapter revolve around change and being ready for the
changes to come. From every employee to every system, innovative approaches and supporting cultures should be encouraged and rewarded. Transformation is not, and never should, be
a big bang; it's a journey with lots of twists and turns. Like a journey through a snow-covered
mountain range needs to be navigated slowly, when transitioning to modern IT you always
need to be ready to adjust based on the data you currently have available and the conditions
that are occurring.

Chapter 3

Azure and Azure Stack

In the previous chapters we talked about strategies for adopting digital and datacenter transformation for an organization at every layer. In this chapter, we shift gears a little bit; we want to introduce to key technologies that will help in the transformation shift and point out the important things to think about as you're getting ready to move. We take a deep look at Azure and elements of the platform, and we look at Azure Stack and what it means for an organization. Each section has links to the main product or FAQ pages. We want to ensure you also have the latest information available to hand, and, given the rapid cadence of cloud computing, the information on the product and FAQ pages is the best place to get the most up-to-date information. Finally, toward the end of this chapter we walk through a scenario for Fourth Coffee and how that company plans to use Azure.

Intelligent cloud and intelligent edge

The first thing you must understand is the principles of Microsoft's vision of the intelligent cloud and intelligent edge. This vision helps shape people's thoughts on the cloud in general but also helps align their future plans for the IT organization they are involved with. Figure 3-1 shows an intelligent cloud at the center of an intelligent edge ecosystem.

Essentially, we have a very broad ecosystem of computers, devices, and anything that you can think of that is connected to a network. With this potential array of technology, we can summarize all these potential categories by calling them devices that essentially generate a vast amount of data. The data can cover anything from the pumpkin pie latte sales processed in a day to customer sentiment about the cleanliness of the restrooms. The intelligent edge gives us a vision of how to collect this data and process it.

The processing of the data happens at the network edge. In some cases the processing may involve data filtering; in other cases, it involves aggregating the data. In most cases it will be both and may also involve more complex data manipulation. The sum of the data that leaves the intelligent edge suddenly becomes very useful to an organization. A broader range of data can give unique insights a company may previously not have had, which enables the company to drive behavioral changes in the business, the people, and the overall culture.

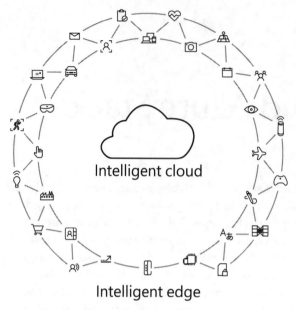

Intelligent cloud

Intelligent edge

FIGURE 3-0   Intelligent edge and intelligent cloud.

However, the intelligent edge is only one part of the chain. Collecting and filtering the data from every source imaginable is a significant task. There is no point in collecting this data unless you plan to do something with it.

The intelligent cloud is at the center of the illustration in Figure 3-0. This signifies the place you send the data collected at the intelligent edge. The intelligent cloud provides the infinite capabilities of technology and power to be able to ingest, analyze, and ultimately drive decisions based on the data sets. The intelligent cloud implies that artificial intelligence is at the core of the analytics and the insights obtained from the data that gets ingested.

In line with intelligent cloud is a maturity model for how organizations apply data to business situations. Figure 3-1 shows the maturity model.

The intelligent cloud maturity model helps organizations understand where they are today with respect to intelligent cloud. We know that the move to the cloud is about more than putting virtual machines in a new place. We even know that it's not just about running PaaS services that can scale on demand and provide virtually infinite processing power. The real draw to the cloud is to capitalize on all of this and drive better outcomes for the organizations.

Let's return to our example of Fourth Coffee, which we're using to discuss strategies for helping an organization to utilize and benefit from the intelligent cloud and intelligent edge. These strategies include everything from technology changes to culture shifts.

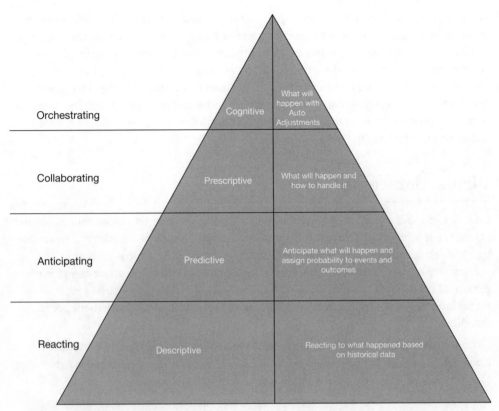

Orchestrating — Cognitive — What will happen with Auto Adjustments

Collaborating — Prescriptive — What will happen and how to handle it

Anticipating — Predictive — Anticipate what will happen and assign probability to events and outcomes

Reacting — Descriptive — Reacting to what happened based on historical data

FIGURE 3-1   Intelligent cloud maturity model.

Let's examine Fourth Coffee and where it is in relation to the intelligent cloud maturity model. Fourth Coffee firmly sits at the bottom of the triangle in the "reacting" space. The company uses the sales data that is collected each month from the stores and analyzes it. If there's a spike in sales, the team tries to understand why it happened and factors that into a plan that is months away. For any current month they are operating in, they have already based their decisions on historical data.

With the business desire to grow the customer base, the current Fourth Coffee locations are offering new incentives for new and existing customers. For this endeavor, the company needs to understand the trend of sales in as near real time as possible. The company also needs to use historical data to predict patterns of behavior.

For example, in Seattle an event happens four times a month. The event organizers change the locations for each event, but Fourth Coffee knows that if the event is near one of its coffee shops, foot traffic in the store generally increases. However, Fourth Coffee doesn't know who the customers are, if they are regular customers, if they have trends? Do the customers from the day of the event frequent the coffee shop after the event, or do they like the Fourth Coffee brand? If Fourth Coffee creates an intelligent edge for its retail shops with the new customer experiences, including the mobile application and customer sentiment stations, the company suddenly has a ton of telemetry data to use to predict patterns. Simply put , Fourth Coffee could place an offer on coffee for the event attendees as the traffic increases. The store could offer new brands of coffee or different food items based on the day and time of the event. The store could increase the staff or set up a mobile coffee station to accommodate rapid foot traffic. The possibilities are endless, and data gives Fourth Coffee the edge over its competitors and satisfaction for its customers.

Virtual datacenter

Now that you have a grasp of intelligent cloud and intelligent edge, let's take a tour of another concept called the virtual datacenter. IT departments over the years have followed two main trends in relation to their IT systems and servers: They have lots of branch-level compute centers, or they have centralized datacenters. The centralized datacenters have been the more popular of the two, but you will find organizations whose applications required a local server for performance or the connectivity wasn't available to reliably connect back to the corporate datacenter.

Corporate datacenters are commonplace. When approaching the cloud, we consider the cloud not as a branch but as a corporate datacenter. With this in mind, we propose a challenge: Starting today start thinking of the cloud as your corporate datacenter.

For this chapter (and all others), we focus on Azure, but the concepts we describe should apply across all clouds. The implementation on each cloud is beyond the scope of this book, but the concepts we discuss are broad enough to map.

Now, if we think about how we build physical datacenters today, there are millions and millions of dollars of investment for the building, the security, the cooling, the power, and the equipment. This is obviously an expensive operation. When we approach clouds like Azure, we don't have to worry about our facilities' hardware costs because a large portion is taken care of by Microsoft.

The customer has a simple task; design the logical layout of the platform that integrates natively into its on-premises systems. Before you design your virtual datacenter, let's take a step back ever so slightly; don't blindly apply the structures and tools that have been implemented on premises. This is truly a time to revisit a lot of past decisions that may have led to inefficiencies in the IT systems and processes.

Also, every time you decide that something is needed, examine how you can do it natively in the platform. For example, if you use a physical load balancer on premises, don't just automatically choose the same virtual appliance in Azure—challenge the requirements and see if you can replace it with a native platform load balancer. We also want to stress the need to be careful because you'll have times that you need the virtual appliance. Taking time to carefully understand your application and its requirements will help you make those decisions.

NOTE When you're thinking of the cloud as a virtual datacenter, the thought process needs to hit globally. Although the major players in the cloud have datacenters around the globe, to an end organization the virtual datacenter needs to be treated as a single logical unit incorporating all regions with singular policies, processes, and tools.

As you think globally about how you interact with a cloud, there are many things that you need to design for on a regional basis. For example, while networking is a globally logical entity that needs to be designed, you need to dive into the individual regions and determine the IP space, subnets, and connectivity models you will implement while considering the global virtual datacenter.

Taking networking again as an example, the current IP space that Fourth Coffee occupies is a 10.0.0.0/16, which offers them 65,535 IPs (this is not a subnetting course, and exact IP address availability assignments are merely a simple example). The full space has been assigned to the corporate datacenter, and it has been further subnetted into VLANS.

The unfortunate thing is the VLAN space has not been contiguously assigned, nor does the allocation have a logical pattern to it. If we want to keep the 10.0.0.0/16 space and use subnets within that range for our global virtual datacenters, it will be a significant undertaking to correct the network.

We also cannot have overlapping address space between Azure and on-premises datacenter. In this example, we could assign the next logical address set to a virtual network in Azure—say 10.1.0.0/16. Before we do, remember that the virtual network is a regional construct, and we want to make sure that we plan globally. In that light, we may say this is acceptable or reduce the allocation sign to a /20 or a /23 (CIDR naming). The point is to plan globally for all the regions we may occupy so that the subnet space is planned out to meet the needs of the business. Figure 3-3 shows a simple contiguous layout with virtual networks to illustrate the point.

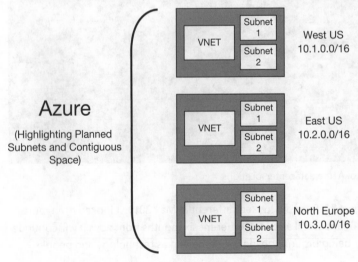

FIGURE 3-2 Sample contiguous global layout for networking.

In the next few sections, we discuss many of the elements in Azure you need to plan for before you deploy production workloads. This is to ensure that your modernization efforts are successful, and your overall transformation succeeds. Remember that designs are logical in nature; therefore, many of the principals should be designed with a level of agnosticism. The technology that will implement the logical design will be unique per cloud vendor and have different capabilities. Therefore, the push for the agnostic design is critical. We will have the principals we want to achieve in our design detailed out. Then, on each cloud, organizations can use the best technology in each arena to implement their vision.

> **NOTE** For more information about Virtual Datacenter visit https://docs.microsoft.com/en-us/azure/networking/networking-virtual-datacenter.

Azure

Now that we have the two base concepts covered, let's talk about Azure. But let's talk about it not in terms of what services it has—because Azure has more than 100 services and is growing—but in terms of what you really need to know to integrate Azure into your IT organization and some of the key choices that help you begin that transformation. First, we start with the diagram in Figure 3-3. This diagram shows the location of every Azure datacenter today.

FIGURE 3-3 Worldwide map of Azure datacenter locations.

This map was from August 2018, and it looked different in May 2018. It looked even more different in September 2017, and it will also look different six months from now. It will continue to grow with more regions being brought online over time and as technology and people develop.

NOTE   Staying up to date on region availability will be important for all organizations. Please visit azure.microsoft.com/en-us/global-infrastructure/regions/ for the latest information available.

The key point right now is to understand the principal of logically designing your IT ecosystem to tap into the global powerhouse that is the Azure datacenters. Think about the benefits to your organization of this global scale.

If your organization isn't ready for the cloud, you probably wouldn't be reading this. If you're not ready for global scale, don't be put off Azure or any cloud; the basic principles still apply to be successful. You can safely target them at a regional level as the logical abstraction mutes where placement occurs.

Azure release cycle

Azure, as previously mentioned, has more than 100 services and is growing. These services are developed and released independently of each other. The cadence for new features or patches can be days but also can be longer as Microsoft often works in sprint cycles of varying times. If you review the Azure Blog Announcements (azure.microsoft.com/en-us/blog/topics/announcements/), you will observe new services being released daily, if not multiple times per day.

It's important for any organization to understand this release schedule because the traditional terms of release to manufacturing (RTM) when a product was ready to be released don't really apply anymore. RTM also meant that the support ecosystem was in place, so that if problems occurred you could interact and obtain support for running the platform in production.

Times have changed, and now the release cycle has three main phases: private preview, public preview, and general availability. Private preview is usually a limited alpha or beta trial of a service; the trial is to validate functionality and whether it fits market sentiment. Customers are generally invited to private previews or asked to register and justify their need for participation. In legacy terms, public preview can be considered the equivalent of beta. You can sign up for most services in public preview; depending on the service, the preview may come with conditions that allow the use of the service in production. Take a look at the following link for the latest services to have a public preview available: azure.microsoft.com/en-us/services/preview/.

NOTE   Please review the supplemental terms for preview use at azure.microsoft.com/en-us/support/legal/preview-supplemental-terms/.

Finally, every organization that requires the use of a service that has reached general availability (GA) needs to plan for an important thing. Azure is a global reaching service, and we're noting this again because you need to remember that although it's a global reaching service, it's also broken into regions. Regions have the infrastructure necessary to support the services being rolled out.

The caveat that needs to be planned for is that not all regions will receive all the services at the same time. This essentially means that a service is rolled out to major regions first and then rolls down to smaller regions.

This roll out is controlled by demand. Say you're in a region with small demand for the service, but it's where you choose to roll out your virtual datacenter. The problem that you need to consider is when the service might be enabled in the region you've chosen.

Planning for the potential that the service may never reach your location is important when you're considering where to place your organization's IT systems and the services you will need to consume in Azure.

Governance

Organizations have invested large amounts of time and money implementing governance models for their current IT systems. Much of this policy and process can be reused; however, there are differences in how we apply the policies to Azure.

In this section, we discuss some of the major differences and areas you need to consider in your design. This may mean in some cases a new approach to implement your governance model or revisiting the governance model and understanding the current validity of what is being dictated. When thinking about Azure, remember that your responsibility has diminished for certain aspects, and that should reflect in your governance. For example, hardware life cycles in Azure are not directly applicable to consuming organizations, whereas Azure virtual machines' life cycles are extremely relevant.

The governance model you adopt also needs to be a living entity with a life cycle attached. This is not to say that every week your organization must shift with whatever is new in the platform. Instead the model must adapt in shorter intervals then before—say every six months rather than every three to five years. There are lots of reasons for this shorter interval of adaptation, but ultimately, they boil down to a couple of simple ones as follows:

- **Cost:** with new generations of technology being released in the cloud, it's usually cheaper to run on newer SKUs.
- **Support cycle** offerings in the cloud tend to have a shorter life cycle compared to traditional software. Windows Server, for example, in Long Term Servicing Channel has five years of mainstream and five years extended support. Cloud Services might announce decommissioning of a SKU after 18 months of service to provide a more robust service for the end consumers.

This is by no means engineered to scare customers, and as we mentioned it usually works out in the consumers' favor as the new SKUs are more cost effective and they run on newer generations of hardware on the backend. We mention this only to demonstrate that an organization that chooses to move to the cloud takes on a more agile life cycle, and it will need to construct or modify its governance model to suit. If it doesn't, the consumer experience of trying to keep something like Windows Server 2003 alive in the cloud for years after its support life cycle will be a painful process, and there will be many disgruntled customers.

Under the topic of governance there are several areas we should discuss in more detail to help understand what is available today and what it means for an organization.

Compliance

No matter the organization, there are rules and regulations that must be followed. Healthcare has HIPAA, U.S. government agencies have FEDRAMP, companies that have credit card processing have PCI-DSS, and, of course, there are many other guidelines depending on what industry you are in and where you are located. Each of these compliance certifications requires organizations to implement IT systems in a manner that meets the needs of the certification but also to protect the systems. Compliance exists to help provide confidentiality, nonrepudiation of data, and trust back to the ultimate end consumers (that is, the customers) of the systems that organizations provide to the business.

The last thing anyone wants is their credit card being used on the dark web to pay for illicit goods because an organization decided PCI-DSS (or others) was not important. Deploying and configuring an IT system to be compliant to any certification is tough, and generally implementation is a significant undertaking for any organization. Maintaining it is also difficult because random inspections during the certified year can be performed to ensure you are still complying with the rules of the certification.

Most organizations generally had to implement a lot of security software, policies, and procedures from the physical layer (that is, the building, doors, fire suppression) right up to the access layers in the software (the web page, end user portal, mobile app). Organizations also had to train everyone who uses information systems about things like password strength and phishing awareness. If you use a cloud platform like Azure, one of the benefits is the investment needed to become compliant lessens. Azure has more than 70 certifications (and counting!) including Industry, Government, Regional, and Global.

> **NOTE** For a complete list of Azure Compliance Certifications, please visit www.microsoft.com/en-us/trustcenter/compliance/complianceofferings.

Why is this important? Well, have a look at Figure 3-4, which is the cloud responsibility matrix.

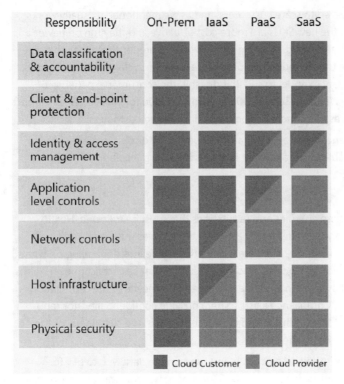

FIGURE 3-4 Cloud responsibility model.

Depending on which option an organization chooses, the level of work it needs to achieve certification is reduced. Take IaaS, for example; the organization no longer must consider physical security from an Azure perspective because Azure has already gained compliance in that area. As we progress from physical security to host infrastructure and network controls, this becomes a shared responsibility model. This is where Azure ensures the underlying platform will be compliant. However, if you run a virtual machine on the host platform, for example, you're responsible for ensuring the virtual machine is compliant. This is important to understand. For example, with PCI-DSS, the Azure Infrastructure is PCI-DSS compliant, but this does not make your virtual machine and application compliant.

> **NOTE** For more information, see the Azure Trust Center at www.microsoft.com/en-us/TrustCenter/Compliance/PCI.

Azure has taken many strides to expose the interfaces required for any third-party system to collect the data it requires to verify compliance to a certification. Azure's own certifications, as well as a large amount of information on how Azure operates and the controls that are in place, are available from the Microsoft Trustworthy Computing Center Website located at www.microsoft.com/en-us/trustcenter/.

Tenants

A tenant represents an organization. It maps to a dedicated instance of Azure Active Directory. Azure Active Directory houses all the organization information, including users, groups, domains, permissions, applications, and so on. Azure Active Directory provides layers of functionality, but, from a tenant perspective, we're aiming to have one tenant per organization. Figure 3-5 shows a sample layout for a Fourth Coffee tenant.

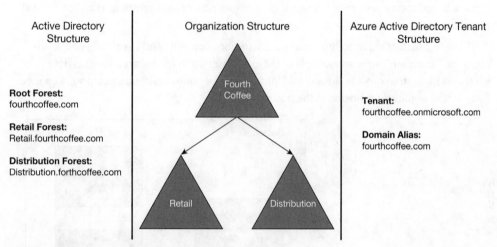

Active Directory Structure

Organization Structure

Azure Active Directory Tenant Structure

Root Forest:
fourthcoffee.com

Retail Forest:
Retail.fourthcoffee.com

Distribution Forest:
Distribution.forthcoffee.com

Fourth Coffee

Retail

Distribution

Tenant:
fourthcoffee.onmicrosoft.com

Domain Alias:
fourthcoffee.com

FIGURE 3-5 Sample tenant layout for Fourth Coffee.

Figure 3-5 shows three structures. On the far left it shows a traditional on-premises Active Directory Forest structure modeled off the middle organizational structure. We have a root forest called fourthcoffee.com and two child domains that represent the retail and distribution businesses.

On the far right, we have a much-simplified structure for our Azure Active Directory tenant. All initial tenants are created with a *<name>.onmicrosoft.com* address; in this case, it's fourthcoffee.onmicrosoft.com. We use a domain alias then, so users can log in with the UPN of *<username>@fourthcoffee.com*.

Tenant structure should be as simple as possible. If you use Office 365 or Dynamics then the same principals apply. In fact, if you create an Azure Active Directory for any of the Microsoft Cloud Services, it will be the basis of use across those services—that is, the tenant for Azure will be the same for Office 365.

However, please note the terminology *tenant* when talking about Office 365 or Dynamics may refer to the region where it gets deployed versus what we are referring to for Azure—in this case, the Azure Active Directory Tenant mapping to the organization.

Subscriptions

Azure subscriptions provide a boundary for two main elements that are important to understand. The first boundary is billing. The subscription provides a method to consume Azure services and report on the cost. The second boundary is limits. We discuss limits in greater detail later in this chapter, but the core of it is that Azure is a shared platform. In the shared platform model there can be only a certain number of resources available to everyone, and we put limits in place to maintain a system of fairness and to ensure no single organization can consume all the resources.

These two factors influence how many subscriptions you will need to operate your environment. Figure 3-6 shows an example of using a subscription for a shared services network, which will be used to provide firewall and intrusion prevention services and corporate connectivity for the applications hosted in the business group.

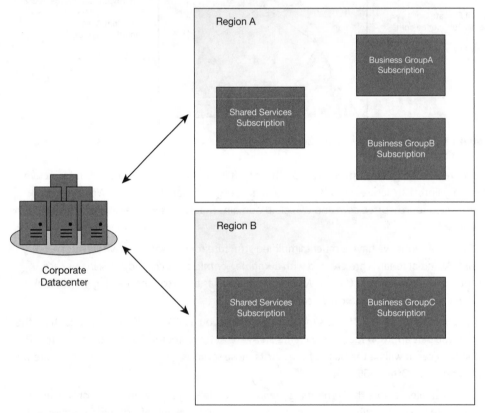

FIGURE 3-6 Sample subscription model.

Each business group has a subscription. In this way, the business group is responsible for its billing and all the applications that help run the business group are clearly defined in its individual subscription. The shared services subscription is run by the IT operations teams, and the cost is divided equally across all business groups. Another aspect to this design is that we separate limits and reduce the risk of hitting any thresholds of the Azure platform.

A caveat to this design is when there are multiple subscriptions and you try to keep each subscription consistent with the same security policies and Role-Based Access Control (RBAC) required by an enterprise. Centralized monitoring and reporting is possible, but it requires some thought. You need to ensure service accounts exist and have access to all subscriptions to be able to report on them effectively.

This is just one example of how to use subscriptions. There is no official design practice because it greatly depends on how an organization is structured, how the IT environment operates today, and how the IT organization is expected to operate in the future.

In the next two sections, we talk about Management Groups and Azure Policy, which are two concepts that allow you to create a structure aligned to the business and to enforce standards across all subscriptions.

> **NOTE** For more information relating to subscription layout, please visit docs.microsoft.com/en-us/azure/architecture/cloud-adoption-guide/subscription-governance?toc=%2Fen-us%2Fazure%2Fazure-resource-manager%2Ftoc.json&bc=%2Fen-us%2Fazure%2Fbread%2Ftoc.json.

Management groups

Management groups provide an organization that will have many subscriptions with a centralized way to manage access, policies, and compliance. Management groups are bound to an Azure Active Directory tenant and allow you to create containers in a hierarchical structure that would represent the organizational structure. Figure 3-7 shows a sample management group layout for Fourth Coffee and its corporate, retail, and distribution divisions.

The structure is simple. We create a root management group that maps to Fourth Coffee's corporate division then create two child management groups—one for retail and one for distribution. We can see that retail will have multiple subscriptions covering its point-of-sale (POS) development, POS production, mobile app development, and mobile app production environments. Distribution will have two subscriptions for its core infrastructure applications and for the development environment. Corporate will have two subscriptions: one for the shared services network and one for its application infrastructures.

The subscriptions will be networked, but the management group structure will allow us to centrally manage access across all subscriptions and implement policies to ensure that all subscriptions under Fourth Coffee will enforce standards so that they remain complaint.

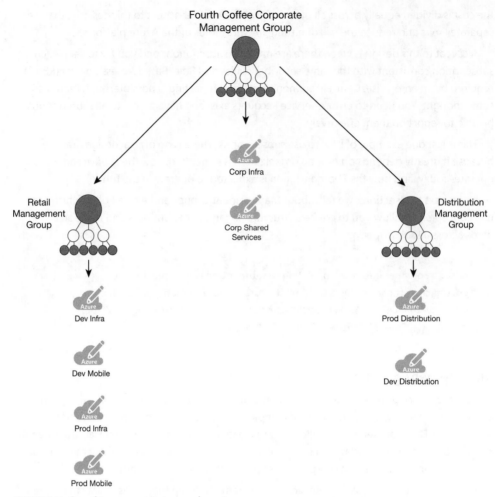

FIGURE 3-7 Sample management group layout.

Role-Based Access Control

Role-Based Access Control (RBAC) implemented in Azure allows organizations to granularly control access to resources based on the role of the administrator or user. Access control can be assigned to users and groups at various levels. Figure 3-8 shows a diagram of the levels at which RBAC can be applied (that is, the scope), which are subscription, resource group, or resource.

Figure 3-8 also includes some sample roles that you can instantly implement to get up and running quickly. The guiding principle for RBAC is least privilege, which mandates that the users are only granted the minimum privileges required to the task they are required to do.

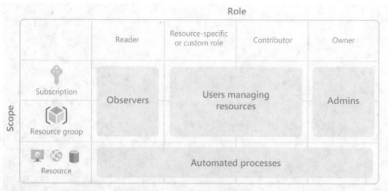

FIGURE 3-8 RBAC scope and roles application.

RBAC design is critical to securing Azure correctly. For example, if you do not secure access to resources correctly then it would be possible for someone to delete a virtual machine or expose the corporate network.

In the example of Fourth Coffee, the shared services network that allows for connectivity back to the on-premises corporate network highlights the need for ensuring security is implemented correctly. If a level 1 helpdesk person had owner access to the shared services subscription, a simple mistake could lead to a security breach that would be very damaging to Fourth Coffee.

You should implement RBAC with groups rather than individual users, and the groups should be applied at the appropriate level. Every owner-level request should be scrutinized, and every request for owner level at the subscription should be denied after subscription provisioning. Owner-level access at the subscription should be reserved only for secured service accounts.

> **NOTE** For more information relating to RBAC, visit docs.microsoft.com/en-us/azure/role-based-access-control/overview.

Azure Policy

Azure Policy enables you to create, assign, and manage policies, which enable an organization to enforce rules across subscriptions so that the resources that are deployed and the resources that may be deployed will stay compliant with the standards that are mandated by the organization.

Azure Policy differs from RBAC. RBAC controls access to the resource, so the user can or cannot manage it. Policy controls whether you can deploy it; if it is deployed, it checks whether the properties of the deployment match the policy that has been implemented.

Azure Policy covers areas like Naming, Compute, Storage, Networking, and many others. Microsoft has provided an array of sample policies in the Azure portal for quick implementation, as shown in Figure 3-9.

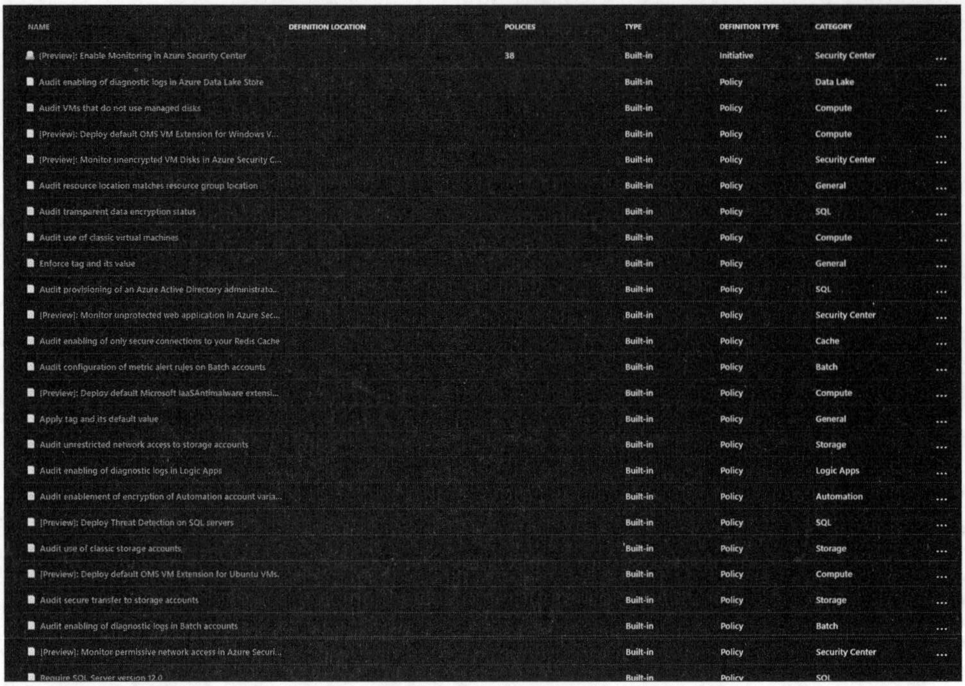

NAME	DEFINITION LOCATION	POLICIES	TYPE	DEFINITION TYPE	CATEGORY	
[Preview]: Enable Monitoring in Azure Security Center		38	Built-in	Initiative	Security Center	...
Audit enabling of diagnostic logs in Azure Data Lake Store			Built-in	Policy	Data Lake	...
Audit VMs that do not use managed disks			Built-in	Policy	Compute	...
[Preview]: Deploy default OMS VM Extension for Windows V...			Built-in	Policy	Compute	...
[Preview]: Monitor unencrypted VM Disks in Azure Security C...			Built-in	Policy	Security Center	...
Audit resource location matches resource group location			Built-in	Policy	General	...
Audit transparent data encryption status			Built-in	Policy	SQL	...
Audit use of classic virtual machines			Built-in	Policy	Compute	...
Enforce tag and its value			Built-in	Policy	General	...
Audit provisioning of an Azure Active Directory administrato...			Built-in	Policy	SQL	...
[Preview]: Monitor unprotected web application in Azure Sec...			Built-in	Policy	Security Center	...
Audit enabling of only secure connections to your Redis Cache			Built-in	Policy	Cache	...
Audit configuration of metric alert rules on Batch accounts			Built-in	Policy	Batch	...
[Preview]: Deploy default Microsoft IaaSAntimalware extensi...			Built-in	Policy	Compute	...
Apply tag and its default value			Built-in	Policy	General	...
Audit unrestricted network access to storage accounts			Built-in	Policy	Storage	...
Audit enabling of diagnostic logs in Logic Apps			Built-in	Policy	Logic Apps	...
Audit enablement of encryption of Automation account varia...			Built-in	Policy	Automation	...
[Preview]: Deploy Threat Detection on SQL servers			Built-in	Policy	SQL	...
Audit use of classic storage accounts			Built-in	Policy	Storage	...
[Preview]: Deploy default OMS VM Extension for Ubuntu VMs.			Built-in	Policy	Compute	...
Audit secure transfer to storage accounts			Built-in	Policy	Storage	...
Audit enabling of diagnostic logs in Batch accounts			Built-in	Policy	Batch	...
[Preview]: Monitor permissive network access in Azure Securi...			Built-in	Policy	Security Center	...
Require SQL Server version 12.0			Built-in	Policy	SQL	

FIGURE 3-9 Sample list of policies available by default in Azure.

Azure policy is no longer assigned only at the subscription level. It can be tied to a management group to further enforce standardization across an organization.

> ***NOTE*** For further information about Azure Policy, visit docs.microsoft.com/en-us/azure/azure-policy/.

Naming conventions

Naming conventions for infrastructure resources can follow traditional organizational standards if they're already well defined. It's important to ensure that the naming convention translates into something meaningful. For example, the name should reflect the location of the machine and the role. A sample of a name might be WUS2FS001. If you breaking this down, you can determine that the machine is in West US 2, it's a File Server (FS), and it's the first node.

Naming conventions span all resources in Azure and should be well planned before implementation. Naming for some resources need to follow standards, or there have to be limitations in the characters or length. Naming conventions can be enforced by using Azure Policy, so you can maintain a corporate standard.

NOTE For more information on the limitations and standards, visit docs.microsoft. com/en-us/azure/architecture/best-practices/naming-conventions.

Resource groups

Resources groups are logical containers to classify resources that share a similar life cycle. For example, an organization would create a resource group to host Application-A components or a resource group to host all the networking resources in an environment. You can apply RBAC to the resource group to control who can perform actions on the resources within. The resource group design doesn't need to be complex, but it needs to be intuitive and keep resources split appropriately with least privilege segmentation in mind.

Azure limits

This might be a strange item to consider as part of governance. However, Azure is a public cloud and has implemented controls so no one organization can consume all the available resources, so it's critical for organizations to understand the platform's limits. Organizations must design to the limits to ensure success on Azure.

NOTE For more information on the current limits on the platform, visit docs.microsoft.com/en-us/azure/azure-subscription-service-limits.

Networking

Designing the governance model to support public cloud architectures is a critical step to ensure its adoption is a success. Fast on its heels, though, is networking. Networking in the cloud is different from networking on premises; it's fully software defined. There are no physical switches for a network administrator to manage or cables to run, yet you need to create something to allow people to connect to the resources that will be hosted in the cloud. So although the cloud is different, there is still a variety of work to be done to provide an organization with connectivity and to ensure security.

Virtual networks

A virtual network is an isolated software layer that allows resources in Azure to communicate with each other. Some examples are virtual machines or exposing PaaS services so that they can be only privately connected to service endpoints by an organization's private resources.

Virtual networks define an IP address space that can then be further divided into subnets. Figure 3-10 shows a sample virtual network layout with subnets defined for a web tier, app tier, and database tier.

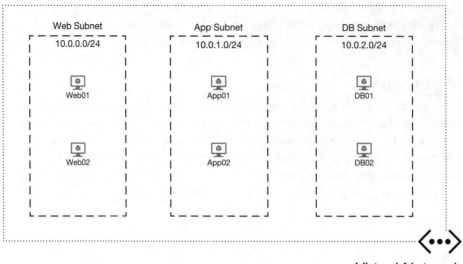

FIGURE 3-10 Sample virtual network layout.

In the example, the virtual network has an address space of 10.0.0.0/16, but you can define any space if it conforms to RFC 1918, which defines standards to assign addresses to private networks. Subnets that are defined must fall appropriately into the address space. For example, we can't define a subnet of 10.1.0.0/24 because it falls outside the address space of 10.0.0.0/16. As discussed earlier in the virtual datacenter section, it's highly recommended that you plan the address space first, and you should make it contiguous with no overlap. If the address space is not planned correctly and you run out of addresses, then it's easy to add an address space to a virtual network, which then becomes part of the routable network.

If you require multiple virtual networks in a deployment, be aware that by default they have no communication capabilities. Of course, you can configure the virtual networks to communicate with each other using technologies like VNET Peering, VPN, Express Route, or Endpoint Exposure.

Another consideration, especially for organizations that require traffic control, is restricting communication between subnets because, by default, if you deploy multiple different subnets, they can communicate with each other. Traffic control is achieved using network security groups with IP access control lists that restrict traffic based on IP address (source and destination), port numbers (source and destination), and priority.

Organizations also can deploy network virtual appliances (NVAs) to control traffic filtering. An NVA is essentially a virtual machine with third-party software installed. Some examples are F5, Palo Alto Firewalls, and Checkpoint Firewall.

You also can use user-defined routes (UDRs) to enable traffic routing to flow routes. You apply UDRs at the subnet level, and they help protect against rogue virtual machines. Generally, you use UDRs to force all traffic through an NVA because, by default, all traffic will flow via an Azure Gateway and out to its destination. Similarly, when we talk about hybrid connectivity, we can use a UDR to force all traffic back on premises.

> **NOTE** For more information on all items that can be deployed into a virtual network, visit docs.microsoft.com/en-us/azure/virtual-network/virtual-network-for-azure-services.
>
> For more information on which PaaS services can leverage service endpoints, visit docs.microsoft.com/en-us/azure/virtual-network/virtual-network-service-endpoints-overview.

Connecting to corporate

Often, an organization's first move to the cloud involves some requirement for connecting the Azure virtual networks to the corporate datacenter to allow intercommunication. If the first move is to lift and shift applications through virtual machine migration, for example, there will be a dependency to communicate with domain controllers for authentication. For that to happen, a communication path must be established. Azure has two main methods to connect a virtual network to a corporate datacenter, which we discuss next.

Virtual private networks

Virtual private networks (VPN) in Azure are implemented by Azure's VPN Gateway service or via an NVA that the organization has deployed. Azure VPN Gateway uses industry standard IPSec/IKE (v1 and v2) protocols.

> **NOTE** For a full list of all IPSec / IKE parameters that Azure VPN Gateway supports, visit docs.microsoft.com/en-us/azure/vpn-gateway/vpn-gateway-about-vpn-devices#ipsec.

Azure VPN Gateways can connect to other Azure VPN Gateways. They also can connect to traditional on-premises VPN hardware. See the Azure VPN Gateways FAQ below to understand the support devices that can connect to Azure VPN Gateways.

> **NOTE** For more information regarding connecting Azure VPN Gateways to on-premises VPN hardware, visit docs.microsoft.com/en-us/azure/vpn-gateway/vpn-gateway-vpn-faq#s2s.

VPNs in Azure can be deployed into two types of configurations depending on your availability requirements and your connectivity requirements. Figure 3-11 and Figure 3-12 show a site-to-site configuration and a multisite-to-site VPN configuration, respectively, that an organization can implement.

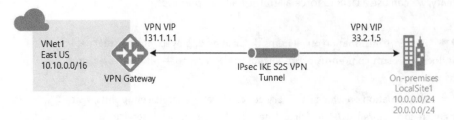

FIGURE 3-11   Site-to-site VPN connection.

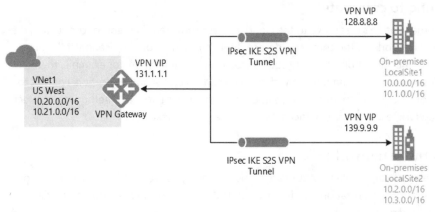

FIGURE 3-12   Multisite-to-site VPN connection.

ExpressRoute

The alternative method to connecting an organization's datacenter to Azure is via the use of ExpressRoute. ExpressRoute is a dedicated, low latency, high bandwidth private connection for an organization to connect to Microsoft Cloud Services (Azure, Dynamic, Office 365, and so on).

Figure 3-13 shows an example of how ExpressRoute can connect from an organization into Microsoft Cloud Services. This connection can be rated up to 10Gbps throughput and comes in flavors of unlimited or metered data throughput.

You implement ExpressRoute via the Azure VPN Gateway service, which means it also can use VPN failover connectivity in case the ExpressRoute has any issues.

> **NOTE**   For more information about ExpressRoute, please see the ExpressRoute FAQ at docs.microsoft.com/en-us/azure/expressroute/expressroute-faqs.

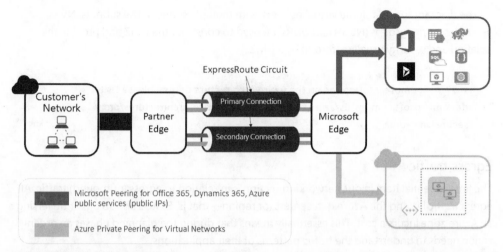

FIGURE 3-13 ExpressRoute circuit.

Building a DMZ

Many organizations have public-facing websites or applications. These applications are usually hosted in a secure network called a *demilitarized zone* (DMZ). This network is locked down to only essential services and usually requires firewall traversal to break out of the network in any direction. We often find that servers hosted in a DMZ are dual-homed with multiple network cards, and IP access control lists are in place to limit traffic to the internal-facing network cards. Figure 3-14 shows an architecture pattern taken from the Azure Architecture center. It describes how to build a DMZ in Azure.

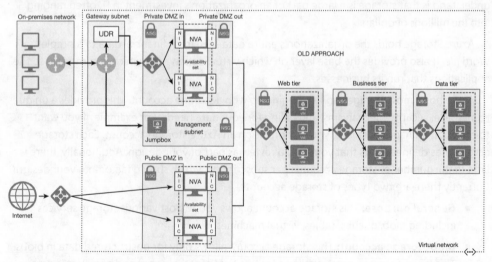

FIGURE 3-14 Sample DMZ Architecture in Azure.

The diagram shows a single virtual network with multiple subnets. The subnets, NVAs, network security groups (NSGs) and UDRs are used to construct the DMZ and provide the isolation and security usually afforded by a DMZ.

> **NOTE** For more information on the Azure Architecture Center, please visit docs.microsoft.com/en-us/azure/architecture/reference-architectures/dmz/secure-vnet-dmz.

Egress traffic

The final, essential item in our networking section is in relation to egress (outbound) traffic. All egress traffic leaving the Azure datacenters (or region—that is, EastUS and so on) or traversing an Azure zone incurs a cost. This essentially means that during the planning phases an organization needs to understand the traffic patterns of their applications.

If they have an application that transfers a lot of data between its tiers then splitting them across regions will be a costly exercise at the very least. There are, of course, many other factors for not splitting across regions, but cost of egress traffic is our focal point here.

Egress traffic counts for VPN connectivity to corporate datacenters and metered ExpressRoute circuits as well. The key for any organization is to minimize traffic transfer as much as possible.

Storage

The next area we need to discuss is storage. Storage to traditional organizations focuses around hard disks, SSD, SMB, NFS, iSCSI, SAN, and many other acronyms. The key point to understand is that storage is a large part of an organization's investment in IT, often ranging into the millions of dollars.

Azure Storage holds the organization's entire data sets, from financial data to a simple Word file. It also provides the base layer on which virtualization runs, which in turn maps to the applications that run its businesses.

Azure hosts most storage services beginning with a storage account. This provides a unique namespace, security mechanisms, and billing for your data needs. For example, if you want to provision an Azure data lake, you first provision an Azure storage account. Each storage account has defined limits that you should review as part of your design. Additionally, there is a limit to the number of storage accounts per subscription, which should factor into your design. Currently there are two types of storage accounts.

- **General purpose:** This storage account allows you to host various storage services including blob, queues, tables, virtual machines, files.
- **Blob storage account:** This storage account allows only for unstructured data in blobs. This type of storage account allows for two tiers of storage: hot and cool. Hot is data that is accessed more frequently, and cold is data that isn't accessed often, so it costs less to store.

NOTE   For more information about Azure storage accounts, please visit docs.microsoft.com/en-us/azure/storage/common/storage-create-storage-account?toc=%2fazure%2fstorage%2fblobs%2ftoc.json.

Security, availability, and performance are key attributes when you're considering storage. Organizations need to ensure their data is protected and ready to be accessed when and where the demand surfaces. When appraising what the cloud has to offer, this attribute is what will drive decisions on what to use in the cloud.

Let's discuss each of the attributes that Azure Storage addresses.

Security

Azure Storage solutions offer encryption at rest as well as encryption in transit. Encryption in transit is handled in the same way as all calls to the storage service are—via authenticated HTTPS connections. Authentication happens in one of three ways currently: via Azure Active Directory, storage account keys, or shared access signatures. You also can restrict traffic via IP ACLs and service endpoints, which ensures that only traffic from validated IP ranges can access the storage account (using the authentication mechanisms).

NOTE   Azure Active Directory authentication is in preview at the time of writing. Please review the following link for more information: docs.microsoft.com/en-us/azure/storage/common/storage-auth-aad.

Encryption at rest protects data by using 256bit AES encryption. Encryption at rest is turned on by default for the following services:

- Managed Disk
- Blob Storage
- Files
- Queue
- Table

Encryption at rest also can use customer provided keys.

NOTE   For more information on customer-provided keys, visit docs.microsoft.com/en-us/azure/storage/common/storage-service-encryption-customer-managed-keys.

Availability

Azure storage accounts are always replicated to ensure high availability and durability. Currently there are three replication offerings, depending on the type of replication you choose.

- **Locally Redundant Storage (LRS):** Storage is replicated within a scale unit (a collection of storage racks) but confined to a single datacenter region and a single availability zone. Multiple copies of the data exist, which are spanned across the scale unit to ensure tolerance from rack or node failures.
- **Zone Redundant Storage (ZRS):** Storage is replicated synchronously within a single region to three storage clusters. A region is made up of multiple availability zones, and each cluster to which data gets replicated will be in different availability zones.
- **Geo-Redundant Storage (GRS):** Storage is replicated within a scale unit similarly to LRS and then asynchronously replicated to different geographic region hundreds of miles away. The secondary datacenter then undergoes LRS replication. The data is available only in read-only state in the event of disaster when the failover is instantiated by Microsoft. There is a variation on this service called Read-Access GRS that allows for organizations to have a read-only copy of their data available at all times.

Choosing which availability mechanism an organization requires will come down to two considerations:

- The SLA on the business application will dictate a level of availability required.
- The application also will influence what availability mechanism you can use; for example, if you use SQL Server, it's recommended to use LRS and leverage SQL Always-On Availability mechanisms.

> **NOTE** For more information on Storage Availability, please visit docs.microsoft.com/en-us/azure/storage/common/storage-redundancy?toc=%2fazure%2fstorage%2fqueues%2ftoc.json.

Performance

Organizations are used to understanding how to optimize on-premises storage to gain the performance targets their applications demand. Azure storage, like networking, is a cloud-scale shared system; like networking, it has quotas and limits applied. You need to understand these limits and quotas before you proceed with any architecture in Azure.

> **NOTE** Storage limits (as with all limits in Azure) are constantly changing as the platform evolves. It is best to visit the following link to review the latest limits:
>
> docs.microsoft.com/en-us/azure/storage/common/storage-scalability-targets?toc=%2fazure%2fstorage%2fqueues%2ftoc.json.

The limits will give the max IOPS an account can perform at and each individual service performance characteristics. If you're going to use Azure Storage Services, ensure that your application requirements do not exceed the platform limits.

Azure VMs and Managed Disks, in terms of performance, are an exception. We discuss this in more detail in the "Compute" section of this chapter. Note that Azure VMs are no longer recommended to be deployed onto unmanaged storage accounts.

Additional Azure storage services

There are many additional storage services in Azure for building global file systems, big data storage, long-term archiving/immutable storage, network file systems, queues, and so on. Each of them has individual architecture patterns and guidelines that need to be reviewed in detail. The link https://docs.microsoft.com/en-us/azure/storage/ is the root page for Azure Storage and includes best practices and descriptions of all services which can be implemented.

Compute

Compute in Azure covers a variety of topics. We briefly cover each area of Azure Compute, but because migrating existing workloads to Azure is the primary focus of most organizations, we discuss that aspect in more depth.

Virtual machines

Virtual machines serve a multitude of purposes, from hosting applications that are legacy or traditional monolithic architecture to running large scale financial systems like SAP. Whatever your requirements, Azure provides various SKUs of virtual machines to meet your needs.

Table 3-1 shows the available SKU types as of March 2019. Utilize the links in the table to view further information about each SKU type.

TABLE 3-1 Virtual Machine SKU types

TYPE	SIZES	DESCRIPTION
General purpose	B, Dsv3, Dv3, DSv2, Dv2, Av2, DC	Balanced CPU-to-memory ratio. Ideal for testing and development, small to medium databases, and low to medium traffic web servers.
Compute optimized	Fsv2, Fs, F	High CPU-to-memory ratio. Good for medium traffic web servers, network appliances, batch processes, and application servers.
Memory optimized	Esv3, Ev3, M, GS, G, DSv2, Dv2	High memory-to-CPU ratio. Great for relational database servers, medium to large caches, and in-memory analytics.
Storage optimized	Lsv2, Ls	High disk throughput and IO. Ideal for Big Data, SQL, and NoSQL databases.
GPU	NV, NVv2, NC, NCv2, NCv3, ND, Ndv2 (Preview)	Specialized virtual machines targeted for heavy graphic rendering and video editing, as well as model training and inferencing (ND) with deep learning. Available with single or multiple GPUs.
High performance compute	H	Our fastest and most powerful CPU virtual machines with optional high-throughput network interfaces (RDMA).

Each SKU type defines a size. Table 3-1 also shows the virtual machine size. The size and the selection you make will define the experience in Azure that is possible.

To explain this further, let's choose two virtual machine sizes from two different SKU types and select a series of virtual machine from each. In this case, we are selecting a DSv3 series virtual machine from the general-purpose type and a H series virtual machine from the high-performance compute type.

Table 3-2 and Table 3-3 list the details relating to each size available in a SKU type and series.

TABLE 3-2 General purpose, Dsv3 series sizes

SIZE	VCPU	MEMORY: GB	TEMP STORAGE (SSD) GB	MAX DATA DISKS	MAX CACHED AND TEMP STORAGE THROUGHPUT: IOPS / MBPS (CACHE SIZE IN GB)	MAX UN-CACHED DISK THROUGHPUT: IOPS / MBPS	MAX NICS / EXPECTED NETWORK BANDWIDTH (MBPS)
Standard_ D2s_v3	2	8	16	4	4,000 / 32 (50)	3,200 / 48	2 / 1,000
Standard_ D4s_v3	4	16	32	8	8,000 / 64 (100)	6,400 / 96	2 / 2,000
Standard_ D8s_v3	8	32	64	16	16,000 / 128 (200)	12,800 / 192	4 / 4,000
Standard_ D16s_v3	16	64	128	32	32,000 / 256 (400)	25,600 / 384	8 / 8,000
Standard_ D32s_v3	32	128	256	32	64,000 / 512 (800)	51,200 / 768	8 / 16,000
Standard_ D64s_v3	64	256	512	32	128,000 / 1024 (1600)	80,000 / 1200	8 / 30,000

TABLE 3-3 High-performance compute, H series sizes

SIZE	VCPU	MEMORY: GB	TEMP STORAGE (SSD) GB	MAX DATA DISKS	MAX DISK THROUGHPUT: IOPS	MAX NICS
Standard_H8	8	56	1000	32	32 x 500	2
Standard_H16	16	112	2000	64	64 x 500	4
Standard_H8m	8	112	1000	32	32 x 500	2
Standard_H16m	16	224	2000	64	64 x 500	4
Standard_H16r 1	16	112	2000	64	64 x 500	4
Standard_H16mr 1	16	224	2000	64	64 x 500	4

In both tables, as the sizes change we see a common thread on vCPU and memory. These values are important to understand because traditional on-premises virtualization stacks allow for more granular manipulation of these specific values. In the cloud, the sizes are fixed.

When examining your workloads, a mapping exercise is required to choose the most optimal size for the workload being run on Azure. The second item to consider is the maximum data disk size. This determines whether the virtual machine series that has been selected can meet the storage capacity needs. The next columns to be acutely aware of are IOPS and Throughput.

This is where you need to take special care. Let's look at an example. Say you have a workload that requires 150TB of storage space and 60,000 IOPS. A quick glance at the chart in Table 3-2 shows that to meet that requirement, you need a Standard_D32s_v3 , at least initially. However, since you're limited to 32 disks on this virtual machine and the maximum size of a disk is currently 4TB then 32 x 4TB = 128TB, leaving you short on storage. In Table 3-3, you can see the H series has support for 64 disks, but this series can support only 500 IOPS per disk, which maxes out at 32,000 IOPS. This stage requires careful planning to ensure all requirements are met.

We have quickly described compute SKU types, series, and sizes. When you review all of them, it appears that there is a level of overlap between some. To help distinguish further between them, especially from a performance perspective, an organization can use the Azure Compute Unit (ACU). This describes the responsiveness of a virtual machine under a typical load. Although the ACU isn't in the preceding tables, you can review docs.microsoft.com/en-us/azure/virtual-machines/windows/sizes, which describes the ACU when you click into each SKU type.

Containers

Part of an organization's modernization journey involves evaluating the potential use of containers. Containers allow for rapid deployment and scaling as well as free movement between IT environments. For example, if an application is migrated from a virtual machine on-premises to a container, first the container image is stored in a container registry and then the application container can be deployed to any system running a container engine. From a container perspective, it doesn't matter if it's an unmanaged service that has been built from the ground up or a managed service like Azure Kubernetes Service (AKS).

However, migrating to a container requires some additional considerations. For example, managing an application's state becomes very important. For the most part, containers are stateless immutable entities. They perform the task they were instantiated for, and when they die, all traces of them disappear. Although you can externalize container state, implementing it requires advanced planning.

Another important aspect to consider is how an application scales and more importantly if it was designed to scale out or scale up. Containers are best suited for scaling out, but if the application was not designed for this purpose then migrating to containers may introduce additional problems.

Understanding the identity and security requirements of an application before container migration enables you to correctly implement the supporting platform or identify legacy authentication mechanisms. For example, if an application requires Kerberos authentication but you've selected a managed service like Azure Container Instances as the platform for running the newly migrated application, then problems will occur. However, if you can change the authentication mechanism to support Azure Active Directory or something similar then you can use Azure Container instances.

When migrating an application to a container, there is a tendency to begin talking about microservices and loosely coupled architectures. If the application in question is a website with multiple subsites, then you have a chance at splitting this workload into multiple containers and achieving a microservices-like architecture.

However, we need to ensure that we address two key fundamentals in relation to this: service discovery and networking. Take the concept of a POD in Kubernetes; a POD is the scale unit within which Kubernetes will run a container. A container itself cannot be instantiated on its own because it requires a POD. Of course, there can be multiple containers in a POD if required, but that's not a common approach.

A POD also has a life cycle, including its associated networking. When a POD is instantiated, it receives an IP address, and a port can be exposed to support application communications. But when the POD dies, the IP address returns to the pool. If we instantiate this POD again, we aren't guaranteed to receive the same IP address. If we have an application broken into multiple containers and we are never sure where the application will be, then this obviously creates problems for the application to operate.

Figure 3-15 illustrates what a POD looks like and that a user will access the POD via its IP address.

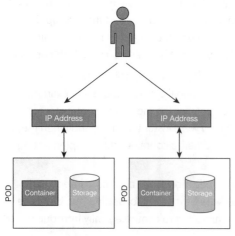

FIGURE 3-15   Kubernetes POD.

We can use services in Kubernetes with POD labels to give us static addressing and port exposure. For example, we know that if the application is broken into three container images, each container image exposes the following ports: 443, 8443, and 9443.

If a service is used, then we can have a service per container image exposing the relevant port and having a static IP address. Given this, each application may be addressed via the service, and the application can function correctly.

A service also can register itself in a DNS server that runs on the Kubernetes Cluster, and then the application can address each service via a DNS name.

Figure 3-16 shows an implementation with a service in Kubernetes and an external load balancer receiving the requests for the web app. Then, depending on which port is being addressed, it routes the request to the specific service, which in turn routes the request to the respective PODs that are responsible for that part of the web app.

Each web app could be coded to support looking for its other components via the DNS name and the port. Traffic routes from each POD through the load balancer into the service, allowing for the application to communicate and operate correctly.

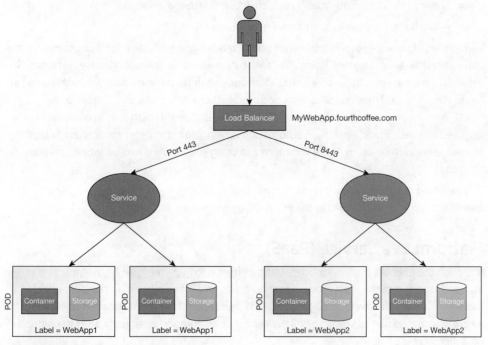

FIGURE 3-16 WebApp on Kubernetes as a service.

Storage and monitoring are other elements that you need to understand. For example, if an application contains state and containers by default are stateless, then it's important that you understand how to externalize state and, more significantly, where the state is stored.

The storage has to be available to all nodes in a cluster because the container could run on any potential node. Monitoring a container ecosystem is a little different than installing an agent on a guest virtual machine and gathering telemetry. In general, for containers we use the orchestrator to provide the monitoring data. A common orchestrator is Kubernetes, which can perform all the tasks we previously described in this section.

Other compute functions

As organizations begin or move further into their modernization journey, other compute functions in Azure start to come into focus. That is not to say that they can't be considered initially, but the more common approach has been to perform a "lift and shift" migration of the existing infrastructure to the cloud before beginning the full modernization and optimization journeys. Either way, this is okay, but here is a list with links to additional information on some of the services you should consider:

- Azure Functions, azure.microsoft.com/en-us/services/functions/
- Azure Web Apps, azure.microsoft.com/en-us/services/app-service/web/
- Service Fabric, azure.microsoft.com/en-us/services/service-fabric/
- Azure Batch, azure.microsoft.com/en-us/services/batch/

You should consider each service when you're modernizing a datacenter. For example, if the application has a web tier, evaluating Azure Web App would be an important step. This way, if the web app is natively deployable or has small code changes it can be deployed and run on an Azure Web App, and modernization has occurred for very little investment. Monitoring, CI/CD, security, and backend integration are all achievable on this platform; in most cases, you just need to check a box. Similarly, if automation is being adopted or an application has lots of small services, then using Azure Functions can bring you forward into adopting serverless compute.

Evaluating the services and the many other features Azure has to offer can quickly and efficiently bring you powerful wins in the modernization journey.

Platform as a Service (PaaS)

Although the ultimate goal in a modernization effort is to implement an IT system that is scalable and stable, uses the most modern technologies, and attempts to maintain cost effectiveness, it is well known that it's a journey. PaaS represents the current state of the end goal, where an organization can leverage all the services available and essentially be at the pinnacle of technology.

This unfortunately is ideological to a degree. Most organizations today have a large suite of applications that aren't easily translated to support this vision. It requires significant investment from vendors and customers to demand the journey and then implement it. The important thing is that everyone understands that the transition is a journey and that changes occur over time with careful planning.

For new applications, you should consider cloud-native (PaaS) or software as a service (SaaS) offerings before considering traditional Infrastructure as a Service (IaaS)–based applications. For existing applications that are being modernized, two key factors determine the ability and pace at which you can modernize them to PaaS:

- **Features:** Many legacy applications are dependent on features and technologies that have a long history—for example, COM objects—but they don't necessarily exist in a PaaS service or a PaaS can't address them. Another example is GUI hooks; some applications inadvertently had dependencies on API call methods that had a dependency on a GUI hook in the operating system. When a switch to PaaS service (which doesn't have these hooks and will never implement them) happens, the application fails. Carefully understanding the feature set available in PaaS Services is critical to success.

  It should be noted that you should challenge the argument for not adopting PaaS service because it doesn't have feature X, especially when you're evaluating an application. Was the feature important in the first place? Can you remove the feature or choose a better way to implement it? That is a small sample of the questions you should ask.

- **Performance:** Performance is important no matter what part of the cloud we talk about. You need to understand the application and its performance characteristics, including how the platform is operating (PaaS service, network, backend storage) and how the code is performing and what it looks like from a user perspective (not the UX but how long it takes to log on, for example). This type of telemetry should be baked into the application from day one, but if it is not currently available on the legacy application, you should endeavor to implement it or implement tooling, which can collect this information rapidly. In the next section, we talk more broadly about systems management and some of the tools in Azure that can help collect this information.

Another aspect of understanding the performance of legacy application is the ability to actually go to PaaS services. If the application is designed in a particular fashion and cannot be easily rearchitected or recoded to use PaaS services in the appropriate way, then it may not be an initial choice for PaaS and have to be implemented on IaaS.

> **NOTE** You also can use the Azure Limits link (https://docs.microsoft.com/en-us/azure/azure-subscription-service-limits) to understand any quota or limits that a PaaS service has that may impact your application.

How these two key factors play will help you to understand the suitability of PaaS. It should be part of the playbook for modernization that the goal is to become as cloud-native as possible. In this light, system/software architectures should be encouraged to come up with logical designs versus product-specific designs.

The logical designs then allow for platform-specific architectures to be drawn up irrespective of where the application will be deployed. For example, I can highlight in my architecture diagram that I need a large data store and a large containers farm.

In terms of an on-premises alternative, this translates to SQL Server Data Warehouses backed by a SAN and a Kubernetes cluster. In Azure, for the first state of modernization, it's a SQL Server Data Warehouse IaaS virtual machine and Azure Kubernetes Service (AKS). Iteration two can use Azure Data Lake and AKS. The idea is to iterate toward a cloud-native architecture.

Systems management

When a modernization journey begins, especially on the cloud, it gives you a chance to challenge the status quo in an environment. It enables you to review your policies, procedures, and technologies that have been implemented over time to determine if they are still relevant and up to the task of what modernization requires. In this section, we look at the main three elements that need to be addressed for most organizations.

Monitoring

Over the past three decades as IT has evolved and become more complex, the need to understand what is happening across the entire IT environment has become paramount. Tooling to understand the environment has evolved as well, with specialist tools being made available by vendors or companies that have created entire businesses out of a promise to give unparalleled visibility into the environment.

If you walk around any IT environment, you will notice the network team has a product that gives them insights, the storage team has a product, and the infrastructure team has multiple products. You could go through most teams and find an array of software that would give visibility into each little ecosystem for which the individual teams are responsible. Often the challenge for organizations is understanding where a problem exists and giving relative visibility to broader teams so they can coordinate troubleshooting activities based on the data.

More importantly, when moving to Azure, you no longer have access to the hardware that runs the infrastructure. If you utilize a PaaS service, then you lose access to the operating system. In the remainder of this section, we discuss the options in Azure for monitoring and what it means for an organization.

INFRASTRUCTURE MONITORING

Azure Monitor is a core monitoring tool in Azure for all resources. It allows organizations to view base-level metrics and logs about most Azure Services. Although there are some services that currently do not report to Azure Monitor, over time this will be remediated as Azure Monitor becomes the unified platform for monitoring in Azure. Azure Monitor will be the central portal to various other platform information, like log information, service health, and alerts.

Figure 3-17 shows a sample metrics dashboard for an Azure virtual machine, with metrics covering CPU, network IO, disk reads bytes/sec, and disk writes bytes/sec. It also shows the menu of available options on the left side, which highlight the key areas for which it will provide insights.

Notice under the Solutions heading that there's access to other tooling. This tooling can provide deeper insights into application operations (app insights), containers, network traffic (network watcher). Additionally provided are management solutions that span best practices and analytic solutions that originated from the solutions gallery, in what was previously known as OMS (and is now Log Analytics).

Azure Monitor also allows for hybrid monitoring. You can use the tooling to provide insights for on-premises infrastructure or alternatively you can deploy the Azure Log Analytics Agent. You can access it from any environment with an outbound Internet connection.

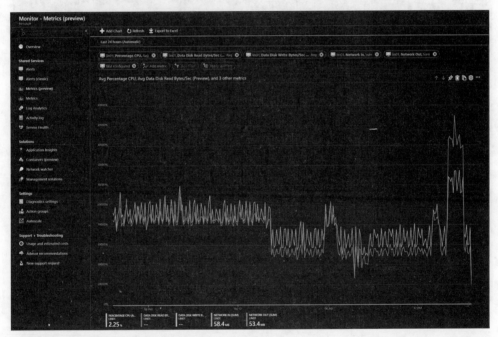

FIGURE 3-17 Sample dashboard for virtual machine metrics.

As important as it is to have insights into an IT environment, it's equally important to get notifications when an event is triggered. Azure Monitor centralizes alerts. This enables you to generate an event query that searches for the data in Log Analytics. If the alert condition is met, it can fire off an alert to the configured party.

Figure 3-18 shows a sample alert for missing updates. The alert is broken into three parts: the condition, the details, and the action group.

The condition defines the query as shown under the search query on the right side. In Figure 3-19, this is a standard log analytics Kusto query. It detects events that have happened within the search time span and frequency. If the condition of a result is greater than 0, an event has occurred, and it triggers an alert.

The alert details allow you to define the additional information about the alert, so it's easier for end users to interpret what has just happened and to set a custom severity based on what the event is.

Finally, the action group allows you to take specific actions and send them to the appropriate team. For example, you can trigger an email to a specific team or you can call an external webhook and include property information so you could log a ticket in a service management system or invoke a runbook for further diagnostics.

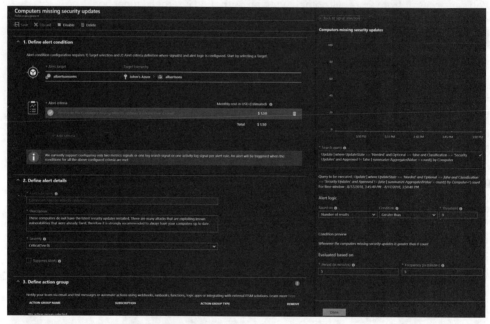

FIGURE 3-18   Sample alert in Azure Monitor.

You can look at metrics and log data for the services in Azure and in any environment if it reports back to Azure Monitor. But what about service health, or resource health in general? The Service Health section in Azure Monitor allows an organization to understand events that affect the Azure platform and that could affect an IT environment deployed in Azure. Additionally, it can give insight into what type of service-impacting event has happened. Figure 3-19 shows a sample screenshot of a virtual machine's resource health.

FIGURE 3-19 Virtual machine resource health.

In Figure 3-19, notice that there are impacting events for the virtual machine. Figure 3-20 shows an expanded alert and the typical information that's displayed to help the customer understand what has happened.

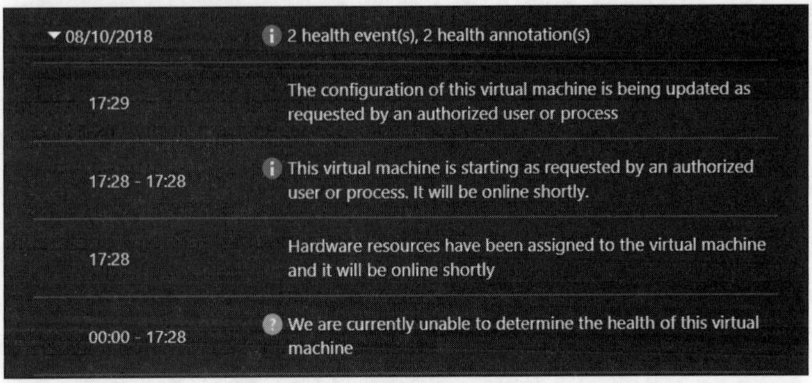

▼ 08/10/2018	ⓘ 2 health event(s), 2 health annotation(s)
17:29	The configuration of this virtual machine is being updated as requested by an authorized user or process
17:28 - 17:28	ⓘ This virtual machine is starting as requested by an authorized user or process. It will be online shortly.
17:28	Hardware resources have been assigned to the virtual machine and it will be online shortly
00:00 - 17:28	❓ We are currently unable to determine the health of this virtual machine

FIGURE 3-20 Virtual machine service-impacting event.

Activity logs in Azure provide insight into the actions that are being performed in a subscription. For example, every time we create a resource in Azure, modify a resource, or perform a typical action that invokes a resource provider in Azure, the activity is registered in the activity log. For example, if a user reads the security keys from a key vault, the action is registered in the activity log. Likewise, if a user resizes a virtual machine, that action is registered.

To understand a little bit more, Table 3-4 shows example actions that can be done from a single resource provider. In this case, we're focusing on a virtual machine in the Microsoft.Compute resource provider.

TABLE 3-4 Sample list of actions for a virtual machine in Microsoft.Compute Resource Provider

TYPE	RESOURCE TYPE AFFECTED	ACTION DESCRIPTION
Action	Microsoft.Compute/virtualMachines/capture/action	Captures the virtual machine by copying virtual hard disks and generates a template that can be used to create similar virtual machines.
Action	Microsoft.Compute/virtualMachines/convertToManagedDisks/action	Converts the blob-based disks of the virtual machine to managed disks.
Action	Microsoft.Compute/virtualMachines/deallocate/action	Powers off the virtual machine and releases the compute resources.
Action	Microsoft.Compute/virtualMachines/delete	Deletes the virtual machine.
Action	Microsoft.Compute/virtualMachines/extensions/delete	Deletes the virtual machine extension.
Action	Microsoft.Compute/virtualMachines/extensions/read	Gets the properties of a virtual machine extension.
Action	Microsoft.Compute/virtualMachines/extensions/write	Creates a new virtual machine extension or updates an existing one.
Action	Microsoft.Compute/virtualMachines/generalize/action	Sets the virtual machine state to Generalized and prepares the virtual machine for capture.
Action	Microsoft.Compute/virtualMachines/instanceView/read	Gets the detailed runtime status of the virtual machine and its resources.
DataAction	Microsoft.Compute/virtualMachines/login/action	Log in to a virtual machine as a regular user.
DataAction	Microsoft.Compute/virtualMachines/loginAsAdmin/action	Log in to a virtual machine with Windows administrator or Linux root user privileges.
Action	Microsoft.Compute/virtualMachines/performMaintenance/action	Performs Maintenance Operation on the VM.
Action	Microsoft.Compute/virtualMachines/powerOff/action	Powers off the virtual machine. Note that the virtual machine will continue to be billed.
Action	Microsoft.Compute/virtualMachines/providers/Microsoft.Insights/metricDefinitions/read	Reads Virtual Machine Metric Definitions.
Action	Microsoft.Compute/virtualMachines/read	Gets the properties of a virtual machine.
Action	Microsoft.Compute/virtualMachines/redeploy/action	Redeploys a virtual machine.
Action	Microsoft.Compute/virtualMachines/reimage/action	Reimages a virtual machine that's using a differencing disk.
Action	Microsoft.Compute/virtualMachines/restart/action	Restarts the virtual machine.

TYPE	RESOURCE TYPE AFFECTED	ACTION DESCRIPTION
Action	Microsoft.Compute/virtualMachines/runCommand/action	Executes a predefined script on the virtual machine.
Action	Microsoft.Compute/virtualMachines/start/action	Starts the virtual machine.
Action	Microsoft.Compute/virtualMachines/vmSizes/read	Lists available sizes the virtual machine can be updated to.
Action	Microsoft.Compute/virtualMachines/write	Creates a new virtual machine or updates an existing virtual machine.

> **NOTE** For a complete list of operations for all resource providers, please visit docs.microsoft.com/en-us/azure/role-based-access-control/resource-provider-operations.

Figure 3-21 shows the activity log for a subscription filtered on the Microsoft.Compute provider and the actions that have been registered.

FIGURE 3-21 Activity Log filtered on virtual machine.

If we click an event and dive further in, we can provide correlation to the event and show the JSON that the platform processes as shown in Figure 3-22.

```
Query returned 61 items. Click here to download all the items as csv
OPERATION NAME                                    STATUS     TIME     TIME STAMP    SUBSCRIPTION                      EVENT INITIATED BY
  ⓘ Delete Virtual Machine                        Succeeded  2 d ago  Wed Aug 15 ...  John's Azure                    johm@microsoft.com
  ⓘ Create or Update Virtual Machine              Succeeded  2 d ago  Wed Aug 15 ...  John's Azure                    johm@microsoft.com
  ⓘ Write Tasks                                   Succeeded  3 d ago  Tue Aug 14 2...  John's Azure
  ⓘ Create or Update Virtual Machine Extension    Succeeded  3 d ago  Tue Aug 14 2...  John's Azure                    Windows Azure Security Res...
Delete Virtual Machine                                                                                                                    ⌄
+ Add activity log alert
Summary   JSON
  1  {
  2    "authorization": {
  3      "action": "Microsoft.Compute/virtualMachines/delete",
  4      "scope": "/subscriptions/b15002ab-6615-4dae-8e2f-2b8d1a41cfc0/resourceGroups/IntroToServer2019/providers/Microsoft.Compute/virtualMachines/Demo01"
  5    },
  6    "caller": "johm@microsoft.com",
  7    "channels": "Operation",
```

FIGURE 3-22 Operation and associated JSON.

The final part we will look at in this section for infrastructure monitoring is the cornerstone of the previous items we have talked about: Log Analytics. Log Analytics could have books written about just that one subject, so we just skim the surface here. In short, Log Analytics allows us to centrally aggregate all the data in Azure and any other environment from which we want to include data. This data can then be analyzed using either solutions or log analytic queries that an organization generates.

Microsoft produces solutions that layer on top of the Log Analytics data. The solutions have analytic patterns, dashboards, and prebuilt queries that target elements of interest. For example, the SQL Server Analytic solution targets performance and configuration items in relation to SQL and provides best practice information if SQL Server is not optimally configured.

Figure 3-23 shows a sample dashboard from a Log Analytics workspace. It displays the base information in relation to the solutions that have been deployed.

FIGURE 3-23 Sample Log Analytics dashboard with solutions deployed.

Figure 3-24 shows a deeper view into the Azure Network Security Group Analytics dashboard. This gives an example of the dashboards available and the analytics that can be provided by a solution.

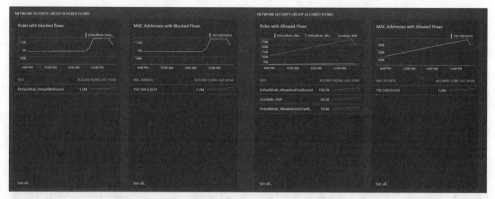

FIGURE 3-24 Deeper view of Azure Network Security Group Analytics.

Application Insights is another tool in the arsenal of Azure Monitor. It can provide granular insights into the operations of an application. Figure 3-25 shows a sample dashboard for an Azure function application. It shows the number of failed requests, the server response time, the server requests, and the availability.

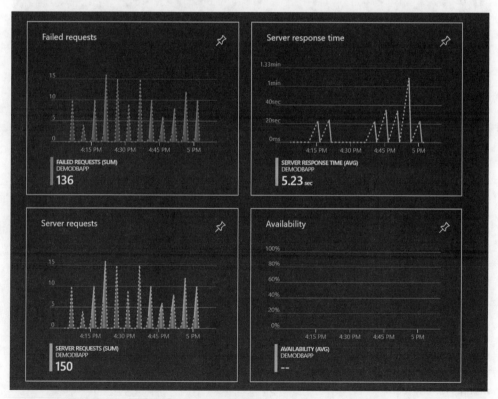

FIGURE 3-25 Sample App Insights Overview dashboard.

Application Insights can provide deep application insights into many aspects of the application both on premises and in Azure. Figure 3-26 shows a deeper drill down dashboard to show further examination.

FIGURE 3-26   Sample App Insights Drill Down Dashboard.

All of the functionality in Application Insights is achieved with an instrumentation key that developers can use to natively build customer telemetry and inject it into Application Insights.

All these monitoring tools are available for organizations to use in their journey to modernization. What makes these tools attractive is that they are cloud monitoring tools that move at cloud cadence. This means you don't need any additional infrastructure or complicated setups; the tools are always ready to monitor the latest releases and provide insights for any team.

NOTE Azure Monitor is an ever-changing service that constantly adds new features. Use the following link to gain access to the latest information available: docs.microsoft. com/en-us/azure/monitoring-and-diagnostics/monitoring-overview-azure-monitor.

Backup

When modernizing an environment and migrating to the cloud, you need to understand how the service level agreements (SLAs) you have made to the business are affected. When the applications are on premises, investments in infrastructure have been made to provide for backup capacity, retention, Recovery Point Objective (RPO), and Recovery Time Objectives (RTO). The infrastructure purchased matches the SLA that was agreed upon.

When migrating infrastructure to the cloud, the backup paradigm changes. The tooling that the organization invested in for the on-premises infrastructure may not be suitable for infra- structure running in the cloud. If you remember the shared responsibility model, in IaaS, PaaS, and SaaS the level of access an organization has to the base infrastructure diminishes, meaning traditional tooling that took virtual machine–level backups with the host hypervisor no longer works, for example.

You need to scrutinize every tool in systems management to ensure it can function in a cloud service and still meet the SLA.

Azure is acutely aware of this challenge and has introduced Azure Backup to assist. Azure Backup is a backup as a service platform that can take image-level backups of a virtual machine. Azure Backup also has a component that can be installed as a server (Azure Backup Server) and perform guest-level backups that can be used to perform application-consistent backups of applications like SQL or Exchange.

Azure Backup natively integrates into the Azure platform and has SLAs of its own in terms of service availability and backup retention. This frees organizations from having to manage another systems management estate just for backup.

When it comes to the wider Azure services, some will have native capabilities for backup built in to the service. Azure SQL is an example of one of these services. For other services it can vary. For example, if a service is deployed from the CI/CD pipeline then using the capabilities for version control in the source control system would be a better option.

For other items like software load balancers or application gateways, you could use and store in source control Azure Resource Manager templates that describe the resource and the rules.

Disaster recovery

When considering disaster recovery in relation to Azure, once again you need first to consider what resources are being consumed.

For example, if you're consuming PaaS services like Azure HDInsight then the first thing you need to understand is how the service stores data. In some cases, the data is coupled into the service, processed, and then injected to a data store. In other cases the data always stays outside the service and it reaches out to the storage account.

Azure HDInsight stores data in a storage account. In this case, to achieve disaster recovery you would need to use geo-redundant storage, so the data is replicated. Then you can spin up a new Azure HDInsight cluster in the disaster recovery region to access the data and continue processing.

In another example it changes again. If the application is IaaS-based and uses Microsoft SQL Server, the argument could be made that you should use native application technology like SQL Always-On with asynchronous commits to replicate the SQL data across regions. You also could use Azure Site Recovery to replicate the application tier virtual machines.

You can use Azure Site Recovery to replicate from on premises (physical, VMware, or Hyper-V) to Azure or Azure to Azure. Be aware that the physical infrastructure also can mean another cloud provider!

Like backup, the SLA for the resources that you've deployed in Azure may need to be adjusted to match the technology in use. A simple example with Azure Site Recovery is staying within the data churn limit that Azure site recovery allows and that your bandwidth can transfer! If you can't replicate your changes due to higher-than-calculated churn and insufficient bandwidth, you won't be able to meet the original SLAs.

> **NOTE** Microsoft has published guidance on building resiliency for the cloud. You can find the information at docs.microsoft.com/en-us/azure/architecture/resiliency/.

Azure Stack

Azure Stack lets you build, deploy, and operate hybrid cloud applications consistently across Azure and Azure Stack. Azure Stack is available as an integrated software and validated hardware platform from vendors like Cisco, Dell, HP, IBM, and others. Azure Stack also has a development kit available to give organizations a feel for Azure Stack and its capabilities.

When a customer purchases Azure Stack, there's an extensive planning phase that happens in conjunction with the implementation partner. This is a detailed process that's beyond the scope of this book. However, we discuss the scenarios that Azure Stack can execute on. First let's show you a list of the current services that can run on Azure Stack:

- Azure IaaS services
- Azure virtual machines
- Azure virtual machine scale sets
- Azure Storage (blobs, tables, queues)
- Azure networking (virtual networks, load balancer, VPN gateway)
- Azure Key Vault

- Azure PaaS services

- Azure App Service (web apps, API apps)

- Azure Functions

- Standalone Azure Service Fabric clusters on IaaS VMs

- Azure Container Service (ACS) Engine

- MySQL RP

- SQL Server RP

As you can see from the services available and as more services will be introduced, it positions Azure Stack as a perfect target for intelligent edge. However, the interesting twist on this is that Azure Stack also can act as the intelligent cloud for an intelligent edge.

In the Intelligent Edge scenario, Azure Stack can be the aggregation and filtration point for various data collection services running across containers, virtual machines, functions, and so on. It can then use the same technologies to intelligently process data and send it to Azure for further processing. Figure 3-27 shows a simple Intelligent Edge scenario with Azure Stack.

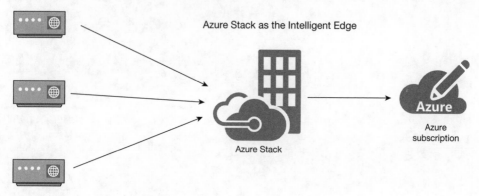

FIGURE 3-27 Azure Stack as intelligent edge scenario.

IoT Hub support in Azure Stack allows it to become an ingestion point for intelligent cloud. It will be giving Azure Stack the potential to receive traffic streams from distributed Intelligent Edges and process them. It's possible for Azure Stack to be running AI deployments on virtual machine scenarios and translate it from being an intelligent edge to an intelligent cloud.

Fourth Coffee and Azure

We have discussed a lot about Azure in this chapter, but what does it mean for our example organization, Fourth Coffee? Throughout this book, we have highlighted different elements of Azure that Fourth Coffee can use and discussed how the organization can evolve to support the new technology and processes required to transition to the modern datacenter. We recommend you explore the "Modernizing IT," "Application Migration," and "Delivering Datacenter Efficiency" chapters to get a full picture of the potential changes Fourth Coffee will go through on its Azure journey.

Chapter 4

Upping your security game

As IT systems become mission-critical elements of running your business, you need to take several steps back and look at your security fundamentals. Security is no longer something you can pay lip service to or put light controls in place to satisfy. A failure in security can translate into a business interruption or the disclosure of sensitive information, which is unacceptable. Security requires planning, implementation, and verification with absolutely no shortcuts. When approaching modernization, it is critical that you understand the potential new avenues that your organization may have to travel, so that you can invest in ensuring that you're protected every step of the way. This chapter discusses what security should mean to you and ultimately how you should up your security game.

The world has gone crazy; protect yourself!

Security is a difficult topic to write about. There's a large amount of ideology in the world about achieving an impenetrable IT system, but anyone who has been involved in IT and has a degree of common sense understands that it is impossible. The balance of trying to achieve a fully secure system while it remains usable remains a never-ending challenge for IT administrators.

So, to write about security we need to make a few things very clear. The first is that no system on the planet is 100% secure, and that's okay. Second, your IT system is only as secure as its weakest link. This means that you can invest in state-of-the-art physical, network, and server security, but a clever social engineer can persuade someone to share their credentials and then bypass the security systems. Notice we mention social engineering and not a mistake like writing the password on the sticky note; having state-of-the-art security involves something like two-factor authentication or smart cards, and a person would have to use the techniques of social engineering to obtain these required items.

Investing in technology is one link, process is the second, and people are the third. In a large number of cases, you will find that a breach occurs because of a lack of understanding. A simple case would be storing company data on an unencrypted USB drive. The person sees no harm in using the unencrypted drive because he just wants to work on the file, and his logic focuses around having no laptop from work, so he plans to catch up in the evening from his home machine. The machine at home, as you can guess, is not secured by the organization's IT system, and the person has been very lazy about antivirus and firewalls. He takes a document home to edit on his home machine. The document gets infected, and he brings the virus back into work.

The IT organization has decided that USB drives are safe because they've educated their staff. Unfortunately this user was sick on the day of the in-person education, and he didn't receive any follow-up training. The user plugs in at work and spins up his document. If he's lucky, his work machine catches the threat. However, if on-access scanning is turned because users' machines have grinded to a halt, then the problem has just become much bigger.

At each step the threat becomes more serious. Now the work machine is infected and connected to the network, and we could imagine a hundred different scenarios that may occur from here. So, what happened? It's simple; the organization modified processes to suit user experience instead of investing in better technology, and no verification was in place. The verification would have caught the modified processes, the uneducated users, and anything else that could happen in the chain of events that we've described.

Here's another example that involves phishing, which is commonplace today. Figure 4-1 shows a pretty obvious example of a phishing email.

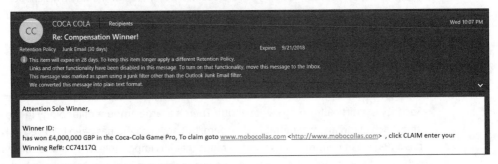

FIGURE 4-1   Phishing email example 1.

While we think getting a wire remittance for money (we weren't expecting) is incredible, it's highly unlikely that this type of notification would arrive via email. Most phishing emails require a mere 30 seconds of objective examination for you to realize that you're looking at a hoax, although phishing emails are becoming more and more sophisticated and require a little more thought.

Figure 4-2 shows a sample email received from "Apple" saying the user's logon has had suspicious activity. The subject of the email would easily grab any Apple user's. However, as we mentioned earlier, taking a moment to read the email carefully will help you see the garbled text.

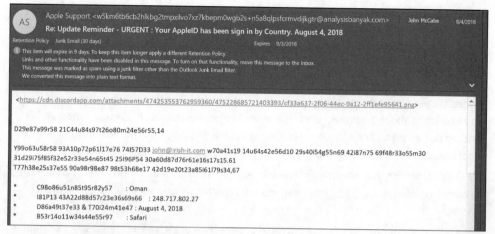

D29e87a99r58 21C44u84s97t26o80m24e56r55,14

Y99o63u58r58 93A10p72p61l17e76 74I57D33 john@irish-it.com w70a41s19 14u64s42e56d10 29s40i54g55n69 42i87n75 69f48r33o55m30 31d29i75f85f32e52r33e54n65t45 25l96P54 30a60d87d76r61e16s17s15.61 T77h38e25s37e55 90a98r98e87 98t53h68e17 42d19e20t23a85i61l79s34,67

* C98o86u51n85t95r82y57 : Oman
* I81P13 43A22d88d57r23e36s69s66 : 248.717.802.27
* D86a49t37e33 & T70i24m41e47 : August 4, 2018
* B53r14o11w34s44e55r97 : Safari

FIGURE 4-2 Phishing email example 2.

Figure 4-3 shows our final example (which comes from www.phishing.org). It shows a phishing email that appears to come from PayPal, and the standard of the email is quite high. It looks professional and has no spelling or grammatical errors. It's only when you hover over one of the links and see that the address is a random website that doesn't match any of the PayPal brands or domains that you understand this is a phishing email. It is these emails we need to strive to protect against through technology, process, and education with verification on each pillar.

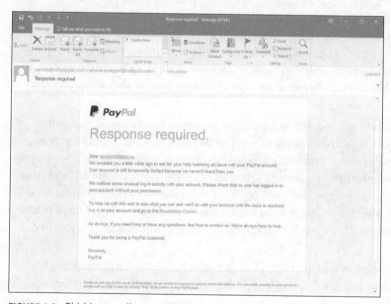

FIGURE 4-3 Phishing email example 3.

We've shown you examples of generic spray-and-pray attacks, but there are many examples of very precise phishing attacks. Attackers monitor sources like blogs, tweets, social networking, and professional networking sites like LinkedIn to gather detailed information about an employee, their organization, their projects, their peers, and so on. The attacker then uses this information to create a very precise attack on a targeted individual. The attacker may acquire a public email address in the name of the person's boss or peer (for example, Tom.Jones13@contoso.com) and send a message about the project the target is working with an urgent request to review an enclosed document and give feedback to the person the message is supposedly from. When the target opens document, which triggers the macros to be enabled, the attacker has won.

Here's something you need to understand: A phishing attack can be thwarted, but a phishing campaign *always* succeeds. You need to plan accordingly and adopt an "assume breach" mindset.

We talked about phishing as one potential avenue for a breach and offered some examples, but there are other approaches. Another practical example involves *tooling*. Consider useful utilities like atomic clock sync applications, or IP scanning tools. Take a system administrator who has for many years downloaded and installed several small utilities that have made her job easier for managing servers. She goes on the Internet, searches for the tool, clicks Download, and installs it. She hasn't checked out anything about the tool because she has used it for years and never had a previous problem. Some of the tools she uses have been compromised, though, or the search results are being influenced to guide people to a rogue download site. The administrator downloads the tools as usual, installs them, ignores the trust messages or that information the installer is not digitally signed, and unwittingly installs malware on the server. The malware proceeds to set itself up as a privileged account and begins infecting other servers. The system has been compromised; and if they are lucky, the IT department detects it quickly. In an unlucky situation, the malware lies in wait until one it does something like encrypting the drive and holding the customer for ransom, deleting all the data, or silently stealing data. Once again technology, process, people, and verification across all pillars will help mitigate this type of situation.

With both the phishing and the utilities installation examples, if the organization had addressed the technology needs, there might not have been the need for the utilities or a reason to turn off on-demand access antivirus scanning. When a process is in place, employees know that installing software from untrusted sources is not allowed and using USB drives that aren't encrypted or company approved is not permissible. Finally, when employees are educated about security, they're better able to be more aware. Verification across all three pillars ensures that any weak spots are identified so additional barriers for protecting IT systems can be put in place.

We've shared some simple examples, but you can begin to imagine the complexity of attacks that are available and see how a lack of proper controls, no matter what the environment, you can get compromised unless you up your security game.

Fourth Coffee: What have they got to lose?

At first glance, you might brush over the security needs of a coffee company. Many people probably think of it as coffee beans + grinding + water = the beverage I order, receive, and consume. What would Fourth Coffee need to secure? However, let's look at the business and IT estate to find potential security traps.

Fourth Coffee's business primarily is a coffee beverage business, although the company also sells other beverages like tea, juices, and water and food items ranging from sandwiches to baked goods. This tells us a variety of things about the company; it has suppliers, stock systems, financial systems, marketing functions, and point of sale (POS) systems. And Fourth Coffee almost certainly accepts credit cards.

Let's start with the suppliers. Fourth Coffee has grown a reputation of having a high-grade coffee blend that has a unique flavor. This unique flavor blend is a closely guarded secret, and Fourth Coffee takes significant efforts to protect the identity of its suppliers and the recipe. There are two potential threat vectors here: the supplier and the internal system. If a supplier gets compromised and an attacker learns the types of coffee beans Fourth Coffee buys, a competitor could also buy those coffee beans and potentially damage Fourth Coffee's edge in the marketplace. The next issue is the manufacturing process that results in the coffee blend. The internal system that controls the process includes the recipe for the blend and roasting time for the beans. If this internal system is compromised (or someone simply takes a photo of the recipe on a cell phone), then Fourth Coffee could again lose its edge. The second threat vector is more complicated to exploit, but the first is easier; given there is a limited number of coffee bean suppliers in the world, they could narrow in rapidly on the internal IT system.

If Fourth Coffee's systems were compromised, an attacker could retrieve the data from supplier invoices, which could be housed in the stock system or the financial systems. These systems could also provide valuable data regarding how Fourth Coffee is performing as a business, how much profit it's making on a product, or how much rent it's paying on a location. All this information could be used to influence nearby competitor's promotions to affect Fourth Coffees business.

Marketing functions might not seem like a point of exposure. However, what if marketing material detailing the next six months of promotions were leaked to a competitor? Fourth Coffee's revenue potential could be affected because the competitors could simply offer a better deal. Also, what if the marketing material leaks sensitive information about the product or potential future products? This would also lead to negative effect. The leaks for marketing material can be something as simple as emailing a PowerPoint presentation to a wrong email address or a poster being leaked by the printer.

Finally, for this set of examples, the retail store could be used as a gateway. For example, if the network team misconfigured the guest Wi-Fi so that the POS system and the guest network are on the same network. This could leak all types of data from sales information to credit cards. If the POS system gets compromised in different ways, all the described data types become exposed.

Even without modernization, Fourth Coffee has a lot to potentially lose. In the remainder of this chapter, we talk about a few different topics that help organizations transform their mind-sets about security. Then we walk through some of the technologies that you can use to begin securing your systems before or after you begin the overall modernization effort.

Assume breach

"Assume breach" is a simple concept, but it's an idea that's different from traditional models of IT security. It puts forward the basic premise that every single endpoint in an environment is already compromised in some shape or form. Pretty simple, right? Well, now apply a security strategy to this, and you begin to understand that it is far from simple. As we mentioned earlier, it's impossible to ensure everything is secure all the time.

All software and hardware have potential vulnerabilities, and it takes only takes a single hacker to understand the vulnerabilities at hand to write an exploit that takes advantage of the vulnerability. If the vulnerability has never been found before then it stands to reason that the systems that generally protect against vulnerabilities will not be aware of them and will simply be unable to protect you. The question you are left with is how to defend against all the potential attacks, from well-known attack vectors to zero-day vectors.

With all this in mind, the assume breach paradigm starts to focus the mindset of ensuring that correct decisions are being made during budget meetings for security investments, architecting the network and IT systems securely, and securing the software being developed to run the business.

Security development life cycle

In today's environments, we often see investments made with a "prevent breach" mindset, which focuses on implementing a security development life cycle (SDL). Figure 4-4 outlines the phases of an SDL and key areas to be addressed per phase.

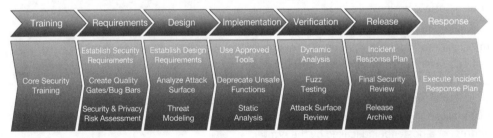

FIGURE 4-4   SDL phases.

Let's dive into each phase to examine how SDL focuses on ensuring that everything is documented, understood, and reinforced, from the person designing and developing code right through to incident response.

NOTE   For more information regarding all the phases we are going to discuss, see www.microsoft.com/en-us/SDL/process/training.aspx.

Phase 1: Training

The first phase is a pre-requisite to beginning a full implementation of SDL, and it involves the education required to ensure everyone in the process of designing, building, and releasing software understands the principles in the SDL. This training becomes mandatory and is executed frequently so that if practices have changed or new threats have been discovered, everyone involved in the process can be aware and implement mitigations sooner.

Phase 2: Requirements

In the requirements phase, you want to establish the baselines for security and privacy. This helps guide the planning and milestones in the further phases. To ensure that these baselines are met, you need to think about and implement two things: threat models and a quality bar. The threat model looks at aspects of the actual practice of coding insecure software and how you can improve it by looking at potential threat vectors. The quality bar ensures that insecure software will not be released to cause potential issues further down the line.

Phase 3: Design

The threat modeling built in the requirements phase plays an important role in this phase as well. As designers are understanding and architecting potential solutions, they apply the threat models to identify all the potential attack surfaces. This can be an iterative approach that is executed until such time that the previously defined quality bar is met.

Phase 4: Implementation

Implementation takes the previous phases and starts looking deeper into the actual code—from ensuring approved tools are being used to develop the software to performing code analysis. The approved software would have undergone the necessary security reviews for the organization to produce secure code. The code analysis would then look at everything from styling to identifying patterns of insecure code within the source code and highlighting prior to compilation.

Phase 5: Verification

Frameworks are great on paper, but you need to ensure that you put controls in place so that what you have defined and are required to meet is verifiable. You need to ensure you have elements like monitoring for security events and abnormalities in terms of user behavior or fuzz testing, where you inject malformed data into applications and see how they respond. You perform verification with a focus on identifying further attack surfaces and then adjusting the threat models so that they adapt and catch threats sooner.

Phase 6: Release

In the release phase, all the outputs previously gathered are scrutinized one last time, and the results are verified to ensure nothing is missed. You also create an incident response plan, or you add it to at this phase. If new threats have been identified or the software being developed opens previously undefined areas, then ensuring that the way to deal with threats and/or breaches is well documented and practiced by the organization.

Phase 7: Response

Practicing the response phase is crucial. The last thing any organization wants is for a breach to occur and then suddenly be unaware of what it needs to do to respond to the incident. Practicing responses to breaches will ensure organizations are ready for these situations regardless of whether they ever occur.

> **NOTE** Microsoft has issued guidelines and tools to help organizations understand and adopt an SDL built from their journey. Please visit www.microsoft.com/en-us/sdl/.

The assume breach mindset adds to the SDL by adding three pillars, which we describe in the following sections.

War games

War games offer an organization a time to perform security exercises on its environment and understand the operational processes and tools in place. These security games deploy two teams: a Red team (Attack) and a Blue team (Defend). The Red team tries to gain access to the system, and the Blue team tries to detect the attack. Both teams produce valuable data that influences the direction the company takes. War games help an organization build better software that's more secure.

Centralized security monitoring

Understanding security in your organization provides visibility into the information being generated. For example, if you don't have full visibility of security logs for Windows in an environment, you may misjudge a failed logon attempt for an administrator. This could in turn lead to a breach and further exposure. If you have centralized monitoring, you could be identifying the failed logon attempt across your Windows environment and respond appropriately.

Live site penetration testing

Live site penetration is the next phase and can be done continuously throughout the life cycle and beyond. New threats are identified every day, and it's important for the security teams to be constantly evolving and testing as they become aware of issues. Live site testing also ensures that when there is not a "game" happening, the controls are still in place and the teams are being effective with implementing and maintaining security policies.

10 Immutable Laws of Security

The Microsoft Security Research Center first published the 10 Immutable Laws of Security in 2000; the laws were updated in 2011. The laws still apply today and help focus the mind on security.

- **Law #1:** If a bad guy can persuade you to run his program on your computer, it's not solely your computer anymore.
- **Law #2:** If a bad guy can alter the operating system on your computer, it's not your computer anymore.
- **Law #3:** If a bad guy has unrestricted physical access to your computer, it's not your computer anymore.
- **Law #4:** If you allow a bad guy to run active content in your website, it's not your website any more.
- **Law #5:** Weak passwords trump strong security.
- **Law #6:** A computer is only as secure as the administrator is trustworthy.
- **Law #7:** Encrypted data is only as secure as its decryption key.
- **Law #8:** An out-of-date antimalware scanner is only marginally better than no scanner at all.
- **Law #9:** Absolute anonymity isn't practically achievable, online or offline.
- **Law #10:** Technology is not a panacea.

Take Law 7, for example; if the decryption key for even military-grade encryption is weak (such as 1234), then obviously the decryption key is an area of exposure. Law 1 applies for software you download from the Internet when you don't fully know the publisher. It could also be applied to phishing emails. Law 6 is interesting because most people believe that their on-premises datacenter is more secure than the cloud. However, a disgruntled administrator will make your security warranty null and void!

For example, If you're using the cloud, there's no physical hardware for administrators to interfere with (such as by plugging in USB keys for booting the server to a different OS), and having no access to the hardware would suggest that the cloud is more secure than your on-premises datacenter. If you have a disgruntled administrator, you have bigger problems, but the example we have just described forces you to look at how security is implemented in your organization, how the laws could apply to your organization, and if you may be weak in areas.

Law 10 reminds you that technology is only one part of the puzzle. People and process are other pieces, and you need to address them equally.

The journey begins on premises

Upping your security does not begin when you decide to modernize. It doesn't begin when you move to the cloud. It begins immediately with your on-premises systems. The previous sections in this chapter that address the mindset of the people and the SDL also apply to your on-premises systems. Once security measures are deployed in an on-premises environment, any modernization journey (or even any migration journey) you take thereafter will be built on top of your strong security principles.

Most organizations have already invested in security in some form. They have firewalls, antivirus protection, intrusion detection devices, and so on. The varying degree of what an organization has implemented depends on the industry of the organization, its size, and the compliance requirements the organization is subjected to, to name a few criteria.

Security is something that no organization can ignore or weakly implement. Also, what major enterprises implement for protection is what small to medium enterprises need to implement as well.

Cost does come into play, and we discuss expense in more detail a little later and show how it is possible for any organization to have affordable world-class security for its environments.

There are plenty of technologies that can help an organization today. For example, Windows Server 2016 and Server 2019 have a plethora of features to help enforce protections and significantly reduce the attack surfaces available in a server deployment. All the features we discuss in the next section are part of the Windows License when you purchase it.

Bear in mind that we're not saying that you should depend only on the technology available in Windows Server, but you should protect your environment using any tool that's available with something you've already purchased. For example, if you use a Windows Server 2016 feature called Device Guard then you can authorize specific applications to run. Device Guard protects against rogue applications that might try to run in your environment. Later in this chapter we talk more about the features in Windows Server and how Fourth Coffee can use them to further its journey in modernization to up its security game.

> **NOTE** For a complete list of all the security features that Windows offers, visit docs.microsoft.com/en-us/windows/security/index.

Security is implemented in layers, a technique that's often called *defense in depth*. This strategy walks the technology stack and ensures that you provide prevention and detection mechanisms to handle and mitigate any type of attack. Although defense in depth isn't infallible, it is one of the best ways to review your implementation to protect against threats. Figure 4-5 shows the layers in relation to defense in depth.

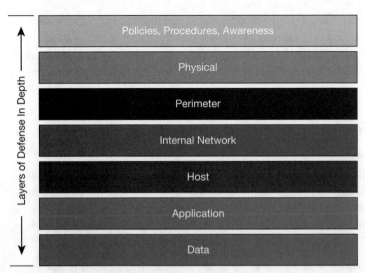

FIGURE 4-5 Layers of defense in depth.

Each layer represents an element you need to protect. The controls you use to protect each layer are up to you, but when you combine all the strategies from all the layers and look at it holistically, you can categorically state that you have addressed defense in depth.

Earlier in this chapter, in the "Fourth Coffee: What have they got to lose?" section, we walked through an example that showed many potential attack surfaces in that organization. If we look in more detail at the infrastructure they have deployed, we find Windows 7 deployed for the desktops and Server 2008 R2 for the systems. Fourth Coffee has a low-end firewall protecting the infrastructure, which also terminates the VPN tunnels from the remote branches. The company uses third-party antivirus protection and patches its systems every six months.

Based on this simple information, you can see Fourth Coffee has layers of security; it uses antivirus protection and has firewalls, and although there's a lengthy period between patch cycles, the company does patch. Although these protections are not sufficient in a modern world, it is a start. If you refer to Figure 4-5, you can see that Fourth Coffee is tackling only part of the defense in depth strategy.

When your security coverage is light, what more can you do? As we said at the start of this section, it begins with your on-premises systems. In the Fourth Coffee example, without doing any upgrades or invoking additional cost, that company could use Windows Firewall to lock down the client and desktop estates, implement User Account Control to mitigate applications requiring administrator privileges from being installed, and implement Windows Defender for antivirus scanning. Fourth Coffee also could implement BitLocker to encrypt its machines and data as well as improve the patch cycle by patching monthly. Now compare this plan to the defense in depth strategy. More layers are covered.

In the next section we cover some modernizations and things that you can do to up your security game. We focus on how you can start on premises, evolve your security, and harness the power of the cloud. The important thing to understand is that it doesn't matter if you have a small organization or a large organization. You can use these techniques and tools regardless of size.

The Fourth Coffee journey: on-premises modernizing and upping the security game

We can break the Fourth Coffee IT systems into three specific parts: the retail stores, the datacenter, and the client base. We break them down like this because each area references different parts of an equation we need to address and solve. Some of our solutions will be specific to one area and others take a more global approach. For example, deciding to upgrade the client base will affect the retail stores and the client base.

To help you understand how to up your security game, we walk through some typical scenarios that Fourth Coffee will encounter and how to solve them.

The Datacenter

Like most organizations, Fourth Coffee has a typical deployment in their datacenter: racks of servers, switches, routers, and firewalls. The company runs Windows Server 2003 up to Windows Server 2012, and its application estate includes mostly traditional .Net monolithic applications running SQL Server as the backend database. Fourth Coffee has invested in virtualization, but it still has a mix of physical machines running parts of its application estate.

In this context, we're gearing our modernization efforts toward IaaS scenarios and/or containers. Later in this chapter we talk more specifically about security and PaaS services.

VIRTUALIZATION TECHNOLOGY REVIEW

One of the first things we need to do is examine Fourth Coffee's virtualization estate and physical estate. Given that the virtualization is from a third-party provider, the first decision is whether to choose to upgrade to the latest version or migrate to a different hypervisor. Fourth Coffee has chosen a Microsoft-centric strategy and has entered into a licensing agreement with Microsoft to ensure that the company can use the latest software and have cross-over benefits when it comes to the cloud. For their future cloud projects, Fourth Coffee has chosen Azure to host its solutions. Knowing this, our conversation is geared toward Windows Server 2016/2019 and the technology contained within.

Windows Server 2016 Hyper-V enables an organization to protect its virtual machine workloads from a variety of attacks. Secure Boot is a feature in Hyper-V for Generation 2 virtual machines that protects from unauthorized firmware modifications, booting different operating systems, or loading UEFI drivers at boot time. To use this feature, organizations must ensure that they use a supported operating system.

NOTE See the following link for ensuring your operating system is supported by Secure Boot: docs.microsoft.com/en-us/windows-server/virtualization/hyper-v/plan/ should-i-create-a-generation-1-or-2-virtual-machine-in-hyper-v.

Next, Fourth Coffee introduced virtual trusted platform module (vTPM) support, allowing a guest virtual machine to encrypt itself using BitLocker. vTPM also supports encrypting the saved state of the virtual machine and encrypting the traffic generated during live migration. Fourth Coffee is implementing Server Core for the hypervisor operating system to reduce the overall footprint. As machines are selected for migration, they'll be brought in line with the supported operating system to be able to use Secure Boot and virtual TPM.

Windows Server 2016 introduces shielded virtual machines. This feature protects a virtual machine from compromised hosts or scenarios in which the storage of the virtual machine has been compromised, or someone has stolen the backup of a virtual machine and attempted to restore it to an unauthorized location. Shielded virtual machines stop the virtual machine from being run on any untrusted hosts. For now, Fourth Coffee has chosen not to implement this feature because it's currently not supported in Azure.

NETWORK TECHNOLOGY STACK REVIEW

Fourth Coffee evaluated using Windows Server 2016 Software Defined Networking to take advantage of features like the distributed firewall for dynamically protecting the network. The work required to change over the current network topology to support SDN, considering that they want to migrate to the cloud, was deemed excessive, so Fourth Coffee won't implement this feature. Instead, the company is implementing a firewall zone for the network traffic coming into the virtualization environment.

MANAGEMENT AND IDENTITY TECHNOLOGY STACK REVIEW

One challenge for Fourth Coffee is its environment, which has a lot of legacy components, and an identity system that's been around for some time. More importantly, the company has had loose security practices, which have led to many users having more privilege than required. Also, there are a lot of privileged accounts that are not in use.

Windows Server 2016 introduced Privileged Identify Management (PIM), which allows an organization to use a known trusted environment for authentication and authorization of privileged accounts. Given that Fourth Coffee isn't completely certain of all the accounts and privileges that exist, implementing a bastion environment like PIM offers would be a viable solution to ensuring that no compromised accounts exist. PIM also enables Fourth Coffee to introduce a concept called Just-In-Time Administration.

In many organizations, system administrators usually have two accounts. One account is the standard user account and the second account is the privileged account. If the user account was compromised, then the administrator could at least be sure that attacker couldn't easily get access to the production systems. However, if a privileged account becomes compromised, a security situation could escalate quite quickly. Just-In-Time Administration enables you to assign access to an account on a system for a specific period. You could technically keep the two accounts and configure Just-In-Time Administration for the privileged account. This is a good start, but you'd need to combine it with another feature in Windows Server 2016 called Just Enough Administration (JEA).

Just Enough Administration restricts the activities a privileged account can perform to the bare minimum necessary to accomplish a task. JIT and JEA complement each other by reducing the need for a privileged account by following the principals of least privilege. It grants the necessary privileges to an account only when they are required and only for a defined period.

Fourth Coffee has chosen to implement JIT and JEA due to uncertainty within its Active Directory. All production workloads will be covered, and the elimination of secondary accounts will begin as workloads are transitioned to the new virtualization environment.

> **NOTE**   For more information on PIM, JIT, and JEA, please see the following links: docs.microsoft.com/en-us/microsoft-identity-manager/pam/privileged-identity-management-for-active-directory-domain-services
> docs.microsoft.com/en-us/powershell/jea/overview.

GUEST OS AND APPLICATIONS TECHNOLOGY STACK REVIEW

Fourth Coffee has made a strategic decision to move directly to Windows Server Hyper-V for its virtualization environment and has chosen to use the long-term servicing channel (LTSC) for the host OS.

The company has decided that upgrade cycles will happen on general availability (GA) of the LTSC branch. For the guest OS, Fourth Coffee will use the Semi-Annual Channel (SAC) as default and only divert to the LTSC channel for application compatibility.

> **NOTE**   For more information about Windows Server releases, please see the following link: docs.microsoft.com/en-us/windows-server/get-started/windows-server-release-info.

By using SAC, Fourth Coffee will ensure that every 6 to 18 months it will upgrade its guest OS to stay in support, which helps make sure the company is moving forward and is using state of the art security features when they become available. As applications move into the new virtualization environment, they will be evaluated and moved to the correct platform. As part of the modernization journey, containers will be considered for applications. Where containers are chosen, they will be implemented in Hyper-V containers to provide hardware-assisted isolation between the runtimes of the containers. This isolates a compromised container and prevents it from affecting the wider system. Figure 4-6 shows a Hyper-V container versus a Windows container.

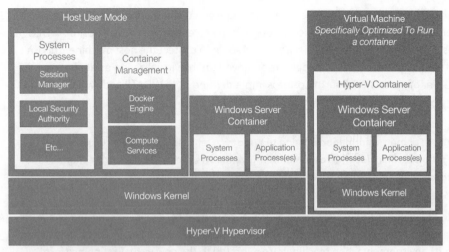

FIGURE 4-6 Hyper-V container versus Windows container.

> **NOTE** For more information relating to Windows containers, please visit
> docs.microsoft.com/en-us/virtualization/windowscontainers/about/.

Fourth Coffee has evaluated Windows Defender and has decided to replace the current third-party antivirus solution. Windows Defender comes enabled on both the LTSC and SAC releases. Windows Defender can be centrally managed via a variety of different tools, including System Center Configuration Manager, Microsoft Intune, Group Policy, PowerShell, and Microsoft Azure.

> **NOTE** For more information about Windows Defender Antivirus, please see the
> following link: docs.microsoft.com/en-us/windows/security/threat-protection/
> windows-defender-antivirus/windows-defender-antivirus-on-windows-server-2016.

Windows Defender Advanced Threat Protection (WDATP) is in the next LTSC release (Windows Server 2019) and in the current SAC release. WDATP provides cloud intelligence against deep platform sensors and provides visibility into memory and kernel level attacks. WDATP also allows us to act against attacks and breaches and collect all the forensic information associated with it. Windows Server 2016 can use WDATP as well, although it does require a separate installer.

> **NOTE** For more information about Windows Defender ATP, please see the following link:
> docs.microsoft.com/en-us/windows/security/threat-protection/windows-defender-
> atp/configure-server-endpoints-windows-defender-advanced-threat-protection.

Windows Defender in the SAC release also introduces a technology called Windows Defender Exploit Guard (WDEG), which is designed to protect against host intrusion. WDEG mitigates attacks from files, scripts, network, and so on to protect the host machine. This isn't reserved for the guest OS either; it could be deployed on the virtualization estate to provide another layer of protection. Fourth Coffee is implementing both WDATP and WDEG during the next major LTSC release cycle (Windows Server 2019).

> **NOTE** For more information relating to Windows Defender Exploit Guard, please see the following link: docs.microsoft.com/en-us/windows/security/threat-protection/windows-defender-exploit-guard/windows-defender-exploit-guard.

Windows Defender Application Control (WDAC) provides the ability to scan and configure a system to allow only authorized applications to run. Fourth Coffee has chosen to implement WDAC in its environment when machines are migrated to the new virtualization platform.

Systems administrators have defined the authorized list of common software per server and have built a golden image from this. Per server, they will update the policy to support the individual application required so they can monitor deviation from the golden image and block any malicious software from executing on the system.

> **NOTE** For more information relating to Windows Defender Application Control, please see the following link: docs.microsoft.com/en-us/windows/security/threat-protection/windows-defender-application-control/windows-defender-application-control.

Windows Defender Credential Guard (WDCG) uses hardware-assisted security to protect the secrets an operating system uses. It stores the secrets in an isolated part of the system to which access is restricted. Traditionally, we would have stored these secrets in LSA (as shown in Figure 4-7), where various elements of the system could access memory or be compromised to access the address space. With WDCG, this is not possible.

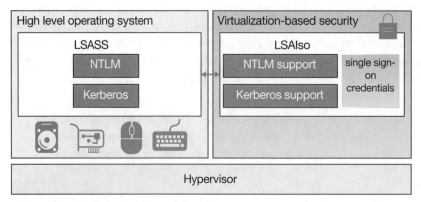

FIGURE 4-7 Windows Defender Credential Guard.

Windows Defender Remote Credential Guard (WDRCG) is an extension of WDCG that protects secrets from being compromised during remote access of a machine. WDRCG only allows Kerberos authentication and prevents NLTM from passing the hash attacks and authentication after a session has disconnected.

> **NOTE** For more information about WDCG, please visit docs.microsoft.com/en-us/windows/security/identity-protection/credential-guard/credential-guard.

Fourth Coffee first will implement all these features on-premises to capitalize on its investment with Microsoft. As the company moves toward either IaaS- or PaaS-based services in Azure, the investments will continue to be worthwhile, and the benefits Fourth Coffee obtains from the agreement—and more importantly, the software—will accelerate the modernization journey. All that we have described with regard to the datacenter can plug into cloud-based software, which gives even the smallest of organizations world-class enterprise protection and peace of mind for operating their business systems.

The client base

The client base in Fourth Coffee is mainly Windows 7. As with the datacenter approach, Fourth Coffee wants to modernize its client base. Windows 10 comes in both LTSC and SAC releases. Windows 10 and Windows Server share a code base, which means that a large amount of the innovations that come in Windows Server also are available in Windows 10.

Given that a threat is more likely to originate from a client than from a server it makes sense for Fourth Coffee to invest in modernizing that estate to gain the security benefits of tools like Windows Defender, BitLocker, Credential Guard, Device Guard, Smart Screen, and so on.

> **NOTE** For more information regarding all the security features in Windows 10, please see the following link: docs.microsoft.com/en-us/windows/security/threat-protection/overview-of-threat-mitigations-in-windows-10.

As clients migrate to Windows 10, the controls are enabled and managed centrally. They cannot be overridden by a client, which helps protect the system. Windows Firewall is enabled by default, which protects clients against inbound connections that in the past have caused havoc for the Fourth Coffee administrators.

As Fourth Coffee upgrades the client base, it begins to unlock other features throughout the Microsoft ecosystem that protect the system. For example, dynamic access control opens a potential avenue for Fourth Coffee to protect its data against unauthorized access. Dynamic access control has been available since Windows Server 2012, but Fourth Coffee didn't have the client base to be able to use it. Even if the company doesn't upgrade to Windows Server LTSC or SAC, with an upgrade to Windows 10 on the client, Fourth Coffee could begin using the technology immediately.

Another aspect Fourth Coffee will implement is using remote desktop farms with its application estate installed. Initially the thought behind this implementation was for disaster recovery, but the IT department concluded that it also will mitigate security events. The applications are centrally hosted in a well-trusted network that requires multifactor authentication for access. The applications run in a secure remote desktop session host, and every part of the experience is locked down and controlled. When cloud migration becomes a necessity, Fourth Coffee can simply migrate the servers to Azure and allow the clients to connect and continue operations.

Given that Fourth Coffee has retail stores, Windows 10 and the remote desktop solution will ensure no sensitive data exists in the retail store. In the event of a compromised (or misconfigured) network, the company won't be at risk of losing data. Similarly, if we modify the POS system to support Windows 10 and use cloud-based payment providers, we automatically use secure connections without exposing the backend payment processors.

Fourth Coffee's journey will bring it to Windows 10. The company will choose the SAC release to ensure the clients always are running the latest operating system and, if necessary, to capitalize on any new security technology. Although it might seem unwise to adopt SAC for server and client, the idea is to force a culture change and drive home to the existing staff (users and system administrators) that IT needs to evolve. Fourth Coffee needs to build a system that's capable of this cyclical evolution.

Cloud—harnessing the power

Fourth Coffee can make a lot of changes before moving a single virtual machine to the cloud. If the company implements the elements we discussed, we can be sure of the integrity of the system when it does move to the cloud.

In this section, we want to go a few steps further and really drive into the statement that any size enterprise can have the same world-class enterprise-grade security. With this in mind, first let's describe a few elements about Azure that are been built into the platform.

Default aspects of the Azure platform

Take a look at Table 4-1. It describes what security features Microsoft has implemented to help secure the Azure Platform.

TABLE 4-1 Azure security investments in the platform

SECURE PLATFORM	PRIVACY & CONTROLS	COMPLIANCE	TRANSPARENCY
Security Development Cycle, Internal audits	Manage your data all the time	Trust Center	How Microsoft secures customer data in Azure services
Mandatory Security training, background checks	Control on data location	Common Controls Hub	How Microsoft manages data location in Azure services
Penetration testing, intrusion detection, DDoS, audits, and logging	Provide data access on your terms	The Cloud Services Due Diligence Checklist	Who in Microsoft can access your data on what terms
State of art datacenter, physical security, Secure Network	Responding to law enforcement	Compliance by service, location and industry	How Microsoft secures customer data in Azure services
Security Incident response, Shared Responsibility	Stringent privacy standards		Review certification for Azure services, Transparency hub

> **NOTE** To dive deeper into each section, please use the following link to access a hyperlinked version of the table, which will bring you to each area and provide in-depth information: docs.microsoft.com/en-us/azure/security/azure-security.

You may have noticed that a large amount of what Azure does is what we suggest you do to run secure systems. Migrating to Azure enables you to capitalize on the journey the Azure platform has already taken.

Take a small business, for example. Running the business on Azure will inherently give the owners access to the steps already taken by the Azure Platform. Although it doesn't cover every base, they can be focused on only the areas that really need attention rather than having to spend time and money on areas that the Azure platform can cover or at least make easier.

Figure 4-8 shows a shared responsibility zone matrix for cloud security. The purpose of showing this before discussing other elements that Azure implements is to remind you that there is always a part the customer must do, and there will be a part that Azure will do. Even when we look at individual services, Azure may provide built-in features and mechanisms, but the customer still must perform some work to ensure the system is secure to the organization's standards. It can be as simple as enabling a security feature or installing an SSL certificate, but it still must be done!

Even when the service is configured, the organization retains responsibility of ensuring it stays securely configured. Azure can't mitigate some rogue administrator opening an insecure port to a service and providing weak credentials to anybody who wants to attack on an open forum.

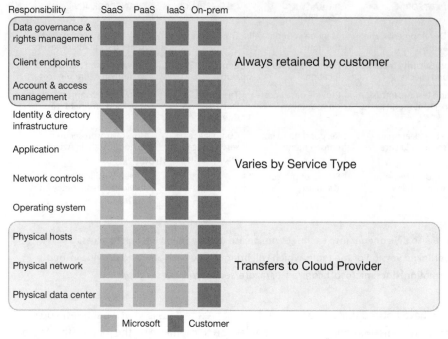

Responsibility Zones

Responsibility	SaaS	PaaS	IaaS	On-prem	
Data governance & rights management					Always retained by customer
Client endpoints					
Account & access management					
Identity & directory infrastructure					Varies by Service Type
Application					
Network controls					
Operating system					
Physical hosts					Transfers to Cloud Provider
Physical network					
Physical data center					

Microsoft   Customer

FIGURE 4-8   Responsibility zones for the customer.

There are two areas we need to highlight to ensure that Azure provides the highest level of integrity and security to our workloads when running on the platform.

Customer data

When customers host their data in Azure, they can rest assured that all data is encrypted at rest. They also can have peace of mind that all data in transit is secure. For example, if a hard drive in Azure Storage or a compute node fails, the disk is encrypted, and it undergoes a certified destruction process because one of Azure's operational procedures is that no hard drive ever leaves a datacenter. Customers also have the choice of implementing additional encryption on some services in Azure. For example, Azure IaaS virtual machines allow you to encrypt the operating system and data disks.

Customers are required to understand where they're hosting their data and whether there are any regulatory requirements for ensuring the data is stored in a sovereign region. Even in the event the customer stores the data in a wrong region, Microsoft will not hand over any data to any authority without prior consent from the customer.

By default, Microsoft engineers don't have access to customer data. They are granted access to data only under management oversight when deemed necessary. All access is logged and controlled. Access follows the Just Enough Administration/Just-In-Time methodology, only so the engineers have the necessary access for the shortest possible time.

Customer isolation

Every customer is isolated in Azure. Initially this is done via the Subscription ID. Most services are bound at the subscription level; as we move forward, this may change to the Tenant/Organization Level. For example, if you create a virtual network in a subscription and another virtual network in a different subscription, they will not be able to communicate with each other. Even in the same subscription, two virtual networks will not be able to communicate without explicit configuration. Azure implements isolation on every part of the platform.

> **NOTE** For detailed descriptions of the isolation provided in Azure, please visit docs.microsoft.com/en-us/azure/security/azure-isolation#introduction.

Additional Azure protections

Azure has a wealth of other elements that protect you. Although we can't explore them all, the following list explains some important ones:

- **DDOS Protection and Mitigation:** Azure provides DDOS protection for all customers in Azure. It implements network devices at the datacenter router to sample traffic, detect patterns, and mitigate accordingly.

- **Filtering Edge Routers/Access Routers:** Azure uses Edge routers and Access routers to provide layers to catch antispoofing techniques. As traffic gets deeper into the Azure network, it restricts further traffic and where it can originate from.

- **Fabric Controller VM Isolation:** The fabric controller in Azure is responsible for your virtual machine placement on a compute cluster. It protects you from a variety of attacks because it blocks all communication unless it comes from the Azure fabric or virtual machines from the same virtual network. It also helps protect against noisy neighbors when choosing to place a virtual machine on a cluster.

Security is fundamentally built into the Azure platform. Running large public estates like Xbox.com or Microsoft.com has taught Microsoft what is necessary to run hyperscale cloud environments and what protections are needed to keep them secure.

Azure has all the knowledge from building and managing these environments baked into it from day one. In fact, the public estates that have migrated to run on top of Azure provide Azure with endless knowledge and help them direct the product development so that any organization that wants to use Azure will also capitalize on the capabilities introduced into the platform by those large public estates.

Microsoft also has embarked on a journey of using artificial intelligence and machine learning to examine all the data it collects, which helps Microsoft make wiser security decisions. The most interesting part of this from a customer standpoint is that after Microsoft has implemented protections or security features as part of the platform, it will refine it and offer it as a service (if not by default as part of the platform). Customers will be able to use the technology to have further protections.

The customer journey to using cloud security

The Azure platform has lots of security technology built in. When you become a customer of the platform, you will naturally inherit the benefits of what has been implemented. However, the customer still is required to do some things. This is where it gets interesting.

Security traditionally has been an expensive investment. When the cost begins to rise, we know most organization begin to trade off and agree on an approach.

With the cloud, you don't have to compromise as much or at all because you can leverage the security in the tools and services that are provided at a much lower cost and use the security you need. Figure 4-9 builds on top of the Shared responsibility model we talked about earlier in this chapter.

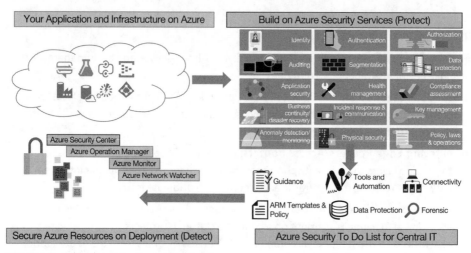

FIGURE 4-9   What the customer can build upon.

The key thing to notice is gearing an organization's application to use the facilities that are provided in the cloud. Let's dive into some of the Azure Security Services and talk about how Fourth Coffee could make use of these technologies to up its security game.

Azure Active Directory

Azure Active Directory is the cornerstone of the identity management solutions. Although it can be an independent authentication platform that uses modern authentication techniques (OAuth2.0, SAML, and so on), it also allows organizations to leverage the work they have created in the on-premises Active Directory to create a unified directory that spans the on-premises system and Azure. This allows for users to maintain a single set of credentials and use them to authenticate to cloud services, including Microsoft 365!

As Fourth Coffee evolves its application estate, it will look at moving away from legacy authentication methods like Kerberos and NTLM to move toward using the authentication providers that Azure Active Directory provides. If Fourth Coffee fully modernizes to SaaS services (third party or Microsoft native) or even creates its own PaaS applications, those SaaS services also can leverage Azure Active Directory.

With the upgrade to Windows Server LTSC and SAC, Fourth Coffee will deploy Windows Administration Center to manage the server estate no matter its location. Coupling this with infrastructure in Azure will push Fourth Coffee to leverage Azure Active Directory to perform authentication services for both Windows Administration Center and Azure with multifactor authentication enabled.

If Fourth Coffee moves forward with its loyalty application, the company can leverage Azure Active Directory to provide authentication services from consumers who use their social accounts (such as Facebook, Google, and Amazon) as credentials. Fourth Coffee won't have to build a complicated authentication and verification system, which speeds up its application development time.

Azure Active Directory also provides Privileged Identity Management Services, which are like what we described for on-premises systems and can be used to provide on-demand access to resources in Azure, Office 365, or Intune. This would help Fourth Coffee by simplifying the accounts that it requires. Also, it would prevent accounts from gaining unnecessary privilege and potentially become a source of a breach.

All the identity capabilities in the platform capture data. This data is fed into machine learning–based tools in the background, which generates reports on what is happening with identity in an organization's environment. The organization can retrieve reports on anomalies, errors, user-specific activities, and all activities that have happened (for example, group changes and password resets). Fourth Coffee can leverage this information to further secure its system and mitigate any potential breaches before they happen, which protects the company from any potential loss of data or revenue. It also protects the company's reputation.

What could Azure Key Vault do?

As Fourth Coffee moves more and more workloads to Azure, it will need a way to securely store secrets, credentials, and certificates. Azure Key Vault provides a cloud-based mechanism to store and generate these artifacts. Azure Key Vault is backed by hardware security modules (HSMs). Microsoft has no access to the information store in a customer's key vault at any time.

Fourth Coffee will implement a mixture of virtual machines that will require encryption and applications that will need to authenticate to each other. Also, Fourth Coffee will implement virtual machine scale sets that will host a web application front end for some of the new systems the company plans to implement.

The virtual machines will contact Azure Key Vault to obtain the encryption key to use for encrypting their disks. The applications will be developed to retrieve the credential information required to authenticate each other, and finally the virtual machine scale sets will retrieve an SSL certificate from the key vault to be able to respond correct to HTTPS traffic and maintain a secure web channel.

What could Azure Activity Log do?

Azure Activity Log records all operations that happen in a subscription. Fourth Coffee can use this per subscription or aggregate the logs into Log Analytics to gain visibility into events that happen on the infrastructure in Azure. For example, the company could use a property on Azure Resources called a Resource Lock. Fourth Coffee could assess the Activity Log, and if a resource lock event is observed, the Activity Log would show what has been done and by whom. Figure 4-10 shows a sample of an Azure Activity Log with a manage lock being deleted.

FIGURE 4-10 Azure Activity Log.

This operation could be linked to a complete ITSM chain, which would alert the operations staff that an unauthorized change may be about to happen. Fourth Coffee also can build lockdown events and implement monitoring and automation to help control this process.

What could Azure Monitor do?

Azure monitor provides a core monitoring service across Azure Services. It collects its data from metrics, activity logs, and diagnostic logs. Fourth Coffee can use this data to examine how a service is performing and then dive deeper into the internals of the service and how it is operating. For example, let us say the company uses Azure VPN Gateway and sees a large amount of failed IPsec tunnels. Azure Monitor gives a quick and easy way to configure the diagnostic and metric settings of most services but also provides the ability to configure a service to send its data to log analytics for deeper analysis.

What could Log Analytics do?

Log Analytics provides centralized aggregation of the monitoring data in Azure and any other environment configured to send information. It allows complex search queries to identify patterns of behavior in an environment. For example, you can identify all machines affected by a specific patch or identify the source of an attack from its IP address to the service and server it's attacking. Fourth Coffee will implement log analytics to collect data from its on-premises estate and Azure. The company wants to understand in detail the events that take place across its IT ecosystem. Fourth Coffee will capitalize on the solutions in Log Analytics to provide assessment services on some of its deployments and bring them in line with the recommendations that are found, which will help identify and reduce its overall attack surface.

What could Azure Security Center do?

Another tool in the arsenal to help Fourth Coffee up its security game is Azure Security Center. This tool has access to all the knowledge gathered by Microsoft from its research of online properties. With all the knowledge and data Microsoft has gathered, it uses machine learning and artificial intelligence to identify patterns of events and detect potential threats. Fourth Coffee will implement Azure Security Center to highlight security risks to the overall IT environment.

Figure 4-11 shows a typical dashboard, which Fourth Coffee would review throughout the day for potential security threats to its systems. This will use the Resource Security Hygiene section of the dashboard to ensure that all machines follow the corporate security policy.

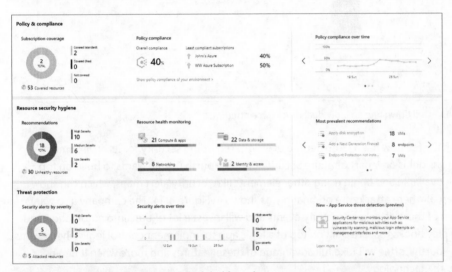

FIGURE 4-11 Azure Security Center typical dashboard.

Fourth Coffee has a suspicion that its competitors are trying to hack its network via brute force attacks. Within a few hours of implementing Azure Security Center, Fourth Coffee has several aggregated security alerts popping up, as shown in Figure 4-12.

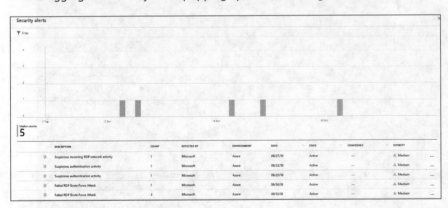

FIGURE 4-12 Security Alerts dashboard.

Using the alerts dashboard, Fourth Coffee system administrators can drill into the attempts and determine which machines are under attack and where the attack originated, as shown Figure 4-13.

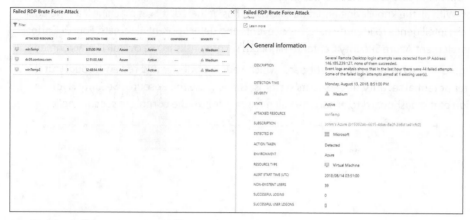

FIGURE 4-13   Drill down into an individual brute force attempt.

Fourth Coffee now has a large degree of insight regarding security for its environment. However, insight is only part of Azure Security Center. Fourth Coffee wants to build on top of what is available and begin using other elements like security alert maps, which can show you a map of where attacks are originating, as shown in Figure 4-14. The company also wants mitigation of these attacks or security events and will invest a lot of time into automation and defining play books that are built on top of a logic app to implement control logic when events happen. Fourth Coffee will take full advantage of these features and more when it begins adopting the technology.

FIGURE 4-14   Security map.

Fourth Coffee also will implement two other features in Azure Security Center. The company will enable adaptive application controls (whitelisting for applications) and just-in-time virtual machine access. This follows what has been implemented on premises, but Fourth Coffee now want to tie into the capabilities of Azure Security Center.

Finally, the company will harness the power of Threat Intelligence, which will give Fourth Coffee the power to identify suspicious processes in its environment or hidden malware and be aware of outgoing attacks—for example, if a legacy host is compromised and acting as a zombie in a denial of service attack.

Network security groups

Network security groups (NSGs) provide a way for Fourth Coffee to filter traffic at either the subnet or NIC level. For example, there could be two subnets that only need to talk to each other on port 1433. NSGs could filter all other traffic entering the subnet and allow only port 1433. Fourth Coffee will be using a combination of NSGs and network virtual appliances (that is, third-party firewall applications) to create the perimeter network required to be secure.

The NSGs also generate flow logs, which will be sent to Log Analytics for analysis using the NSG Flow Logs Analytic Solution. This will provide insight on the traffic attempting to traverse a subnet and what is allowed and blocked.

Application gateway/web application firewall

Fourth Coffee will want to deploy web applications that will be public facing—for example, the loyalty application. The first iteration that Fourth Coffee will attempt will be on virtual machines. The application gateway with web application firewall will allow Fourth Coffee to publish its application securely and provide protection with the OWASP Core Rule Set (CRS)

> **NOTE** You can find the OWASP Core Ruleset information at owasp.org/index.php/ Category:OWASP_ModSecurity_Core_Rule_Set_Project.

Figure 4-15 shows an example of what a web application firewall will mitigate against, for example, attacks like SQL injection attacks or cross-site scripting.

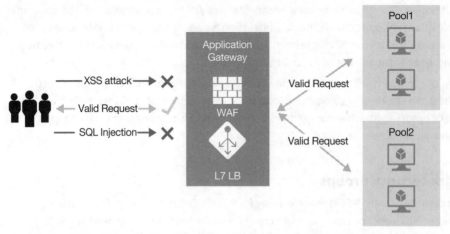

FIGURE 4-15 Web attack mitigation with web application firewall.

SSL Termination is another feature that Fourth Coffee will use as part of this service to perform network captures for the traffic going to the backend servers. The company can choose end-to-end encryption, but the initial scenario is to perform analysis on the traffic stream unencrypted to the backend.

Azure Firewall

Fourth Coffee wants to be as cloud-native as possible and has steered clear of the network virtual appliances. Instead, it has decided to use Azure Firewall. Azure Firewall provides a fully stateful firewall that is highly available and can scale as the business requires it. Figure 4-16 shows the expected placement for Azure Firewall in a network design.

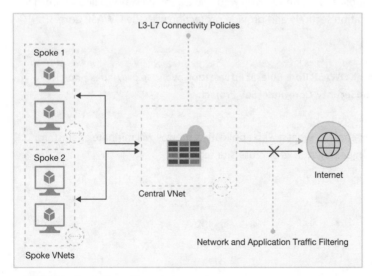

FIGURE 4-16 Azure Firewall.

The firewall gives Fourth Coffee the control needed to enforce network and application connectivity policies across all subscriptions, which negates the need for a third-party firewall.

Anomaly API

Fourth Coffee will generate a large amount of data from a variety of applications. While the company leverages a large amount of Azure services and the native capabilities to identify the security threats to the environment, it wants to investigate how it can identify potential threats in its applications.

In the future, as the application estate begins to develop, Fourth Coffee will use the Anomaly API service in Azure to assist in identifying patterns in the data the company sends.

For example, the company may use the Anomaly API to identify customer trends or to sample the telemetry data collected from the coffee machines to detect behavior patterns that aren't normal to its operation, which would preempt a failure. There are a bunch of other scenarios in which Anomaly API could be used for including security events in Fourth Coffee's applications.

Web application vulnerability scanning

Fourth Coffee expects to have several web applications. Although the initial plan is to host the apps on virtual machines, the end goal is to move them to Azure App Service. The Azure Web Application Firewall will help mitigate external attacks. It also can be enabled for internal attacks. However, if Fourth Coffee needs to understand what other potential vulnerabilities exist in the web apps, then it needs to be performing vulnerability scanning. Azure Security Center can integrate with Qualys to perform vulnerability scans for virtual machines and display the results in Security Center, as shown in Figure 4-17.

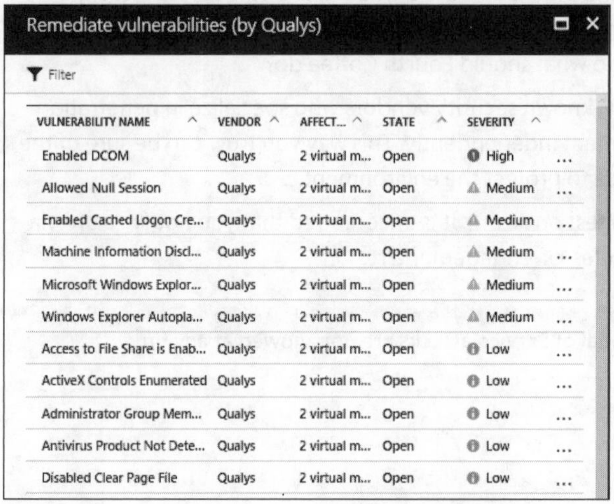

VULNERABILITY NAME	VENDOR	AFFECT...	STATE	SEVERITY	
Enabled DCOM	Qualys	2 virtual m...	Open	High	...
Allowed Null Session	Qualys	2 virtual m...	Open	Medium	...
Enabled Cached Logon Cre...	Qualys	2 virtual m...	Open	Medium	...
Machine Information Discl...	Qualys	2 virtual m...	Open	Medium	...
Microsoft Windows Explor...	Qualys	2 virtual m...	Open	Medium	...
Windows Explorer Autopla...	Qualys	2 virtual m...	Open	Medium	...
Access to File Share is Enab...	Qualys	2 virtual m...	Open	Low	...
ActiveX Controls Enumerated	Qualys	2 virtual m...	Open	Low	...
Administrator Group Mem...	Qualys	2 virtual m...	Open	Low	...
Antivirus Product Not Dete...	Qualys	2 virtual m...	Open	Low	...
Disabled Clear Page File	Qualys	2 virtual m...	Open	Low	...

FIGURE 4-17 Vulnerabilities discovered by Qualys Scan.

However, Fourth Coffee wants to do something similar for web applications, then choose a tool which integrates into the Azure App Service and is supplied by Tinfoil Security.

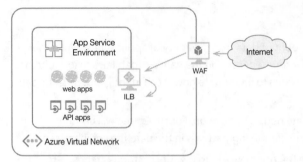

FIGURE 4-18 Deployment of Azure App Service and Web Application Firewall.

Fourth Coffee has access to such a vulnerability scanner that will identify security gaps in the web apps and allow the developers to understand what they are required to change to make the application more robust and secure. As shown in Figure 4-18, Fourth Coffee will deploy a web application firewall and implement the vulnerability scanning in Azure Web Applications.

Penetration testing: Validating the environment

Fourth Coffee thinks it has all its security bases covered with the built-in protections of the platform and the external services (like the vulnerability scanning) it can enable. However, it lacks one specific thing: third-party penetration testing.

Although implementing the Red and Blue teams are a good idea because it stresses the system and identifies gaps, it's also an expensive effort for organizations to sustain. The value they provide is incalculable, though, so what should Fourth Coffee do?

In this case, it's best to engage well-known security vendors who specialize in penetration testing so they can audit the environment independently. This way you truly can be sure of the safeguards that have been put in place to protect the environment.

Before beginning any penetration test on Azure, it is encouraged that you notify Azure via microsoft.com/en-us/msrc/pentest-rules-of-engagement?rtc=1.

> **IMPORTANT**   Be aware that Denial of Service attacks are not allowed at any time!

The Security Game has been upped!

We've talked a lot about services in this chapter, and we've even slightly duplicated information from other areas. One thing that is obvious is that even if you are a small organization (or a large one or something in between—it doesn't matter), if you adopt an assume breach mindset and use defense in depth principals, you can implement a wealth of technologies that will cross IT ecosystems and give organizations the protection, detection, and visibility into the darkest corners of the systems.

Security doesn't end with the tools we've mentioned throughout this chapter. We could include other tools like Azure Backup and Azure Site Recovery as services that help protect data and allow quick recovery in the event of a breach. It's imperative that every organization defines strong mandates to ensure security is well defined, maintained, and verified.

Fourth Coffee feels confident in its approach of choosing the Microsoft platforms to modernize its environment. The company has a wide choice of tools to pick from, the control required to achieve the business requirements, visibility into its systems, and the ability to act on security threats rapidly to minimize any potential impact. It's Fourth Coffee's goal to wrap security into the DevOps process with SDL being a major talking point for all applications, whether developed in house or outsourced.

> **NOTE** If your organization is thinking of moving to the cloud, review the Cloud Services Due Diligence Checklist as part of your evaluation process: microsoft.com/en-us/trustcenter/compliance/due-diligence-checklist.

Chapter 5

Application migration

When companies think about how to take advantage of the cloud, the question of application migration inevitably raises its head. This subject alone could have thousands of pages written on it. In this chapter, we look at the framework Fourth Coffee used for thinking about application migration. This chapter provides tangible guidance to help you achieve efficiencies while evolving to the cloud. We include some of the tools that you can leverage to accelerate your journey.

The Five R's

The new CIO of Fourth Coffee, Charlotte, found herself responsible for hundreds of small and large line of business (LOB) applications. Keeping these running was critical to Fourth Coffee, but it also was consuming the bulk of her budget and most of her peoples' time. To pursue digital transformation and save the company, she needed to reduce the resources she spent on these LOB applications so that she could invest in new applications.

In discussing the situation with her staff, Charlotte was greeted with all the reasons why change was impossible and why things had to stay the way there were. When she brought up the possibility of rewriting an application using a cloud architecture, her staff picked an example application and explained why rewriting it was nearly impossible. They recounted previous efforts to improve things and articulated all the reasons why those had failed. She quickly realized what she was dealing with, something psychologists call "learned helplessness," which is a condition in which people feel powerless due to a history of previous failures.

Charlotte ended the meeting early and said to the team, "I understand there will be challenges and difficulties, but we can, and we will, succeed with this transformation. We don't control everything, but we control the critical things. We control our thinking, our attitude, and our actions. I'm going to send you the Gartner Five R's model for moving to the cloud. I want you to read it and internalize the fact that we will be moving ahead with changes. Our challenge is to prioritize our actions and determine the right path forward for our applications."

Charlotte diagnosed two misconceptions her team had that would lead them to failure if left uncorrected:

- They considered moving to the cloud to be an all-or-nothing proposition.
- They thought that all applications would move to the cloud in the same way.

The Gartner 5 R's model provided Charlotte's team with a conceptual framework for migrating applications to cloud computing. Not every application needed to move to the cloud, and the ones that did could move there using one of the 5 R's: Rehost, Refactor, Revise, Rebuild, and Replace. Each of these approaches provide different costs and benefits.

Let's explore these different approaches in more detail.

Rehost

Rehosting allows us to redeploy the application to a different environment—that is, physical to virtual (IaaS) or on-premises IaaS to Cloud IaaS. Sometimes this is called *lift-and-shift*. The advantage of rehosting is that it allows very quick migration to the cloud because there are almost no changes required to the application. The disadvantage is that it does not leverage the cloud to the maximal degree.

As Isaac Newton taught us, a body at rest wants to remain at rest. One of the smartest things Charlotte did was to insist that the team take one LOB application and rehost it in the cloud as soon as possible. That got things moving. Here team had gotten their cloud accounts set up, they were using the Portal and getting connected the documentation and the community. Charlotte made a point to start small and celebrate each victory the team had. Fourth Coffee was now in the cloud.

After the application was running in the cloud for a while, one of the team members pointed out that they could take advantage of several free management capabilities that the cloud provider made available. Fourth Coffee used Azure, which includes inventory management, change management, update management, and other things. When something went wrong with the application, the team went to the change management tool and discovered a modification that someone had made that broke the application. They'd never had a function like that before; now they not only had it but it was free, and they didn't have to evaluate, purchase, or deploy a management tool. The team started warming to the cloud.

Figure 5-1 shows an example of the rehost scenario and the changes that happen in moving from an on-premises system to IaaS. The management of the hypervisor and host becomes the responsibility of the cloud provider, but the rest of the stack does not change.

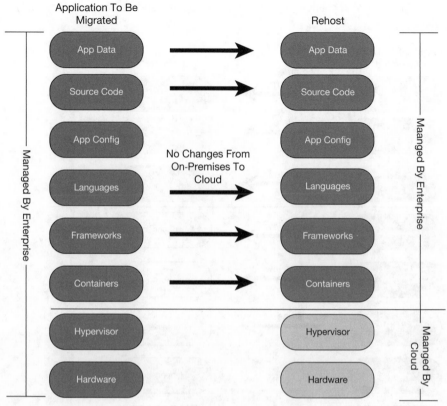

FIGURE 5-1 Rehost.

Refactor

Refactoring an application moves it from its existing infrastructure to a PaaS cloud infrastructure. Developers can use existing frameworks that they previously have leveraged with the applications and take advantage of updated versions of these frameworks, which can then extend the application to use native cloud capabilities. This R scenario highlights a few inherent problems with PaaS; for example, a feature implemented on premises does not have a modern cloud-native feature to match. It also highlights vendor lock-in because you have to code for the cloud platform–specific features. This scenario's end result uses the cloud in the most cost-effective manner; however, the journey through the refactor scenario often is the most expensive to achieve.

Figure 5-2 highlights what changes, transformations, updates, and new components apply in this scenario.

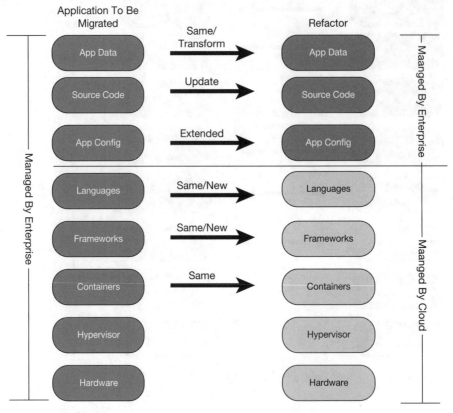

FIGURE 5-2   Refactor.

Revise

The revise scenario attempts to take existing code bases and extend them to support modern cloud concepts. This can be a costly procedure. Depending on the complexity of the application, it also can be lengthy.

For example, breaking apart a monolithic application can be complicated, and the level of complication depends on how it was coded. It may require a rearchitecting of the code base to break it into smaller applications and well-defined interfaces to let the code begin to be extended to support cloud concepts and become optimized for the cloud.

Figure 5-3 highlights the changes, updates, and new elements for the revise scenario.

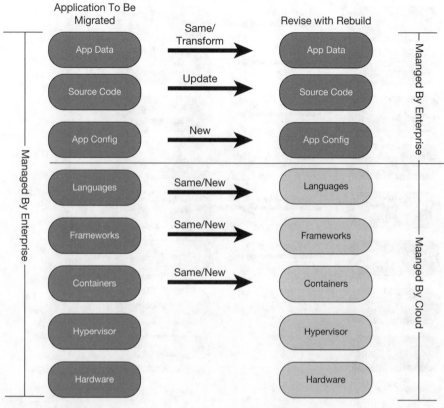

FIGURE 5-3   Revise.

Rebuild

The rebuild scenario involves moving away from any existing code base that has been written and starting from scratch. This involves rearchitecting the application to support all the innovative features of the cloud provider. Vendor lock-in is a key drawback of this scenario, but it also ensures that the application will fully capitalize on the capabilities of cloud.

Figure 5-4 highlights the changes required in the rebuild scenario for the application.

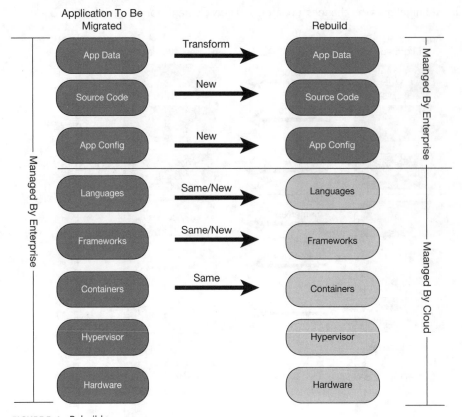

Application To Be Migrated

Rebuild

App Data — Transform → App Data

Source Code — New → Source Code

App Config — New → App Config

Languages — Same/New → Languages

Frameworks — Same/New → Frameworks

Containers — Same → Containers

Hypervisor — Hypervisor

Hardware — Hardware

Managed By Enterprise

Maanged By Enterprise

Managed By Cloud

FIGURE 5-4 Rebuild.

Replace

In replace, you again move away from an existing code base (as in the rebuild scenario); however, instead of rewriting an application, you decide to use an application that meets the needs of the organization but is delivered as-a-service (that is, SaaS). Replace also can mean retire if there is no other path; it's necessary to make this hard choice to phase out old applications.

For example, let's say you're using a CRM system that was custom built 15 years ago. This system was built on old .Net frameworks and gets functional patches from the development team. Its architecture is tightly knit with no well-defined interfaces. To adopt any of the other patterns listed for the 5 R's would be a significant undertaking for any development team. The organization can use a cloud-based CRM system to avoid modernizing the old system and synchronize the old data to the new system.

Figure 5-5 highlights the transformation the application and management will undergo in the replace scenario.

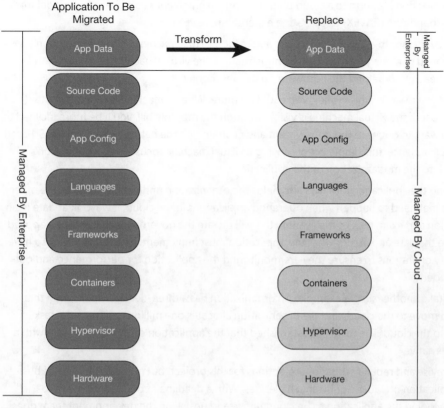

FIGURE 5-5 Replace.

Getting to the cloud to drive optimization

In this section we discuss moving to the cloud to help you drive optimization. When you look at the 5 R's and the paths they present, it's immediately obvious that you need to spend a lot of time deciding which one fits best to the application and organization's needs.

In general, the business needs to evaluate each application with an in-depth analysis and determine the best course of action.

But what if we suggest that you focus on the R scenario for rehost, at least initially. This may seem like a crazy idea at first, but moving an application to the cloud, no matter which scenario you choose, is no trivial task. There are many steps still to get ready for the move to the cloud, but regardless of the steps or tasks involved, moving to the cloud in the rehost scenario does one explicit thing.

One of the key drivers for the cloud is reducing cost. Lifting-and-shifting an application at first doesn't seem like much of a cost reduction because you're placing a virtual machine from one virtualization platform to a cloud platform and changing your cost operating model from capital expenditure (CAPEX) to operating expenditure (OPEX).

Now every month a bill arrives for that application virtual machine. However, you don't have the overhead of managing the physical infrastructure, the virtual machine used to run on, or the overhead of upgrading the hardware, so it saves money.

While you're saving this money, you could do more. When a machine is running in the cloud and the cost of the virtual machine is visible through the monthly bill, you'll be more inclined to examine ways to optimize this deployment and capitalize on the nature of PaaS- or SaaS-based services. In essence, this simple act of moving a virtual machine focuses the organization's approach to the modernization of the application.

Moving the application into IaaS also helps the organization understand some of the other changes that need to happen when operating applications in the cloud. If we look at data in an application and examine its classification, this will dictate the governance that must be applied to secure the data and in turn what the application must implement. Additionally we also have to modify operations to ensure they are monitoring the application for performance and outages properly.

Let's take another simple example. An organization has a three-tier LOB application that needs to move to the cloud, and the organization allocates one million dollars to the task of getting to the cloud. The team has established that the application cannot be replaced with a SaaS alternative.

The revise and rebuild scenarios are options for this project, but recoding this line of business application provides significant challenges. With a deadline of one year to move to the cloud, recoding the application to be cloud native and upskilling the development team does not seem feasible.

Undoubtedly as the developers would begin to recode the application, they would find that translating some of the core code is significantly harder than anticipated, and the time required would almost double what had been budgeted. They have consumed the million dollars allocated to replatform the code and need an additional investment before reaching the cloud. Let's say this additional investment is another 500,000 dollars to complete the project. They will have invested 1.5 million dollars, and only now will they begin to operate in the cloud and make use of the benefits.

In the rehost scenario, they get the application to the cloud in a matter of weeks, they begin the process of understanding how to operate in the cloud, and they can start building abstract interfaces that begin to decouple the application. The application can start leveraging the right pieces of the cloud and further promote driving down the cost of running the application. For example, they can use native cloud backup or native cloud disaster recovery and native cloud monitoring.

As we previously mentioned, it may seem a little crazy not to push toward revise or refactor scenarios first, but it begins to make sense when you evaluate the additional benefits and other challenges that moving to a rehost scenario enables you to address while upskilling the development team and implementing the necessary organizational changes to support effectively moving to the cloud.

DevOps the cornerstone of application migration

A cornerstone of moving your application to the cloud is to ensure you get DevOps right. We discuss DevOps in greater detail in Chapter 7, "Supporting innovation."

In the context of this chapter, we need to quickly discuss DevOps and ensure you have the right models in place to support moving to the cloud. It's no secret things change when you move to the cloud no matter what R scenario you ultimately choose, but it's also clear that you need to drive efficiency and automate as much as possible, from deployment to monitoring to remediation.

DevOps provides this foundation for organizations to move their application estates to the cloud. It redefines the processes, the tools, and the people to support applications in moving to the cloud. DevOps doesn't necessarily have to start with the cloud; you can begin long before any application move to the cloud is considered, but DevOps is an absolute requirement before you begin the journey of migration or modernization.

Take DevOps in stages. It's a life cycle that drives improvement and learning from mistakes. For example, in the case of the three-tier application we mentioned earlier, we could begin simply by automating the build process from source code into a staging environment and then releasing into production the first and second tiers of the application. As we examine what we learn from applying DevOps to each tier we begin to understand that no matter where the application tiers are to be deployed they can be deployed by the DevOps process.

We can improve on this by integrating application telemetry and infrastructure monitoring data, so operations and developers can look at this information in unison and make more intelligent decisions about how they need to progress. If they choose to evolve the application on the first tier to either a web app or a container running a web app, they would follow a process of changing the source code and following the automated deployment process, which would target the new environment of choice.

DevOps is the cornerstone of the application migration process. Without it in place, the result would end up bringing archaic practices to a modern cloud infrastructure, which would hinder an organization's capability of fully attaining the benefits of the cloud.

The migration process

In this section we discuss the process for application migration, including demonstrating some of the tooling to help you collect the information about your environment and the tooling to help move your application to the cloud. The migration process is broken down into various phases as shown in Figure 5-6. Each phase's data is used as input into the next phase to help guide decisions and have a successful migration project.

Each phase's method of collection and tooling should drive a standardized process from performing application migrations to ultimately building the concept of an application migration factory.

Each phase as it's being designed should derive the required data that needs to be collected from all key stakeholder teams. Examples of key stakeholders include the operations, development, and security teams. These teams can define the "important" information they need to assess an application, not only from an application migration standpoint but also in terms of performance and security, which will dictate some of your choices in the migration life cycle.

You also can use the information that the teams require to guide how you build your cloud infrastructure and how you construct the migration factory. It allows you to have a minimum bar that already meets the requirements of these teams, so when an application goes through the migration factory you know things will be in the correct order, and you don't expect any blockers from going to production with these applications.

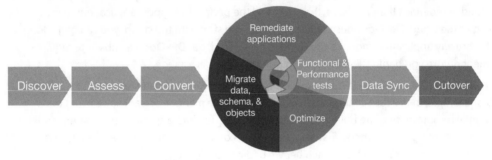

FIGURE 5-6 Application migration life cycle.

Discover

In the discover phase of the application migration life cycle, you need to gather as much information as possible to make the appropriate decisions for migrating your applications. This involves creating a large amount of standardized workshops and questionnaires and selecting the right tooling to gather the appropriate information for the organization's decision-making.

Application selection

Application selection is paramount. Selecting the wrong application at the start of this life cycle can considerably hinder the migration to the cloud. However, selecting an application that doesn't represent or touch enough points to ensure that the migration life cycle is appropriately comprehensive could lead to a disaster down the line.

Factors for looking at applications can be broken into two main categories:

- **Business factors** Business factors look at the mission criticalness of the application, any regulatory governance it must meet, and potentially the sensitive nature of the data contained in the application. A great place to start would be applications that aren't mission critical, have low regulatory governance, and contain a low level of sensitive data. These would be the low-hanging fruit and would enable you to begin building the standardization process required to achieve a successful application migration.

- **Technical factors**   Technical factors look at the hybrid requirements of the application (that is, does it require access to data sources that have to remain on premises), its monitoring requirements, the location of the monitoring tooling, any custom connections to other business software, how "chatty" the application is, and how latency sensitive the application is. A great starting point would be with applications that have no custom integration, little or no latency requirements, low monitoring requirements, little or no hybrid requirements, and are not very chatty.

As we mentioned earlier, you need to find an application that's representative of the application estate and has a nice blend so that you can build the standardization procedures. However, since this is also a life cycle, you can start with the simple applications and evolve the procedures as you cycle thru the application estate.

INFORMATION GATHERING

There are three main methods for information gathering in relation to application migration. It's preferable that you perform the information gathering methods in the following sequence: questionnaires, tooling, and then workshops. We discuss each method in the follow sections.

QUESTIONNAIRES

It's necessary to build a robust questionnaire to obtain the data you require from an application. This helps you make decisions about that application—for example, whether you should migrate it at all and which R scenario best fits with the application today and its future state.

In Table 5-1 we show you a list of basic sample questions (and some example answers) that you could use as the start of your questionnaire.

TABLE 5-1   Basic questions for the questionnaire

BASICS	ANSWERS
Application name	Time Management
Who is this for?	HR
How long has this application been around?	> 8 years
Are there applications serving similar needs in your portfolio?	Yes, potential to consolidate
Are there SaaS options in the market that might meet your needs with or without customization?	Yes
What's your team's timeline for the cloud journey?	2 years
Are you looking to actively leverage and contribute to the open source community?	No
What's the expected number of concurrent users per month?	2,000

Table 5-2 highlights the basis of some business driver questions, which further help you to prioritize and select the best type of applications to start with.

TABLE 5-2 Business driver questions for the questionnaire

BUSINESS DRIVERS	ANSWERS
What is the primary objective to migrate to the cloud for this application?	Provide multichannel access, including mobile
What is the secondary objective to migrate to the cloud for this application?	Free up datacenter space quickly
Is this application critical to your business?	No
Do you expect this application to handle large traffic?	No
How often do you plan to update the app?	Once every 1 to 3 years
Do you expect this app to add breakthrough capabilities like intelligence, IoT, Bots?	No
Do you have a pressing timeline (DC shutdown, EoL licensing, DC contract expiration, M&A)?	No
How important is it to leverage your existing code and data?	Important
If you were to decide on a migration/modernization strategy, which one would you pick?	Refactor: Minimally alter to take better advantage of the cloud
What are the least efficient aspects of this application?	Infrastructure

Table 5-3 includes some sample questions that are more aligned to the development of the application and its evolution.

TABLE 5-3 Development and architectural questions for the questionnaire

ARCHITECTURAL AND DEV PROCESS CONSIDERATIONS	ANSWERS
What's the next architectural milestone you want to achieve for this app?	Good with monolithic for this app
Does this app require you to access the underlying VM (that is, to install custom software)?	No
Does this application involve extensive business processes and messaging? Is it chatty?	No
Does this application involve custom integration with other web and cloud apps via APIs or connectors?	Yes
Have you adopted SOA for this application?	No
Are you interested in moving your application's database to cloud as well?	No
What is the primary objective you want to achieve with data storage for this application?	Ease of management
How important is Big Data/AI capability for this application?	Nice to have
Is this application highly connected with or dependent on on-premises applications/systems?	No
If you were to assess the level of changes you are willing take to move this application to the cloud, what would they be?	Moderate: no core code change required
Is your app sensitive to latency?	Yes

Table 5-4 shows sample questions relating to regulatory requirements.

TABLE 5-4 Regulatory questions for the questionnaire

REGULATORY, COMPLIANCE AND SECURITY REQUIREMENTS	ANSWERS
Are there specific compliance or country-specific data requirements that can affect your migration and architectural strategies?	No
Does the application need secure authorization and authentication?	Yes
Does the application require firewall, app gateway, or advanced virtual network and related components?	Yes

These questions are the basics. You can go deeper and gather more information relating to the application and the surrounding infrastructure. Some additional areas for which you may want to build questionnaires include

- Compute
- Networking
- Storage
- Database

Questionnaires on these topics give a more robust picture than the information we provide in the tables.

BASELINING

Application baselining collects data on the normal state of the application and how it operates during normal and off-peak business hours so that you can establish a pattern and provide a comparison when you move to the cloud. Baselining really should be an ongoing thing rather than being focused on a point-in-time migration because it will help you understand application characteristics that will be useful for determining problems during operations.

Gathering this data enables you to make accurate predictions of the types of services you consume within your cloud provider and helps you build budgeting and financial models from that data. If you don't understand how the normal state looks then you can greatly affect the IT budget by making inaccurate decisions.

Baselining requires collecting two main types of data: performance and configuration.

Performance data   Performance data gives you a view on how the application is responding to the workload it's being put under. Reviewing this data for a wide period rather than using a single time capture of only a couple hours will give you a more accurate profile of how the application works. Ultimately you can compare the performance data when you move the application to the cloud.

You can handle collecting performance data in a variety of ways:

- **Performance monitor**   Performance monitor is natively built into Windows and helps you capture and visualize performance data for any performance counter available in Windows and its applications.

  Logman is a command-line utility that allows you to build performance counter sets (a collection of performance counters in a file) and invoke them to collect performance data.

  Here's a simple way of creating a file and invoking a timed capture for performance data.

1. Open Notepad and copy the following content into it:

```
"\System\Processor Queue Length"
"\Memory\Pages/sec"
"\Memory\Available MBytes"
"\Processor(*)\% Processor Time"
"\Network Interface(*)\Bytes Received/sec"
"\Network Interface(*)\Bytes Sent/sec"
"\LogicalDisk(C:)\% Free Space"
"\LogicalDisk(*)\Avg. Disk Queue Length"
```

2. Save the file and call it **windowsperf.conf**.

3. Open an administrative command prompt and copy the following code into the window. This code requires you to change the data and time windows between the -b parameter and the -E parameter:

```
logman create counter baseperf -f bin -b 03/04/2018 09:40:00 -E 03/04/2018
09:45:00 -si 05 -v mmddhhmm -o "c:\perf\baseperf" -cf "c:\perf\windowsperf.conf"
```

4. Open **Performance Monitor** (type **perfmon** and press enter). As shown in Figure 5-7, you will observe the data set after its created on the left-hand menu. Notice the data set baseperf.

5. Go back to the command prompt windows and type the following:

```
logman start baseperf
```

This will begin the data collection for the prescribed time period you entered in the previous steps.

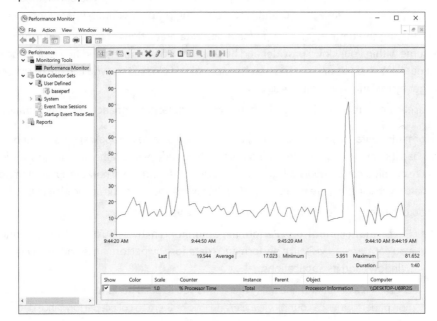

FIGURE 5-7 Performance Monitor data collection.

After the data is collected, you can use Performance Monitor to view the data. The same procedure can be used across multiple machines, and you could wrap these in scripts to further automate the process.

- **PowerShell** PowerShell can help automate the collection of performance counter data using the Get-Counter cmdlet. Here is a sample script for collecting performance counter data via PowerShell:

```
$CtrList = @(
        "\System\Processor Queue Length",
        "\Memory\Pages/sec",
        "\Memory\Available MBytes",
        "\Processor(*)\% Processor Time",
        "\Network Interface(*)\Bytes Received/sec",
        "\Network Interface(*)\Bytes Sent/sec",
        "\LogicalDisk(C:)\% Free Space",
        "\LogicalDisk(*)\Avg. Disk Queue Length"
        )
    Get-Counter -Counter $CtrList -SampleInterval 5 -MaxSamples 5 | Export-Counter
-Path C:\PerfExample.blg -FileFormat BLG -Force
```

- **SCOM** Microsoft System Center Operations Manager (SCOM) is traditionally an on-premises monitoring tool created to give deep insight into your IT environment. You can use SCOM to collect long-term data about your environment, (using management packs and/or scripts) and it gives you insight on what the application's normal state is.

> **NOTE** For more information regarding SCOM, please visit this page: https://docs.microsoft.com/en-us/system-center/scom/welcome?view=sc-om-2016.

- **OMS&S** Microsoft Operation Management Suite and Security (OMS&S) is a cloud-based tool that can span multiple environments (cloud and on-premises) via agent-based collection to aggregate large amounts of data—including performance data—into a single repository for analysis. You can collect any performance counter on Windows and Linux and determine an application's normal state from this and a variety of other data.

  OMS&S can collect multiple sources of data and provide service mapping to help identify interdependencies and/or communication paths you may not be aware of. Figure 5.8 shows an example of adding Windows performance counters to Windows.

FIGURE 5-8 Performance counter configuration in OMS&S for Windows.

NOTE For more information regarding collecting performance data in OMS&S, please visit https://docs.microsoft.com/en-us/azure/log-analytics/log-analytics-data-sources-performance-counters.

- Third-party tools

  There are many third-party tools beyond the scope of this book. Here's a small sample:

  - Splunk
  - Nagios
  - Spiceworks
  - HP OpenView

Configuration data   Configuration data enables you to look at how the application is configured at a point in time. This point-in-time view enables you to correlate its normal state of operations in conjunction with the captured performance data. Application vendors often have many settings that you can tweak for improved performance depending on the environment where the application is deployed.

When you are capturing the configuration data you can review it before moving to the cloud so you can determine any potential problems. A simple example involves authentication. If the configuration of the application requires Kerberos authentication but you haven't planned your network around support for a Kerberos authentication method in the cloud, the application will fail.

Additionally, if you choose to step a little into the modernization of the application—for example, containers—you need to ensure you can allow the containers to connect securely to other systems using some identity model. If it is a Windows container and you haven't stepped into modernizing the authentication methods to something like OAuth2.0, then the application still requires Kerberos and the supporting infrastructure to allow Kerberos to operate successfully.

You can collect configuration capture in a variety of different ways. Manually capturing the configuration data is an option, of course. However, using automate tools, such as capturing performance data, simplifies the process. We discuss some of these tools in the next section because some of the discovery tools or migration assistants also capture the configuration data you need.

SERVICE MAPPING

When looking at applications, you need to gather as much information as possible about the application to have a successful migration project. However, the information needs to be validated, as is always the case when you're collecting information.

Applications that are candidates for migration usually have the original architecture diagram and protocol flows drawn up at the start, but as the development process occurs this information tends to not be updated as regularly as you require. (For application developers who do make updates, that's great!) But the lack of information updates or inaccurate updates still can lead into the scenario in which the app was "designed" to do X, but it does Y. This becomes more important when you're about to migrate an application.

Take a simple example of a LOB application. The vendor has described in the architecture and supporting documentation that the app uses a built-in authentication process. When you move it to the cloud, even in a rehost scenario, the application breaks! No one can log on.

You troubleshoot and discover that the application requires Kerberos authentication. Now you must either change the network configuration to support hybrid connections to your on-premises network or you must use Azure Active Directory Domain Services (if your application can support the associated Kerberos versions!).

Service mapping is the technique of taking the architecture and protocol flows and discovering whether your application is indeed operating in the capacity the specifications have defined. This will help you identify how your application is working, what processes it instantiates, how it communicates with other systems; you essentially have almost all the information you need to understand which way the application is working on the network.

Not only will service mapping help you with your application and how it communicates, you can use it to help you design your network infrastructure in a Cloud environment. From the information you can determine if you need to open additional ports or firewall rules, or you can find out if you can move the application to Cloud.

During your service mapping, if you discover an application that communicates using multicast technologies or broadcast technologies, then you will have problems moving to a cloud platform like Azure. because at the time of writing, Azure doesn't support those technologies.

Oracle RAC is an example of one of these database platforms whose technology currently uses multicast technology in its clustering mechanisms. So, for now at least, you can't bring it through application migration in the rehost scenario.

You can handle service mapping in a variety of ways, and it builds on the information you have collected in the previous sections of this chapter. You could use network traces in tools like Network Monitor or Wireshark. Figure 5-9 shows a sample network trace in network monitoring. We show the communications that happen normally (you will see a lot), and then we show that we can map this to a process.

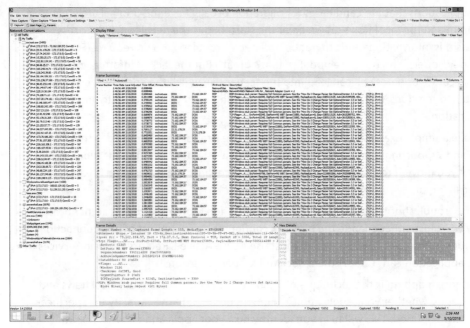

FIGURE 5-9 Network monitoring.

Figure 5-10 shows Service Map that's built into OMS. It shows the application server, where it's talking, and on what ports it's talking. On the right side we drill into process information and event details down to the DLL versions. Service maps, which has a helper agent on it, collects this data alongside the OMS agent and injects it into our log analytics workspace, so we can produce these views!

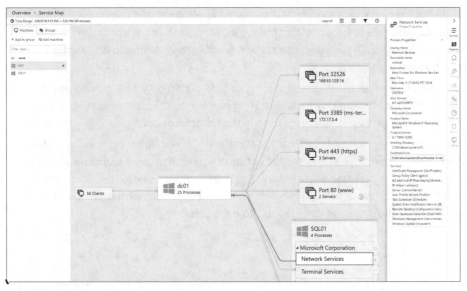

FIGURE 5-10 Service map.

Data

Data is usually the most important part of the application. If we lose the application, we can restore the front-end components and connect back to the data stores. More importantly, we need to profile our data in the correct way. Identifying our data stores and understanding the sizing requirements, its security requirements, and its performance requirements will help us build an appropriate map to the cloud.

For example, an Azure Standard Storage account can hold up to 500 TB of data and has a 20,000 IOPS limit. If we have an application that has 400 GB of data then the storage account is perfect, but if the IOPS count required is 30,000 IOPS then the storage account won't meet the needs. Also, an application that requires an NFS interface to the storage also discounts the Azure Storage Account. Finally, if the data stored in that data store has been classified as High Business Impact or Personal Information, we potentially need to enable encryption or more to host the data in that storage account even if its other needs have been met.

Similarly, if the data happens to be a database, the same information about performance, sizing, and so on is still required, but support also comes into play. Does the vendor support the datastores that are available in the cloud, and what are its conditions on items like blob storage and latency, for example.

TOOLS

An organization needs to select the correct tools to gather the depth information related to an application to aid in their decision-making process. In this section, we discuss some of the free tools available today. These tools will help you gather a lot of the information we have talked about in your environment.

Microsoft Assessment and Planning Toolkit

Microsoft Assessment and Planning Toolkit (MAPS) provides a powerful tool to collect an inventory. It's an assessment and reporting tool to gather the information required to help you migrate your applications to the cloud.

> **NOTE** You can get the MAPS tool from https://www.microsoft.com/en-us/download/details.aspx?id=7826.

The installed tool collects an inventory of the machines you want to target. Targets are called scenarios, and they include the following:

- Windows
- Linux/Unix
- VMWare
- SQL
- Oracle

An inventory contains the operating system, configuration, and performance data for the machine to be able to assess it for scenarios later. One of the scenarios we are most interested in is the Azure Migration Platform Scenario, which collects information to build an inventory that consists of the hardware information, OS information, IIS instances, SQL information, and web applications. Figure 5-11 shows the inventory discovery process in MAPS.

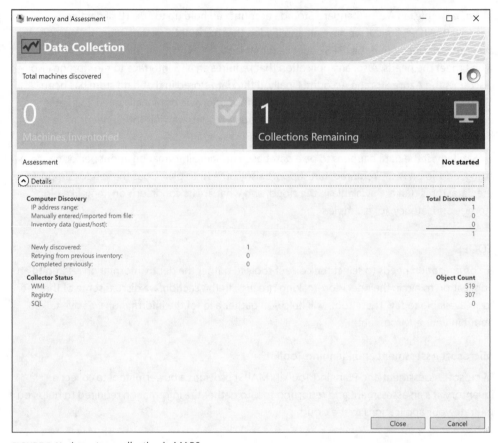

FIGURE 5-11 Inventory collection in MAPS.

After the inventory is collected, the next step is to collect the performance data. You can run some reports prior to doing this, but collecting the performance data gives you a complete picture of how your system performs over a period of time The performance data collection should be left for as long a period as possible during normal business operations to get an accurate representation of how it performs and also to contribute to the sizing report for an Azure VM. Table 5-5 shows the output of a sizing report after the inventory and performance data have been collected.

TABLE 5-5 Output of an Azure VM sizing report

MA-CHINE NAME	OS	TYPE	AZURE VM SIZE	EST. MONTH-LY SMALL COM-PUTE HOURS	EST. MONTHLY NETWORK USE-OUT-GOING (GB)	EST. MONTH-LY STOR-AGE USE (GB)	VM CPU UTI-LIZA-TION (%)	VM MEM-ORY UTILI-ZATION (MB)	VM DISK I/O UTILI-ZATION (IOPS)	VM NET-WORK UTILI-ZATION-OUT (MB/S)	VM NET-WORK UTILIZA-TION-IN (MB/S)	DATA DISKS
dc01.fourth-coffee.com	Microsoft Windows Server 2012 R2 Datacen-ter	Virtual	B1ms	11520	5.19	15.63	0.72	1371.3	2.69	0	0	1

> **NOTE** For more information, check out the FAQ for MAPS at https://social.technet.microsoft.com/wiki/contents/articles/1643.microsoft-assessment-and-planning-toolkit-frequently-asked-questions.aspx.

Azure Migrate

Azure Migrate is a cloud-based service used to discover, assess, and migrate from n-premises networks to the cloud. This tool is targeted toward a virtual machine migration or a database migration and leverages existing Microsoft tools within Azure Site Recovery and the Database Migration Service. As of March 2019, this tool is scoped only to VMware environments with a planned roadmap to support additional environments. Hyper-V support is currently planned.

Azure Migrate runs an appliance that you can download via the Azure Marketplace. It connects to vCenter and scans the environment to build an inventory and assess it for migrating to the cloud.

After analysis, Azure Migrate guides you to the process of migrating your applications to the cloud.

> **NOTE** For more information on Azure Migrate, please visit https://azure.microsoft.com/en-us/migrate/.

Azure App Service Migration Assistant

Although it's not an official Microsoft tool, the Azure App Service Migration Assistant looks at a variety of information related to an on-premises web app and determines its suitability for the cloud, specifically the Azure App Service. The Azure App Service Migration Assistant inventories and collects configuration data around an app's binding, authentication, extensions, and so on. You receive an assessment and report based on the findings from the inventory and determine if you can easily move to the Azure App Service. The tool also performs the migration if you want.

This tool is not officially supported by Microsoft, but it's a valuable tool in the arsenal.

> **NOTE** For more information, please visit https://www.movemetothecloud.net/.

Third-party tooling

There are plenty of third-part tools available today. It's outside the scope of this book to highlight all available tools or provide in-depth guidance about them, but here is a short list of some of the major tools available. You can visit their websites for further information.

- BitTitan (https://www.bittitan.com/)
- Movere (https://www.movere.io/product/)
- CloudPhysics (https://www.cloudphysics.com/)
- Cloudamize (https://www.cloudamize.com/)

WORKSHOPS

The workshop is considered the final point in the chain of the discovery phase. It requires the participation of all the teams—infrastructure, support, operations, security, and development. Using all the information collected in the previous stages of the discovery phase, you can review each application and have a complete end-to-end discussion to determine each app's viability for the cloud. You can use the information to agree on the appropriate R scenario to map to for migrating the application to the cloud.

These workshops also can cover the assessment work that we cover in more detail in the next section, but that assessment work is not the end purpose of the workshop.

Assess

The assessment phase builds on top of the data collected in the discovery phase There is overlap between the two phases, especially regarding the applications you begin to target and how you prioritize which application goes first.

In this section, we introduce two items that help you prioritize the applications and map them to the cloud in the appropriate way.

Prioritization tables

You can break prioritization into three areas to help you define a weighting system that you can use to determine the sequence of which applications move first:

- By type
- By business value or criticality
- By complexity and risk

BY TYPE

Breaking applications into their respective types can help you discover whether there are SaaS alternatives or native PaaS frameworks that you can leverage. Figure 5-12 shows a breakdown of how you might segment applications by type.

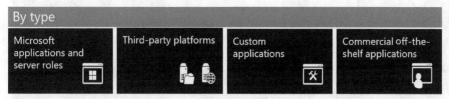

FIGURE 5-12   Segmenting applications into types.

BY BUSINESS VALUE OR CRITICALITY

Understanding the business value and how critical it is to the organization also helps you prioritize an application for migration. If it is a mission-critical application which the business cannot operate without and requires absolute stability, this might lead to a delay in bringing the mission-critical application to the cloud until lessons are learned.

Figure 5-13 shows an example of how you might segment the applications by business value.

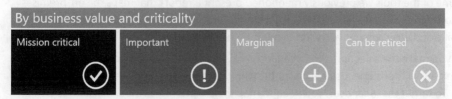

FIGURE 5-13   Segment applications into business value and criticality.

BY COMPLEXITY AND RISK

Finally, you can break applications into segments of complexity and risk. If an app has low risk and low complexity for the migration, it receives a high score for being approached. Figure 5-14 shows how you might segment based on complexity and risk.

FIGURE 5-14   Segment applications into complexity and risk.

You can score each area and bucket and use the cumulation of those scores to build a prioritization table. Figure 5-15 shows a sample prioritization table derived from the segments and the discovery data. It also includes other potential factors you may weigh in the decision of prioritization. The weight factor is from 1 to 5: 1 is not important or low, and 5 is very important or high.

				Performance				Architecture							Financial		Risk		Operations		Security and compliance		
								UI	Application			Data		Infrastructure									
App ID	Application name	Include	Capability type	Elasticity	Scalability	Latency	Throughput	Complexity	Size	Complexity	Life expectancy	Structured mag.	Complexity	Hardware life expectancy	Operating cost	Business value	Organizational	Technical	Business continuity	Tools/integration	Jurisdiction	Regulation	Encryption
1	App 1	Yes		5	5	5	5	5	5	5	5	5	5	5	5	5	5	5	5	5	5	5	5
2	App 2	Yes		1	1	1	1	1	1	1	1	1	1	1	1	1	1	1	1	1	1	1	1
3	App 3	Yes		3	3	3	3	3	3	3	3	3	3	3	3	3	3	3	3	3	3	3	3

FIGURE 5-15 Prioritization table.

This table holds a list of all the applications in an organization. You use one like it to determine the path and a timeline of events to migrate the application estate to the cloud.

Target

The final stage before you enter the migration factory is targeting the application to Azure Services. Some of the tools we previously mentioned present a report that maps the on-premises applications to services available in the target cloud. Target selection starts when you select the actual cloud environment you want to migrate the application to.

After you make the selection, the R scenario drives the services in the cloud environment you ultimately will consume. Using an example with the rehost scenario, we target IaaS services in Azure. To target these services, you need to map the on-premises virtual machine to an Azure virtual machine size. These sizes determine the CPU cores, the memory, and the amount of data disks you can attach to.

For other services—that is, if you need to monitor the application inside the virtual machine—you need to identify the monitoring needs, which would have been established in the discovery phase, and what cloud services can meet the monitoring needs. If the requirements are for operating system information then you could leverage OMS&S. If the requirements are for deep application telemetry then you might leverage application insights.

Cloud Map

When you migrate to the cloud, remember that not all features may be available. Consequently, it's important to create a cloud map table. The table shown in Figure 5-16 maps the features consumed by the on-premises network to what's available in the cloud. We also include roadmap data on our map to help teams determine when the support for the services they require will become available in the cloud. Figure 5-16 shows a table for database services consumed on premises and what they map to in the cloud. You could further iterate this to include the individual services each database source uses and what features map to Azure Database Services.

Source	Azure Target					
	Azure SQL DB	Azure SQL DB-MI	Azure DB for Postgres	Azure DB for MySQL	Azure DW	Azure Cosmos DB
SQL Server 2005+	Dec 2017	Dec 2017			Q2 CY18	
Oracle	Dec 2017	Dec 2017	Q2 CY18	Q2 CY18	Q2 CY18	
SAP ASE/Sybase	Q2 CY18	Q2 CY18				
DB2	Q2 CY18	Q2 CY18				
MySQL	Q1 CY18	Q1 CY18		Q1 CY18		
PostgreSQL			Q1 CY18			
Oracle Exadata					Q2 CY18	
Teradata					Q2 CY18	
Netezza					Q2 CY18	
Amazon Redshift					Q2 CY18	
MongoDB						Q1 CY18
Other NoSQL						

FIGURE 5-16 Cloud map table.

Building a migration factory

Perhaps the most important part of migrating applications to the cloud is creating a concept called the migration factory. The migration factory principal outcome is that after we've collected the information from discovery and assessed it correctly, it enters the "factory" and moves to the cloud, ready for cutover.

The factory has a lot of responsibility in the migration life cycle chain. It needs to ensure that the application works *as expected* on the cloud platform of choice when it exits the factory. It also generates an important output of how to do the final migration over to the cloud.

To achieve these results, in this section we dive a little deeper into each phase of the migration factory and begin why the data we collected in the discovery, assess, and target phases are so important.

Testing

A core concept of DevOps involves testing. The testing produces valuable feedback to determine whether the application running on the relevant cloud platform works. This testing should not be manual; it should be heavily automated. Building this automated test system ensures that the application is tested consistently against the rules that have been agreed upon by the business and IT organization.

FUNCTIONAL TESTS

In the functional testing phase of the migration factory, you validate that the application operates as expected. You can do a variety of tests, including synthetic transactions with validate data queries or logon procedures. Other elements including cross-platform integration points and reports. You also would test for component upgrades of an application. The tests are constructed with IT operations and end-user scenarios in mind, and the scores must be 100%. Any failure should be fed back into the remediation phase of the migration factory. Table 5-6 shows a sample definition for a functional test for an application.

TABLE 5-6 Functional Test Sample

ITEM	DESCRIPTION
[Test Case Name]	Log in Test
[Test Case ID]	12334234
[Test Case Author]	Joe Bloggs
[Testing Phase]	Functional / User Testing
[Description]	This test validates that a user can log to the system via the front-end portal.
[Test Case Steps]	1. Open the web page for the application: http://crm. 2. Enter the username and password for end user. 3. Validate the default status page of Dashboard A. 4. Log out. 5. Repeat steps 1–4 using an administration account and verify. Dashboard B is default.
Screenshots	\<Dashboard A Screenshot\> \<Dashboard B Screenshot\>
[Test Case Results]	Pass/Fail
[Test Case Feedback]	Test passed for end-user scenario, administration scenario loads Dashboard C

> **NOTE** You can find further samples at http://download.microsoft.com/download/8/ D/9/8D995CB3-2C3E-43B4-97D3-B372FBF6C7EF/STARTS%20Quality%20Bar%20 FY2016.pdf.
>
> The sample details functional testing originally designed for Windows Phone.

PERFORMANCE TESTS

In the performance testing phase of the migration factory, you validate that the application operates equally or better than the on-premises infrastructure. Testing performance covers standard end-user scenarios, including reporting, login times, querying for new data, and creating records. Testing also should cover internal application metrics that aren't traditionally visible to a user but can be used to correlate reported events. The performance testing can be validated against the baselines previously performed in the discovery phase. Application architectures may change because of the performance testing during the remediation phase.

Performance tests can be defined similarly to functional tests. They should focus on performance metrics for the application. Table 5-7 shows a sample performance test you could start with to document and then build the automation test from.

TABLE 5-7 Performance test sample

ITEM	DESCRIPTION
[Test Case Name]	Log in Test
[Test Case ID]	12334234
[Test Case Author]	Joe Bloggs
[Testing Phase]	Performance Test / Login Time
[Description]	This test validates that a user log takes less than 3 seconds.
[Test Case Steps]	1. Open the web page for the application: http://crm. 2. Enter the username and password for the end user. 3. Collect metrics from Application Insights. 4. Validate the login metric is less than 3 seconds. 5. Repeat steps 1–4 using an Administration Account.
Performance Requirements	<3 seconds
[Test Case Results]	Pass/Fail
[Test Case Feedback]	Login was within specified parameters.

Performance testing also will describe load scenarios and expected performance. Here are some sample expectations under load testing of a web app with a load of 500 users.

- **Throughput** 100 requests per second (ASP.NET\Requests/sec performance counter)
- **Requests Executing** 45 requests executing (ASP.NET\Requests Executing performance counter)
- **Avg. Response Time** 2.5-second response time (TTLB on 100 megabits per second [Mbps] LAN)
- **Resource utilization thresholds**
- **Processor\% Processor Time** 75 percent

Hopefully by now, you might begin to understand that these tests can be duplicated from the original application build and testing process. This is the whole point of DevOps—to simplify and automate while maintaining the same or better coverage as before. You may also find that the testing from the migration factory feeds back into the original testing scenarios and improves them at the initial build so that each functional upgrade undergoes a rigorous end-to-end test.

Remediation

In the remediation phase, the output of the functional and performance tests are analyzed for patterns and remediation takes place. The remediation sets output back to the teams running discovery and assessment in case there is additional data that should be collected up front before an application enters the migration factory. The remediation phase also ensures that the application incorporates the changes, so they do not reoccur in subsequent testing. Remediation may identify areas or scenarios in the testing phases that are not covered and drive change to ensure more complete coverage in the application testing.

Data migration

Data migration has a specific phase in the migration factory because it identifies and details the most effective method of getting data to the cloud. In some cases, the tooling may migrate the data for you; in other cases, you may have to export the data to a storage unit, encrypt it, and ship it to a cloud datacenter. Whatever the method, the data migration phase highlights this for you and begins to shape the process you will require when it comes to switching over to production.

Data Sync

Data sync happens both during the migration factory and after as you prepare for cutover. In fact, one of the choices that will appear during the migration factory is whether you offline sync your data and incur an outage or use an automated method of having the data consistently in sync so you have no downtime.

There are many types of data, of course, and you must establish the methods of getting data to the cloud. For example, if the data is that of a database and is hosted with in SQL, you can look at items like SQL Replication or SQL Always On, which enable you to have a constant data stream of replication moving to the cloud to make cutover easier. Azure has tools like the Database Migration Service, which can replicate and cut over the data for an application's database.

If you have an application that doesn't have native replication, you can look into third-party tools that can replicate the data. However, you also might look deeper into the cloud platform. Azure Site Recovery is a tool on the Azure Platform that can replicate a virtual machine and its data to Azure and allow for a smooth cutover.

Offline Data sync is a potential option as well. With it, you back up and restore the data and schedule an outage for the period of the cutover.

Cutover

The last phase of the migration life cycle is the cutover. The cutover involves bringing the application to production, and it's the final gate of application migration. This final gate gives an organization its last chance to stop a migration from happening if there are problems and a final chance to ensure all elements of the application are thoroughly tested and all supporting processes and operational technology have been put in place.

You may have noticed that at the start of the application life cycle migration we suggest you involve a variety different teams to ensure that you have representation of interests across an enterprise to ensure an application is secure, stable, performant, and recoverable. However, we haven't directly called out those groups in the migration factory. We also haven't called out any specifics about support systems for the application—for example, how you monitor the application in the new cloud environment or how you back up the application.

This is the one of the reasons we have the cutover gate. The cutover gate enables you to ensure that you have all the tools in place so that when the application gets cut over you can monitor the application appropriately. You make sure that you can back up and restore the application in the cloud and still recover using the legacy backup catalog. You also ensure that all the security criteria have been put in place, including governance, regulatory, and privacy requirements.

Building a detailed checklist to ensure all these requirements are met is essential! When components go live in Azure, they need to meet fundamental requirements which have been determined during the discovery phase. If they don't meet this quality bar for production then the component can't go live!

The quality bar for each application may be slightly different in terms of whether the application can scale, what availability mechanisms are in place, how you monitor the application telemetry, and so on. The pillars shown in Table 5-8 help define what that quality bar should be generically across all applications. If the quality bar can't be met, you can raise and approve exceptions, but you should document and revisit them periodically to rebalance the quality bar for them.

TABLE 5-8 Quality Bar Questionnaire

SCALABILITY	AVAILABILITY	RESILIENCY	MANAGE-MENT	DEVOPS	SECURITY
Can the application handle the load? Does the application infrastructure increase the node count with increased demand?	Do you have multiple instances of the application across regions and geographies? Can the application sustain a node failure? Can the application sustain a path failure?	If the application fails, how is a new instance instantiated? If the application fails, how does the final transaction get replayed? If you failed to a different geo region, how do you recover from the last checkpoint?	How do you back up the application? How do you monitor the application telemetry? How do you monitor the operating system telemetry? How do you monitor performance problems? How do you gather logging data?	How do you capture fault information and integrate it into the bug/triage/remediation process? How do you deploy new updates to the cloud deployment? Have you translated your applications and infrastructure to use infrastructure as code?	Do you have encryption turned on for data at rest? Do you have encryption turned on for data in transit? How do you rotate encryption keys? Do you have firewalls in place? How do you monitor audit data from machines and cloud services?

The table itself is not a definitive checklist for creating that cutover quality bar, but it gives you some suggestions of the types of questions to ask to ensure all elements are in place for an application before it moves to production.

The cutover process itself doesn't just finish with the quality bar. The methods for bringing an application live must be defined. Figure 5-17 shows a sample application that has been through the migration factory and is ready to be cut over so the cloud service takes the load.

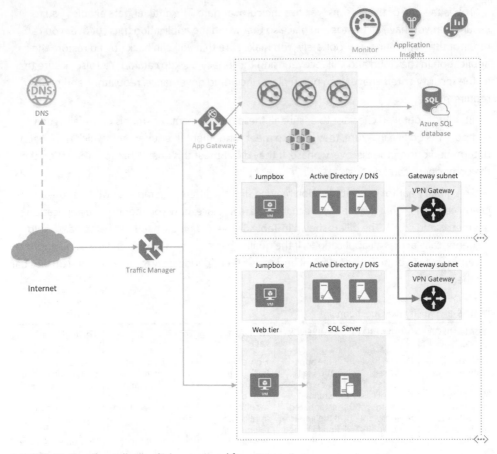

FIGURE 5-17 Sample application being prepared for cutover.

Figure 5-17 represents a web application in a traditional two-tier architecture (web and database). The application was accessed via a URL that presented the interface to the application. After going through discovery, the web application was migrated from a full web virtual machine into a container and was deployed into a Kubernetes cluster. The DevOps pipeline was created to support the application being deployed directly from source code into a container and then into the Kubernetes cluster. The database was migrated to run in Azure SQL Database. The migration factory validated all the test scenarios for functionality and performance, and we met our cutover quality bar for moving to production.

To perform the final cutover for this application, we must consider a few steps.

Consumer access to the application

We must consider how consumers access the application. As we mentioned earlier, the consumers access the application via a URL, but knowing only this is not enough. We must understand what state that URL is in. Is it a short URL like http://app01 or is it a FQDN URL like http://app01.fourthcoffee.com? We need to understand where the application is being accessed from: internally or externally? Do we have any proxy servers in place? Do we access the URL over HTTP or HTTPS?

These are all relatively basic questions, but they can greatly affect cutting over. For example, if we have an internal-facing application, customers access it over HTTP, and we decide to use an approach as shown in Figure 5-15, how do we translate a short URL to a long URL? How does that impact our network? How do users authenticate to the application if we haven't modernized to authenticate to OAuth2.0? How does the application respond if we use HTTPS? Was it designed to handle HTTPS?

The questions keep building, but you will begin to see that they help us build additional functional tests that can be integrated into the migration factory. For now, let's say we're moving from a short URL to a long URL as previously detailed, and we maintain Kerberos authentication.

It will be necessary to explain to the staff that we will begin requiring them to access the application via the FQDN. We also can create a CNAME for http://app01 to redirect to the FQDN. In our scenario, we can create a traffic manager URL that all clients will be sent to before they're appropriately directed back into the application. The traffic manager URL gives us some breathing space as well. We can expose the app on premises to the internet securely and have the traffic manager send the stream to the on-premises network while we get ready to cut over. The traffic manager has a failover profile that allows us to seamlessly redirect the traffic to Azure. The application gateway will ensure that even if clients attempt to access the application via the unsecure http endpoint, they will be redirected to the secure https endpoint. In theory, we also could support http://app01 pointing to the internal VIP of the application located on the Kubernetes cluster if we don't want to expose the application or modify access policies.

In our case, we need to make DNS modifications to support this new traffic redirection. These will include CNAMEs, but it also involves reducing the TTL of the DNS records so clients don't cache the results for long and will get updated quickly to the new site. Ensuring network configuration is in place to support these paths is also a requirement, but this can be completed as part of the infrastructure building and the final cutover testing.

The data sync in our case will be an offline cutover. The SQL Server on premises will be drained of connections and will have restrictions put in place for accessing it by any tier or consumer except the Database Migration Service. The data will be migrated, and then the traffic manager profile will be redirected to the cloud. Consumers then will begin to access the system as normal, and the cutover will be complete. We can begin to retire the on-premises system.

Creating the teams to support the migration factory

Creating a migration factory requires having a migration factory team in place to support the endeavor. The team is tasked with performing all the functions we have discussed so far in this chapter—from discovery to cutover. Building the overall teams to support this starts with building PODS.

Pods

Pods represent a group of people who fall into a particular skill set. For example, you may create a pod of .Net developers, a pod of Java developers, or a pod of people who have VMware-specific skills. Figure 5-18 shows a sample of pods forming a bigger migration team.

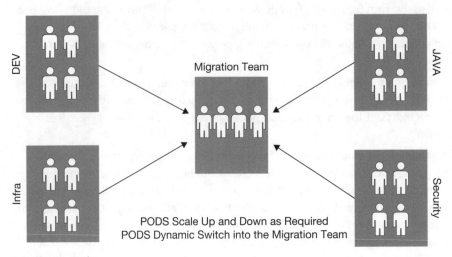

FIGURE 5-18 Pods.

The pods combine to create bigger teams to support the migration of particular applications. The pods can flex based on the demand during the application migration. For example, if this a Java application, the Java pods might increase its members to support migrating that application. Then if the next application is .NET heavy, the Java pod will downsize, and the .NET pod will scale accordingly. Notice that the infrastructure and security pod may stay the same size.

TEAMS

Pods form teams. Although there will be a core migration team to support the effort, there also will be a variety of other teams to support the overall migration factory. Figure 5-19 shows some of the additional teams (which can also be made up from pods).

Our approach is to have a core migration team that will run our factory and get our application estate to the cloud in the quickest but best way possible. Our app team will be responsible for discovery and profiling our applications. Our advance team is responsible for ensuring the migration team knows what needs to change in its processes to support any new types of applications, especially if the advance team has predicted or identified a pattern in the applications still to come.

The exception team handles the one-offs in the applications, which have pretty unique circumstances, or applications that have entered the factory and have been identified as having unique characteristics that don't conform to a standardization process. The QA teams ensure that the applications have been validated correctly in the cloud and are the guardians of the cutover.

The teams shown in Figure 5-19 work closely together. As in the DevOps life cycle, they feed into each other with valuable feedback to improve the overall migration factory.

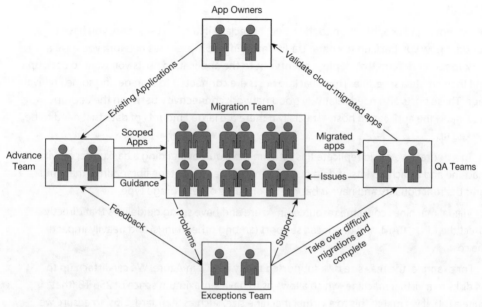

FIGURE 5-19 Teams.

Beyond migration

We have walked through the processes and systems you need to put in place to complete application migration. After it's been implemented and you successfully start moving applications to the cloud, the conversation will eventually divert to the question, "What next?"

Optimization

What's next is optimization. At the start of this chapter, we highlighted that you often will have to get to the cloud first and then drive optimization rather than trying to drive optimization and then move to the cloud. Refactoring an application takes an enormous amount of effort, and items usually pop up unexpectedly, and time to delivery of the refactoring slips, which delays the whole project. If we move using the rehost scenario, we get to the cloud rapidly and begin the process of optimization with focus on cost optimization and using cloud efficiency.

Optimization covers a variety of different possibilities some of which we will discuss here.

Management optimization

Let's start with how you can approach the management system that enterprises use to control their environments and how different areas within that management ecosystem can be optimized.

BACKUP

When moving your application to the cloud, especially in a rehost scenario, you have to consider how you back up the data. Traditionally, in an on-premises network you have a backup server or farm that deploys agents out to the application hosts you want to back up and then create a schedule. These backup hosts are connected to storage and some archival tape. These hosts also need relatively good network connectivity between the backup server and the application host, especially if there are large amounts of data that need to be backed up.

To a degree, we could replicate this setup in the cloud by building a backup server virtual machine and attaching lots of data disks. Then install a virtual tape library drive that emulates the functionality and have it backed up on some other storage type.

Virtual machines consume resources in Azure and have sizing guidelines that directly affect the CPUs, RAM, and disk it can support (among other things) and heavily impacts the cost.

For example, the max size disk supported today is 4 TB in Azure. We can attach up to 64 disks to a virtual machine, which allows us to have a maximum space of 256 TB (that's quite a lot). If we match this to a virtual machine size, such as Standard_L16s, to ensure we get the IOPS and throughput needed to meet our RPO and RTO for our backup, our estimated monthly cost runs into $33,000 USD per month. What's interesting is that this is just for the data; it's not a complete virtual machine backup!

> **NOTE** Pricing will vary. Please look for the latest information available on the Azure pricing calculator at https://azure.microsoft.com/en-us/pricing/calculator/.

That solution isn't cost-effective, and we shouldn't implement it. If we take an optimized approach to backups, we would look at a native cloud service. Azure has an integrated backup platform called Azure Backup. If we want to back up the virtual machines with all the data and applications installed in a snapshot consistent method, the cost for 256 TB of storage for Azure Backup is estimated to be $11,000 USD per month. If we still require guest OS–level backup, the cost rises because we must include a virtual machine to run Azure Backup Server. Figure 5-20 shows a sample virtual machine blade with Azure Backup integrated directly into it. You can see job information and the recovery points available. This shows the default policy of one backup per day.

Another example scenario involves SQL backup. SQL can export the backup data directly to an Azure storage blob, so we could use the Azure Backup service to get a full virtual machine backup and then run a SQL backup job to export the data to Azure Storage. SQL also can restore from Azure Storage as well.

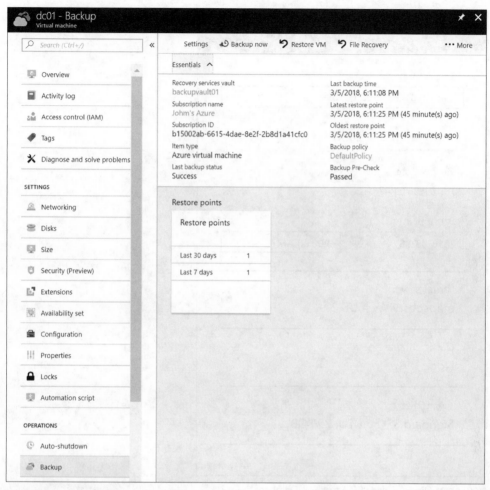

FIGURE 5-20   Azure Backup natively integrated into a virtual machine blade.

Backup also changes when you consume Azure PaaS services. If you use Azure SQL Database, for example, you don't have an agent-based backup available; you do not get access to the "host" server. You select the backup options that the PaaS service makes available with the appropriate SLAs.

In the case of Azure SQL, the native backup runs every five minutes and creates a restore point automatically. Depending on the tier of service you select, you can retain data for 35 days and then integrate it into a recovery vault for longer-term retention.

Figure 5-21 shows a sample of the restore recovery point blade for an Azure SQL Database. Notice that we have the oldest recovery point available and then a restore point selected. You can modify the date and time of the restore point to any date going back to the oldest recovery point.

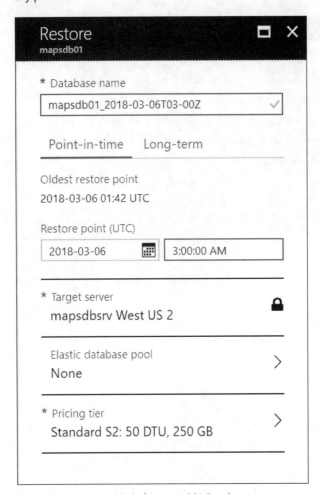

FIGURE 5-21 Restore blade for Azure SQL Database.

MONITORING

Monitoring can be different when it comes to the cloud, with different technologies in the cloud, with different cost structures (i.e. charging for egress traffic). You need to spend time thinking of what you need to know and how to achieve it in cloud. If you choose the standard rehost scenario then you can use existing tooling to monitor the virtual machines you have migrated as long as you have the appropriate connectivity between the virtual machines and the monitoring system. If you choose a refactor scenario then the monitoring system that's currently in place has to be examined to determine whether it's still fit for the purpose.

The deeper and more cloud-native your network becomes, the less effective the existing tool becomes. For example, if you have an agent-based monitoring system and you move away from virtual machines to a serverless architecture, where do you deploy the agent? How do you determine the health state and provide alerts when problems occur?

Another problem with trying to maintain an existing monitor system is that you're not receiving the latest updates of the latest services that are happening in cloud. If you think at the pace at which the cloud evolves and look at the vendor's update cycle, it's generally significantly behind where the services are today. Even with the updates you can't take advantage of the powerful machine learning and AI algorithms that cloud monitoring solutions are implementing to detect more sophisticated threats.

Figure 5-22 and 5-23 show two different security-related dashboards that are built from Microsoft rulesets; those rulesets have been built from the knowledge that Microsoft has attained while running global cloud services.

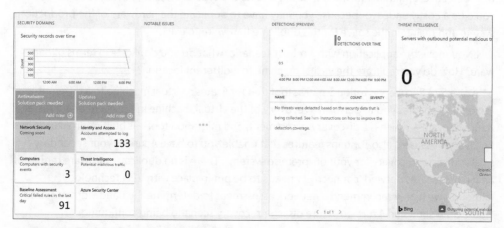

FIGURE 5-22 Security and Audit dashboard.

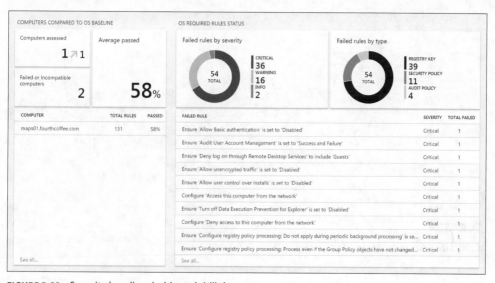

FIGURE 5-23 Security baseline dashboard drill down.

OMS&S is an example of a cloud monitoring tool that can collect data native from Azure virtual machines and native PaaS services.

Microsoft takes the information it has obtained from running its global services and creates rules and patterns to detect erroneous events. You can build customer-specific rules and export data to PowerBI to build visually striking dashboards. This tool can collect data from any internet-connected source via a variety of methods, including the agent-based collection.

DISASTER RECOVERY

When you migrate your application to the cloud, how you recover the system in the event of a critical failure has to change. Traditionally you would define a recovery point and recovery time objective, and that information would dictate the type of system you had to build. This could be a costly endeavor because you may have to duplicate the hardware of the production system and maintain the space for this duplicate hardware to exist.

If you move the application with a rehost scenario, what do you duplicate in terms of hardware? How do you replicate the virtual machine to a different location?

Azure Site Recovery is a cloud-native tool that replicates a virtual machine to a different region and enables you to perform a recovery of the virtual machine in the event of a disaster. Azure Migrate—which is a discovery, assessment, and migration tool—is built upon Azure Site Recovery because it also contains features that enable you to have Azure as your secondary site for disaster recovery for your on-premise systems. There is no duplicate hardware required, and in most cases network connectivity needs to be put in place with VPN technology (although we highly recommend a network assessment to determine the bandwidth required). Figure 5-24 shows an Azure-to-Azure disaster recovery scenario being configured.

FIGURE 5-24 Azure-to-Azure site recovery.

Azure to Azure Site Recovery reduces the cost of having to maintain secondary datacenters and secondary hardware. If you use the "playbook" scenarios available in Azure Site recovery, you can greatly reduce the human touchpoints required to recover from a disaster.

Application optimization

The ultimate end goal in application migration is to maximize the benefits of running in the cloud. For most enterprises, the rehost scenario will be the first one to approach. After this scenario is performed you can begin looking at how you can optimize the application. In this section, we discuss a few of the options and approaches you might take when examining the next steps.

AZURE WEB APPS

If you have an application that has a web-tier front end, an easy way to optimize the application is to move the web app to an Azure Web app. This ensures you can benefit from the scalability, reliability, and availability of the Azure App Service platform. It also removes another virtual machine that you must manage.

The authentication methods and frameworks the application consumes may need to be updated before it can be hosted on the platform. You can integrate Azure Web app deployment mechanisms into your DevOps frameworks, so you can make changes and deploy and test rapidly.

CONTAINERS

If the application you migrated has a web tier, you also could migrate it to a container to reduce the overall footprint. With containers, you can integrate the packaging and deployment into a DevOps pipeline and have end-to-end deployment. You can use a managed container service (AKS) to run your container estate. Containers give you the chance to optimize in a lift-and-shift manner from a virtual machine to a container.

When you use containers, you become less worried about some management concepts like guest OS monitoring. Your monitoring footprint changes, and you can gather telemetry from the managed service rather than having hooks into a custom-built platform.

AZURE FUNCTIONS

Azure Functions provide even more opportunity for shrinking the size of a deployment and using native PaaS systems and serverless compute as much as possible. If your application had background web jobs or you had a "processing tier" in the application, you could migrate in source code these jobs to Azure functions that would execute the jobs. The job is only charged for the length of runtime, and Azure Functions provide all the necessary resources to execute that job.

In comparison, if you had to run a virtual machine to execute these jobs, you would constantly be paying for a virtual machine even when it had no work to do. You could also run into scale issues if the virtual machine ran out of resources.

POWERBI

This is one of the simplest optimizations you could do, and the benefits that an application would receive are also unquantifiable! You could use PowerBI to generate reports for your application or your business. This would reduce the need for a reporting server. PowerBI scales on demand because it's a cloud service, and it can integrate directly with Azure SQL as a data source (as an example, it can also connect to other data sources).

AZURE SQL MANAGED INSTANCES

If your application requires a SQL database, rather than provisioning a dedicated virtual machine you could optimize and use a SQL Managed Instance in Azure. Managed instances provide all the functionality of a virtual machine with SQL installed but have none of the management overhead because it's handled by the platform.

Chapter 6

Delivering datacenter efficiency

In this chapter, we take a deep dive into some examples of datacenters in action, look at existing frameworks for delivering datacenter efficiency, explore examples of good, efficient IT practices in action, and walk through a scenario for moving a workload from your on-premises infrastructure to Azure while maintaining a process framework.

Snowflake datacenters

Take a moment and ask yourself, "When was the last time I worked for an organization that didn't have a datacenter?" Explore that thought and reflect on how good or bad it was. Think about whether you had structured cabling; if so, was it labelled correctly? Did you have regular hardware refresh practices, and what was it like to deploy new servers? Also what have been the common elements of all the datacenters you have worked with?

It's no secret that enterprises all over the globe have datacenters—big, small, or globally distributed. In fact there are an infinite number of different types of datacenters, and every single one is slightly (or in some cases significantly) different. In fact, datacenters are like snowflakes—each one is unique!

Why is uniqueness important? Well, because each datacenter is unique, we need to try to identify key components and pillars to help you focus on what datacenter efficiency looks like for you and give you a path that you can follow with slight deviations to begin to achieve efficiencies.

Before you embark on the journey, let us clear up one thing that's ingrained in every fiber of every aspect of IT: Change is scary, and change is hard. However, as we continually mention in this book and chapter, change is required to get to modern IT and to delivering datacenter efficiency.

As we alluded to in Chapter 1, change becomes the focal point of delivering datacenter efficiency. It becomes the one challenge that you need to conquer above all else. In fact, through every iteration, change can take on a different formation that you need to conquer all over again. Change can shapeshift based on the problem you need to solve, and you need to potentially change your approach in whatever form that may take.

Datacenter efficiency isn't only about improving the hardware or using the latest, greatest next-gen piece of software. It's more fundamental, and a good comparison is exercising the human body.

If you try to run a 5-mile race on day one of exercising, would you be able to that? (If you can, you're lucky!) Chances are that you would need to train your body to have sufficient stamina and lung capacity to run a race. The training required to be successful is pretty specific. What about a boxing match? Would you be able to last 15 rounds based on the same training you did to run 5 miles? Or would you even be able to run 20 miles on the same training that you did to be able to run 5 miles, or would change be required?

The point is that to meet the goals you need to change, and unfortunately you can't entirely map out changes, and you will work off wire frameworks to achieve your goal.

Try thinking of change in terms of levels. As you recognize and build efficiencies into one level, you proceed to the next. But change also is bidirectional; sometimes you need to go down to the original level to fix areas to deliver the efficiency in the next higher level.

Figure 6-1 shows an example levels in respect of delivering datacenter efficiency.

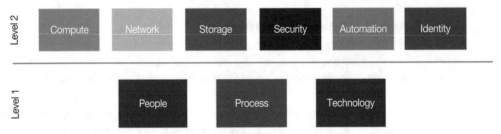

FIGURE 6-1   Building blocks of delivering efficiency

If you start on Level 1, you can train people in the newer technologies and modern modes of administration, and you can give them challenges to meet enthusiastic service level agreements (SLAs) for the business. You can review and improve on how a service is delivered or optimize the tasks done in a process, and you could implement new technology to help you achieve items within people and process.

After you have some of these foundations, you can proceed to level 2 and start improving your compute, network, storage, and so on environments using the newly skilled people, the updated processes, and the updated technology. When something in level 2 is proving difficult to deliver efficiency on, review the foundation components in level 1 and decide whether there is more you could do at that level to strengthen delivering efficiency in level 2. As you walk through all aspects of the IT organization, start at level 1, examine and scrutinize what is in place, and start the change.

Datacenter transformation versus digital transformation

In almost every executive briefing, whitepaper, or blog post about modern IT, you see something about digital transformation. Digital transformation is critical for modern IT, and it's absolutely critical for businesses in general to go through digital transformation because the potential of becoming stagnant and missing a large percentage of markets is too great.

However, among all this digital transformation exists a core problem much like the chicken and egg scenario. Which should come first: datacenter transformation or digital transformation? Given that datacenters run businesses, to be successful at digital transformation you need to at least begin addressing the topic of datacenter transformation. If we play devil's advocate, though, we suggest that maybe you need to begin digital transformation to be able to have datacenter transformation.

The truth is that you need to examine both paradigms of transformation and map out intersecting paths. For example, in recent years customers have begun looking at their aging datacenters, specifically their secondary (usually disaster recovery) datacenters. These secondary datacenters typically incur almost equal amounts of cost to build when compared to the primary datacenter, often ranging into the tens of millions of dollars. They also require significant budgets to maintain and operate. In theory, as the production IT system grows, so should the investment into the secondary datacenter. If a disaster rolls in, you might find that the multimillion-dollar investment can't meet the RTO/RPO defined in the financially backed SLAs the company has written. This is a significant problem.

Now introduce a public cloud technology like Azure and a need to digitally transform, which makes life for the IT organization easier, makes the business always available, and makes recovering from a disaster easier. The IT organization could essentially drop its entire secondary datacenter, replicate the entire infrastructure to Azure using Azure Site Recovery, and have a fully automated failover capability that can be tested and refined through each pass.

The company has begun to achieve datacenter efficiency through both a digital transformation (the introduction of automation and education for their employees) and datacenter transformation (using Azure as the secondary datacenter), which saves millions of dollars annually.

There are a million examples that we could use. Let's take a look at our case study and focus on a challenge that IT staff at Fourth Coffee had, and let's work toward solving that issue with practical implementations.

Fourth Coffee—eating their elephant

We've frequently referred to eating the elephant throughout this book, but it's for a good reason. It's the reminder that regardless of the subject of the chapter or section, the work involved isn't easy, and it takes time to achieve. It is a step-by-step process often done as little changes (or bites).

You might remember from Chapter 2 that Fourth Coffee wants to undergo a transformation project. The project encompasses a vast array of goals, both business and IT related. To help you understand delivering datacenter efficiency a little more, we're looking at some of their items and breaking them down further so that we can give some practical advice on how the company might achieve the goals.

If we look at some of the items Fourth Coffee wants to achieve and distill them into one specific item that we can used as a beacon for delivering datacenter efficiency, we would say that Fourth Coffee wants to deliver a better customer experience. This focal point allows us to break down the problem further by trying to understand the elements that would make a better customer experience. In Chapter 2, we established that items like a mobile ordering experience, always having the right stock so the customers can have their beverages, bringing more venues to the customer, and providing customized experiences would go a long way to achieve this.

Stop and think about whether this is a digital transformation, a datacenter transformation, or just a matter of delivering datacenter efficiency? In our opinion, it's all three. Why? Because to achieve anything on the list, Fourth Coffee has to involve aspects of level 1 and level 2 as we outlined earlier in this chapter.

Now let's take one single item from Fourth Coffee's transformation goals: the mobile ordering experience. This gives us a framework for the other items we want to achieve. If we think about potential architectures that would support the goal, the technologies and/or entry points would be like others.

We have two problems for FC to achieve the goal of a mobile ordering experience:

- The infrastructure is not built to handle it.
- The IT team are not skilled to support it.

If we don't address these two issues, this project would fail—maybe not on day 1 but very soon into the project because the complexities of building a system, let alone modifying a datacenter to support it, can be overwhelming.

Let's take the problem into the two parts and walk you through how we could digitally transform to achieve this goal, perform some datacenter transformation, and achieve efficiency during the course of the project.

The infrastructure is not built to handle it

We've mentioned that Fourth Coffee has aging hardware and old software. The company has complicated managing their environment by piecing the components together over the last few decades. Adding the infrastructure to host a mobile ordering experience would likely tip the infrastructure into oblivion. The real question we need to solve is how can Fourth Coffee do more with less, or how does Fourth Coffee operate this infrastructure efficiently?

Remember one thing, terminology and your viewpoint can lead to making poor choices. An example is negatively judging words like "aging hardware and old software." If you have a negative attitude, ultimately you start thinking about replacing hardware and software, which leads to extra cost, and you might not think of it as efficiently as you need to. If you take those kinds of terms at face value and realize that the hardware and software are still tangible assets with value, then you can look at efficiency in a very different manner.

Here's a practical example: a server that was bought three years ago still has use. It can help you in building a resource pool, for example. Unfortunately, sometimes to drive efficiency, you must incur costs. Everything must be assessed for its end need and from there you decide what can be done.

In the Fourth Coffee scenario, we have a couple of items we must examine and understand how we can become more efficient. Let's take the aging fiber channel SAN; it was purchased seven years ago and hosts hundreds of gigabytes (GB) of data. It runs at 4 GB/s and has reached its capacity for additional trays. Its extended warranty is expired, and it's becoming a liability for the company. There is only one sensible thing for Fourth Coffee to do: replace it, which incurs cost. The challenge is deciding what to replace it with. SANs have been a cornerstone of enterprises for decades, but they also introduce dependencies on vendors, storage types, storage cards, special administrators, and so on.

To drive datacenter efficiency, you must take a step back and look at a straightforward concept: standardization. Standardization helps drive datacenter efficiency by using commodity hardware with no specialization to reach the demands of the business. Standardization simplifies the administration patterns, the support process, the maintenance cycles, and coverage in disasters.

What does this look like for Fourth Coffee? In the Windows Server 2016 world, we introduce the Storage Spaces Direct feature, which enables us to create highly reliable, scalable, and performant storage solutions built on commodity hardware. Rather than spending millions of dollars on specialized SAN hardware, Fourth Coffee could purchase a solution at a fraction of the cost. The company also could build a Storage Spaces Direct solution in virtual machines in Azure., which lends portability to the solution (that is, build it on premises and migrate to Azure later).

The administration concepts are based on PowerShell. The technology is Microsoft and is already a large percentage of Fourth Coffee's IT estate. The hardware is commodity; if the company can't get the previous type of disk, it just needs to match the speed and choose a different vendor. If Fourth Coffee loses a node in a storage spaces direct cluster, it can build a new one again with commodity hardware. Connectivity is provided by ethernet rather than special fiber card. Storage Spaces Direct also provides a large degree of redundancy across nodes by replicating data synchronously. Fourth Coffee also can implement a highly converged infrastructure that drives more efficiency with this technology. Figure 6-2 shows a layout of Storage Spaces Direct.

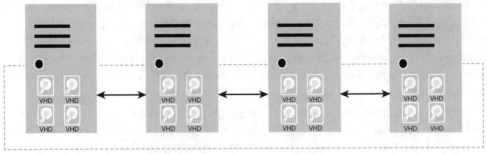

Storage Spaces Direct Storage Pool

FIGURE 6-2   Storage Spaces Direct system

The efficiency is driven from not having to get specialized knowledge to manage a system and not having to pay a premium for specialized hardware. Efficiency is also realized by simplifying the management experience, using interfaces that lend themselves to automation, reducing the power consumption of the storage, and so much more.

Fourth Coffee also should review its database solution for the point-of-sale (POS) system and force the upgrade to the latest edition of SQL Server. This allows us access to better features for performance and high availability. Straight away Fourth Coffee can migrate away from a physical cluster and use SQL Always On technology.

This new database system can be built in virtual machines. SQL Always On also allows for third-leg asynchronous copies for disaster recovery. In combination with Hyper-V, Scale-Out File Services, and Storage Spaces Direct, Fourth Coffee can build a highly efficient infrastructure to host the SQL database. Include Azure in the equation, and we can span our database to the cloud for an asynchronous disaster recovery copy.

Figure 6-3 shows the sample solution, including the spoke for the public cloud. It demonstrates a fully hyper-converged infrastructure that uses commodity hardware delivering unparalleled performance and reliability. The sample uses SQL Server in virtual machines for flexibility and availability sets to ensure that the SQL nodes will be available in the event of a physical node failure. The databases reside on the storage spaces' direct pool with multiple copies spanned across the nodes for high availability with a 10 Gbit Ethernet Remote Direct Memory Access (RDMA) enabled backbone.

All this drives efficiency in the datacenter from hardware usage to energy to solution cost. Then we look at the benefits that updated modern software will deliver, like SQL Always On and the asynchronous replication or Hyper-V replication to make our disaster recovery process easier. What becomes even more useful is that no matter its location, the administration experience remains similar, and that reduces the learning curve required to adopt this technology.

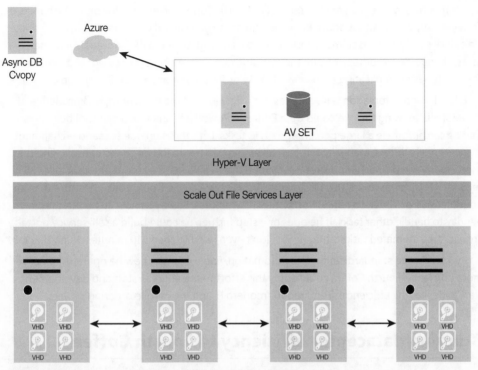

FIGURE 6-3 Hyper-converged infrastructure with SQL AlwaysOn and third spoke to Azure

We could keep examining the infrastructure and highlighting how we could deliver more efficiencies; however: we need to take a look at another aspect of delivering datacenter efficiency in the next section. We will of course revisit this later in practical examples of achieving our goals and provide more details to expand on the delivery of a mobile ordering system.

The IT team is not skilled to support it?

Although updating hardware and software and reprovisioning existing assets will deliver some efficiency to our datacenter, those things are only part of the journey. Efficiency can be driven from standardization and, more importantly, automation. We could spend a lot of time automating elements of the infrastructure and deliver a large degree of efficiency from that alone.

Remember, a person's time has a cost, and although it's a cheesy saying, time is money! Saving someone's time will save money, and if the person has more time to work on better tasks to improve IT then it will help deliver more services to the business with fewer resources. Standardization levels the playing field and simplifies our challenge of delivering efficiency and automation, and it helps save you the time to perform mundane tasks that are highly repetitive.

We mentioned in an earlier chapter that at Fourth Coffee the administrator for Exchange, Eddie, is a superstar. Although we know he's great, no one can fully understand what he does. He's always busy and has so many tasks to help users with their mailbox quotas, set up new users, change email address, ensure the message queues are being processed, and make sure the databases are replicating in their availability groups (database availability groups).

Eddie has no automation skills and has not invested the time to increase his knowledge of PowerShell. Knowing this, we could train Eddie on PowerShell and teach him tool building so that he can automate a large percentage of his tasks. Let's focus on one scenario—changing a user's email address. Manually this task takes five minutes to log on to the console, find the user, modify the property, and save the changes. With a PowerShell script, the task takes 30 seconds. If Eddie has to run this task manually 20 times a day, it would consume more than an hour of his day! With automation, it consumes 10 minutes. Eddie has now 70 minutes more per day to handle other tasks. If he goes one step further, he could build a self-service portal around the automated task so that he wouldn't even need to spend 10 minutes doing that job.

By introducing standardization and automation, Eddie changes how he operates to deliver more efficiency. Fourth Coffee could apply this effort to the entire IT staff and development staff to deliver the efficiencies required for modern IT and the mobile ordering project.

Bringing datacenter efficiency to Fourth Coffee

Take a quick look at Figure 6-4, which shows Fourth Coffee's current POS architecture.

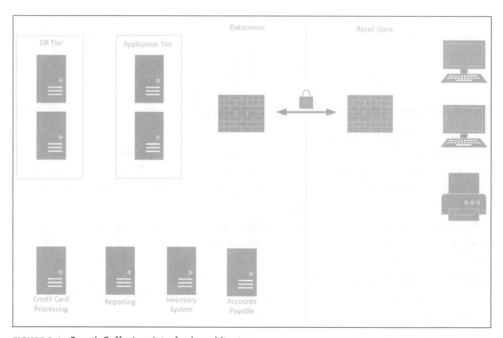

FIGURE 6-4   Fourth Coffee's point-of-sale architecture

In this section, we take you through the practicality of looking at the three basic pillars of people, process, and technology and showing you how to achieve efficiency across areas like compute, network, storage, and so on, starting from the current state of the POS system and evolving to the mobile ordering system.

People investment

Before tackling any technology, you *must* invest in people and their skills. It's common in an enterprise for a team to get stuck and not necessarily be aware of all the latest and greatest improvements and features from a technology or vendor group. They often can get siloed into what they have to deal with day to day.

Investing in people is a matter of fact. If you don't do it, someone else will, and there has to be some expectation on the people that they keep themselves relatively up to date.

Here's an example: An organization gives the employees some time every Friday to identify new technology that could help them into their daily activities. If no new technology can be identified, there's an opportunity for the employees to identify how they can improve on the area and to give critical feedback.

The skills we want to encourage organizations to develop can be broken down into two main areas: soft skills and technical skills. We discuss items within each as we move through this chapter.

Soft skills

There are many skills an IT organization requires investment in. We highlight a few key areas where training employees can lead to greater productivity and efficiency for the IT organization:

- **Feedback:** Teaching people to give concise, relevant feedback is not an easy task, but doing so leads to treasure! The rewards are simply too great to count when you have a method of getting the right information to affect positive changes in the business.

- **Presentation skills:** Developing your team's ability to articulate and deliver a message to the correct audience can be critical for the success of any project. When people successfully deliver a message, they can win the investment they require. When they're ineffective in delivering the message, it can set the IT department back.

> **NOTE** James Whittaker provides a great reference for developing presentation skills. You can find some of the amazing material he has released at the following link:
>
> news.microsoft.com/stories/people/james-whittaker.html

- **Unconscious bias:** This is a curious skill to develop. It involves helping people understand that they can unknowingly judge conversations and ideas based on the people involved. Training people to recognize this behavior and correct it can lead to greater efficiency in team collaboration.

Technical skills investment

Unfortunately, developing soft skills is only half the battle! Technical skills help the IT organization perform tasks more efficiently and build out tools that can be reused by the rest of the organization, allowing cross-pollination of skills throughout the IT silos.

In this section, we identify and dive into some of the technical skill areas that we feel greatly benefit organizations. We try to break down each area of investment to help describe what is it, what it looks like, and what can it do to help you make priority decisions on where to spend time.

GRAPHIC USER INTERFACE (GUI) TOOLS

What is it?

Windows Server has long shipped with a set of GUI tools to perform administration tasks for managing servers. Some of these tools work on local and remote systems, but others work only on local machines.

What does it look like?

There have been numerous attempts to standardize the look and experience of GUI management tools, including the Control Panel, Microsoft Management Console (MMC), Server Manager, and, more recently, Honolulu. The result is that there is no single coherent GUI experience for managing Windows Server. But that is not why we don't use GUIs in this book. If you want to pursue modern IT, we strongly recommend against using GUIs to do management for the following reasons:

- **Quality control:** If you have a change you need to perform on 100 servers and that change involves 100 mouse clicks, what are the chances you'll reproduce those mouse clicks in order 100 times? (Hint: 0)

- **Lack of productivity:** Imagine the effort required to run a GUI on 100 machines to perform an operation. Now image the effort required if you have 1,000 machines or that you need to do this work for the thousands of test VMs that you create every week.

- **Lack of peer review/auditing:** How confident are you giving a new-hire admin privileges to 100 production machines and having perform arbitrary GUI operations? Can you peer review or audit their mouse clicks?

What can it do?

GUI tools are great tools for learning a technology or running a single server for a small business, but they have minimal to no role in modern IT.

Where do I learn more?

Don't.

POWERSHELL[1]

What is it?

PowerShell is a powerful automation framework that is cross platform. Companies can utilize this framework to build tooling to help them more effectively administer their entire IT Enterprise.

What does it look like?

PowerShell is built around cmdlets, which perform actions and are stored in modules. The actions in the cmdlets are usually in the format verb-noun.

For example, if you want to get all the processes on a system, you use the Get-Process cmdlet as follows:

```
Get-Process
```

Or

```
Get-Process -Name lsass
```

Another example would be if you want to retrieve the last 10 events in the security event log for a Windows server. You would use the cmdlet Get-Eventlog as follows

```
Get-Eventlog -LogName Security -Newest 10
```

The output is shown in Figure 6-5.

```
JPS> get-Eventlog -LogName Security  -Newest 10

  Index Time          EntryType  Source           InstanceID Message
  ----- ----          ---------  ------           ---------- -------
  275302 Nov 29 16:01  SuccessA... Microsoft-Windows...    4648 A logon was attempted using explicit credential...
  275301 Nov 29 16:01  SuccessA... Microsoft-Windows...    4648 A logon was attempted using explicit credential...
  275300 Nov 29 16:01  SuccessA... Microsoft-Windows...    4648 A logon was attempted using explicit credential...
  275299 Nov 29 16:01  SuccessA... Microsoft-Windows...    4648 A logon was attempted using explicit credential...
  275298 Nov 29 16:01  SuccessA... Microsoft-Windows...    4648 A logon was attempted using explicit credential...
  275297 Nov 29 16:01  SuccessA... Microsoft-Windows...    4648 A logon was attempted using explicit credential...
  275296 Nov 29 16:01  SuccessA... Microsoft-Windows...    4648 A logon was attempted using explicit credential...
  275295 Nov 29 16:01  SuccessA... Microsoft-Windows...    4672 Special privileges assigned to new logon....
  275294 Nov 29 16:01  SuccessA... Microsoft-Windows...    4624 An account was successfully logged on....
  275293 Nov 29 16:00  SuccessA... Microsoft-Windows...    4648 A logon was attempted using explicit credential...

JPS>
```

FIGURE 6.5 Output of Get-Eventlog

If you used the optional -*ComputerName* parameter on Get-Eventlog, you could target remote computers. You could even wrap this in a script and collect log data from 100 machines automatically, search for a pattern in the data collected, and trigger an alert somewhere if a condition is detected!

PowerShell is all about a set of small tools that can be stitched together using the pipeline character (|). It's designed to create an environment where you can *think* about what you want, *type* it, and *get* the results. Imagine that you want to **Get** all the **Processes Where** the

---

[1] Most of the things we'll be doing with PowerShell require Administrator privileges, so start PowerShell by right-clicking the icon and selecting Run As Administrator.

HandleCount was **greater than 2000**, **sort** them by **HandleCount**, and then **Format** it as a **Table** showing the **Name**, **ID**, and **HandleCount**. Here is how you do that in PowerShell:

```
Get-Process |
  Where HandleCount –ge 2000 |
  Sort HandleCount |
  Format-Table Name,ID,HandleCount
```

> **NOTE** There is a lot of PowerShell in this book, so let's make sure you know what you're looking at when you see the examples. The examples show cmdlet parameters using three forms:
>
> - **No quotes: Get-Service -Name ALG**
> - **Single quotes: Get-Service -Name 'Time Broker'**
> - **Double quotes: $x = 'Broker'; Get-Service -Name "Time $x"**
>
> Here is what is going on:
>
> - When a parameter value is a single word with no spaces, it does not need quotes, and we don't include them to make it easier to read.
> - When a parameter value is multiple words and does not have a variable to be expanded, we use single quotes. This suppresses variable expansion and is best practice to avoid unintended actions.
> - When a parameter value includes a variable name to be expanded (for example, $n), we use double quotes, which allows the parameter to be expanded.

What can it do?

You can use PowerShell to manage your environment that spans across multiple clouds. For example, you can use it to manage creating users, creating virtual machines, failing over a database, and many other tasks. PowerShell can reduce the amount of time required to do standard day-to-day administration tasks to improve the efficiency of the IT team.

Where do I learn more?

The help that ships with PowerShell is amazingly good. Start by using the Get-Help cmdlet and take it from there. If you to prefer watching videos, many people have successfully used a series of Microsoft Virtual Academy video talks to learn PowerShell. The best way to find these are go to the Microsoft Virtual Academy (mva.microsoft.com) and search for "Snover PowerShell." Look for the following:

- Getting Started with Microsoft PowerShell
- Advanced Tools & Scripting with PowerShell 3.0 Jump Start

POWERSHELL DESIRED STATE CONFIGURATION (DSC)

What is it?

Desired State Configuration (DSC) is an essential part of the configuration, management, and maintenance of Windows-based servers. It allows a PowerShell script to specify the configuration of the machine using a declarative model in a simple standard way that is easy to maintain and understand. This is a subset of PowerShell; in a sense, you could consider this the next level of PowerShell skills.

What does it look like?

Following is a sample DSC configuration layout that installs the IIS Role on servers dedicated to being a web server and Hyper-V on servers dedicated to being a VM Host:

```
Configuration Lab1 {

    Node $AllNodes.Where{$_.Role -eq 'WebServer'}.NodeName
    {
        WindowsFeature IISInstall {
            Name  = 'Web-Server'
            Ensure = 'Present'
        }


    }
    Node $AllNodes.Where{$_.Role -eq 'VMHost'}.NodeName
    {
        WindowsFeature HyperVInstall {
            Name  = 'Hyper-V'
            Ensure = 'Present'
        }
    }
}

$MyData =
@{
    AllNodes =
    @(
        @{
            NodeName  = 'Web-1'
            Role      = 'WebServer'
        },
        @{
            NodeName  = 'Web-2'
            Role      = 'WebServer'
        },
        @{
            NodeName  = 'VM-2'
            Role      = 'VMHost'
        }
    )
}

Lab1 -ConfigurationData $MyData -Verbose
```

The very last line does the following:

- It creates a subdirectory using the name of the configuration **'Lab1'**.
- It generates a set of Managed Object Format (MOF) files, one for each node to be configured into that subdirectory (for example, **.\Lab1\Web-1.mof**).

The MOF files are compiled versions of the configuration and are read and interpreted by the Local Configuration Manager engine on the machine to be configured. At this stage, you have defined the configurations you want. Later we show you how to implement those configurations using the Start-DSCConfiguration cmdlet.

What can it do?

PowerShell DSC is a very powerful tool that can help you deploy software and maintain state on machines in a standardized manner. You can use it to integrate into the CI/CD process to ensure that when a piece of software gets updated you can update the DSC configuration scripts to deploy the new software.

Where do I learn more?

Again, the help that ships with PowerShell is your best starting point. Type

```
>   help about_DesiredStateConfiguration
```

and take it from there.

If you to prefer watching videos, many people have successfully used a series of Microsoft Virtual Academy talks on PowerShell to learn PowerShell and DSC. The best way to find these are go to the Microsoft Virtual Academy (mva.microsoft.com) and search for "Snover Power-Shell." Specifically, look for the following:

- Getting Started with PowerShell Desired State Configuration
- Advanced PowerShell Desired State Configuration (DSC) and Custom Resources

CLOUD SHELL

What is it?

Cloud Shell is the ability to run a console window in a browser. It's currently available from the Azure Portal but also will be available from other websites in the future. Cloud Shell enables you to run a Bash/Linux or PowerShell/Windows session.

Each environment includes the latest version of the Azure tools and other tools, including gvim, git, and sqlcmd. Interestingly, the PowerShell/Windows environment allows you also to run Bash, and the Bash/Linux environment allows you also to run PowerShell.

The PowerShell environment mounts Azure as a drive, which allows you to navigate and interact with Azure resources the same way would a file system. For example,

```
> dir azure:\*\VirtualMachines\* |group PowerState
```

NOTE Although they were designed to make it easy to manage Azure Resources, these are fully functional environments. You could install the AWS PowerShell cmdlets and manage AWS using Cloud Shell.

What does it look like?

Figure 6-6 shows the Cloud Shell in action directly from the browser. It looks and feels like traditional PowerShell Windows! We are listing the status of the Virtual Machines in our Azure Subscription.

FIGURE 6-6 Cloud Shell in action

From Cloud Shell, you can administer your Azure Resources and perform tasks as necessary.

What can it do?

Ultimately Cloud Shell gives you the ability to use familiar tooling like PowerShell to manage a complex environment like Azure.

Where do I learn more?

Visit docs.microsoft.com/en-us/azure/cloud-shell/overview to get more information about Cloud Shell.

AZURE AUTOMATION

What is it?

Whereas PowerShell is a task automation and configuration management framework, Azure Automation (AA) is a task automation and configuration management solution built on top of PowerShell. AA is a product designed to be used by teams to manage production environments. AA runs as a cloud service in Azure but can manage any Windows, Linux, or MacOS machine anywhere—whether it is running in Azure, in AWS, in GCE, or on premises (via an Azure Automation Gateway).

AA is the solution that transforms ad hoc scripting into formal production management. It enables teams to create formal repositories of production scripts under source code control (no more losing track of your scripts, accidental deletions, or questions about who/when/how did this production script change). It provides a secure central repository for managed assets (for example, credentials to be used to manage systems, common parameters to be used by all scripts). It provides scheduling and integration with other products/web services so that scripts can be run on regular intervals or in response to events. It also provides logging and output management so that you know when scripts were run, and you can look back on previous runs to examine the script results.

What does it look like?

AA has many different sections to it, including source control, DSC, runbooks, and assets. Figure 6-7 shows AA and some demo runbooks. The figure also shows the menu of other options you could potentially configure and use.

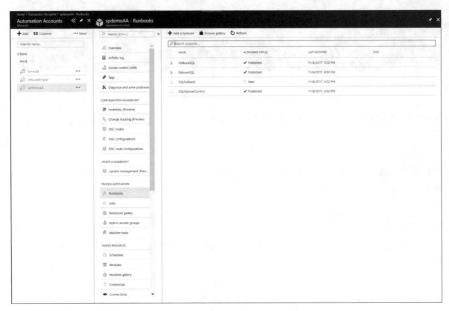

FIGURE 6-7   Azure Automation

What can it do?

AA was built to automate processes that can be executed in PowerShell and Python across private and public environments! You can use it to create users, provision infrastructure, and do an endless number of other tasks. You also can integrate AA with Microsoft Operations Management and Security Suite to respond to alerts and trigger actions based on the data. You can use it via webhooks, which opens up another significant amount of potential integration points. AA also can leverage DSC and enforce configurations to act as a pull server across private and public clouds.

Where do I learn more?

Visit azure.microsoft.com/en-us/services/automation/ for more information.

Process investments

Every organization strives to build procedures for administration tasks that are performed. We have built hundreds of procedures for organizations that try to standardize how something is done. IT departments need this standardization so they can ensure that if they have 500 servers to deploy, each one gets deployed in the same way. This leads to stability in the environment and reliability of the service the IT team is offering.

However, something almost always happens to the process. It gets defined, it gets implemented, and eventually it gets ignored.

Why? In our experience, process gets ignored because it never had a life cycle applied to it. Like all things we talk about throughout the book, a life cycle is required to build successful processes.

The life cycle of a process

Life cycle is cyclical. It must feed itself to continue to be useful and meet the needs of why it was defined. As with most life cycles, we can identify four main pillars that you can map to the DevOps pillars (review Chapter 2 for the DevOps life cycle):

- **Documenting a process:** Documenting the process is simple; you record the steps taken to complete the task. However, there is a twist, which is understanding why you are performing the task. Each step in the process should have a reason for why it is done. This helps you shape an efficient process and can also lead to being objective about what you are trying to develop.

- **Evaluating a process:** When the initial process is "built," walking through the process becomes important. Does it meet the needs of what you are trying to achieve? Is it effective in achieving these tasks? And finally, what can you automate (what steps could you script or have a workflow take over)?

- **Feedback:** Remember that although you can create great processes for people to follow, if they don't reflect how it is actually done or how it evolves, the cool thing you've created will be useless. You need to get feedback regarding how it operates in the wild, whether it meet its needs, and what issues it doesn't take care of during the feedback process.

- **Improvements:** Implementing improvements is the process or widening the scope or automating more tasks because we have changed the governance. Building improvements leads to efficiencies not present today.

As we mentioned, process requires a life cycle, which you should review regularly to ensure it is still meeting the needs. When talking with customers, we often refer to process building as being like writing a script. Today we can write a script to perform a task, and with the knowledge we have today it will be written in a particular way. As our skills improve in scripting, we revisit the script and improve on its performance and reliability. We may even increase the scope of the script. Over time if we examine script v1 versus script v5, we'll see that it has become a very different entity.

Technology investments

One of the promises of this chapter is to help you deliver datacenter efficiency. We have talked about two of our level 1 (or base) layers: people and process. We can invest in people, and we can build amazing processes, but if we don't have the technology to support them, our datacenter transformation and delivering any type of efficiency will be hampered.

In this section, we show you how you can eat the elephant with technology by giving you lots of practical examples that will save you time and money and deliver efficiency. Each time you approach and implement one thing, you take another bite of the elephant.

You might be wondering what this has to do with the mobile order solution example. Well, to implement a modern solution like a mobile ordering system, we need modern people to manage and maintain it, modern processes to support it, and modern technology for it to be implemented on. We discuss it in more detail later in this chapter, but first we need to demonstrate how we can achieve efficiency in our pillars described in level 2.

Each area we focus on highlights some common areas you can target with examples to improve efficiency.

Automation technologies

Fourth Coffee used to use a wide range of GUI tools to manage its environment. The problem was that the productivity and quality of IT operations was very low. Now Fourth Coffee has adopted a "script everything" culture that slowed things down at first but then rapidly paid for itself as the productivity and quality of IT operations soared and the willingness of the team to take on big initiatives increased.

The point of this section is straightforward: simply decide on your automation tool and implement it! Automation should translate the processes you have defined and improved upon into items where you can give IT staff back time and reduce the amount of unnecessary hands required by tasks.

There are many tools available; we focus on PowerShell in our examples because of its general portability between systems and environments and the extent of its ecosystem.

When working with PowerShell, an important concept to bear in mind is related to toolmaking. Every PowerShell script you create should take the form of a tool for reusability!

Take this example:

```
Get-Service -Name Spooler
```

If you save this to a script, it will only ever be able to query the Spooler service. Now, if you change it to the following:

```
Param
(
    [string]$serviceName,
    [string]$computerName
)


Get-Service -ComputerName $computerName -Name $serviceName
```

In the example, the **computerName** and the **serviceName** are parameterized so that you can query potentially any service on any computer. Although it's a simple example, it demonstrates the principal of examining a simple one-liner and translating it into something reusable for a wider purpose.

Identity investments

Fourth Coffee used to manage identities using GUI tools. The problem was that this was inefficient, error-prone, and ill-suited to bulk operations or certain operations. Now Fourth Coffee does all of its identity management via PowerShell, which allows the company to enforce corporate identity policies, ensure consistency of operations, automate bulk operations, and quickly produce novel solutions to unique problems or opportunities.

Managing users and groups is critical to the proper operations and security of an enterprise. It also can be a painstaking, error-prone process if you perform it manually. For example, it can take up to five minutes for a user to get created as you log on to the domain controller, open the Active Directory Users and Computer tool, navigate to the organization unit you want to create the user in, and then run through the user creation options. If you also include other systems like Exchange and a login for a point-of-sale system, it can take longer; five minutes can extend to 30 minutes if you don't get distracted. Now consider what happens when you hire a bunch of people.[2]

---

[2] The cmdlets work on Active Directory, so you have to have the ActiveDirectory module installed on your machine. If you don't have these on your machine, you have to install them. On a Windows 10 Client machine, you need to find, download, and install the Remote Server Administration Tools (RSAT). On Windows Server 2016, you can install them with the command **Install-WindowsFeature RSAT-AD-PowerShell**.

Modern IT required Fourth Coffee to get very good at automating identity so that the company could keep up with the needs of the business and to address security concerns.

CREATING USERS

Creating a user in PowerShell requires a few cmdlets to complete the entire process.

First, you use the cmdlet New-ADUser with the following syntax:

```
New-ADUser -Name 'Joe Bloggs' -UserPrincipalName Joebloggs@fourthcoffee.com
```

The user is created, but because of the way New-ADUser creates the account, it does not have a password and therefore can't be enabled. You need to use the Set-ADAccountPassword cmdlet as follows:

```
Set-ADAccountPassword -Identity 'Joe Bloggs'
```

This prompts you for a new password to set for the user. If you want to get fancier, you can encode the password as a secure string and use it as part of the command as follows:

```
$securePW = ConvertTo-SecureString -String 'Password01' -AsPlainText -Force
```

If we use the **$securepassword** variable now, which stores the secure string we need, we could use the *-newpassword* parameter for the Set-ADAccountPassword cmdlet to include the password rather than being prompted for it. Now the syntax will be as follows:

```
Set-ADAccountPassword -Identity 'Joe Bloggs' -NewPassword $securePW
```

You also could use the *-AccountPassword* parameter for New-ADUser cmdlet as well and eliminate this line completely.

Finally, you use the Enable-AdAccount cmdlet to enable the account as follows:

```
Enable-AdAccount -Identity 'Joe Bloggs'
```

These are the individual steps and work! Now you make this useful by building a tool script to create an AD user with extra properties. Take the following code and save it to a file named New-TeamMate.ps1:

```
param
(
    [string]$GivenName,
    [string]$Surname,
    [string]$EmployeeID,
    [string]$Department
)
<# Make this script more readable by creating a hashtable whose names match
   match the parameters of New-AdUser and then 'splat' them.
   Get Details by typing:
   > Help about_Splatting
#>
```

```
$pw = 'Password123!'
$accountPassword = ConvertTo-SecureString -String $pw -AsPlainText -Force

$param = @{
    GivenName    = $GivenName
    Surname      = $Surname
    Name         = "$Surname, $GivenName"
    SamAccount   = "$GivenName.$Surname"
    EmployeeID   = $EmployeeID
    Department   = $Department
    Office       = '41/5682'
    City         = 'Redmond'
    State        = 'Washington'
    Company      = 'Fourth Coffee'
    Country      = 'US'
    AccountPassword = $accountPassword
}


New-AdUser @param
        Enable-AdAccount -Identity $param.SamAccount
Write-Verbose "Added $GivenName $Surname"
```

When you execute this script, you can run the script with the parameters as follows:

```
./New-TeamMate.ps1 -GivenName John -Surname Doe -EmployeeID 12345 -Department IT
```

This creates a user with a default password and default settings for office, city, and so on.

Once Fourth Coffee delivers its new customer-focused applications, the company will be hiring a lot of users, so you should modify this script to be able to work against a CSV file like this:

```
JPS> cat .\NewHire.csv
GivenName,SurName,EmployeeID,Department
Mary,Breve,3000,IT
Sandeep,Java,3001,Development
Sarah,Bean,3002,Accounting
```

All you need to do is modify the parameter block and wrap the rest of the script in a process script block:

```
param
(
    [Parameter(Mandatory=$true, ValueFromPipelineByPropertyName=$true)]
    [string]$GivenName,
    [Parameter(Mandatory=$true, ValueFromPipelineByPropertyName=$true)]
    [string]$Surname,
```

```
        [Parameter(Mandatory=$true, ValueFromPipelineByPropertyName=$true)]
        [string]$EmployeeID,
        [Parameter(Mandatory=$true, ValueFromPipelineByPropertyName=$true)]
        [string]$Department
    )
    process
    {
    <# Make this script more readable by creating a hashtable whose names
       match the parameters of New-AdUser and then 'splat' them.
       Get Details by typing:
       JPS> Help about_Splatting
    #>
    $PW = 'Password123!'
    $accountPassword = ConvertTo-SecureString -String $PW -AsPlainText -Force

    $param = @{
        GivenName   = $GivenName
        Surname     = $Surname
        Name        = "$Surname, $GivenName"
        SamAccount  = "$GivenName.$Surname"
        EmployeeID  = $employeeID
        Department  = $department
        Office      = '41/5682'
        City        = 'Redmond'
        State       = 'Washington'
        Company     = 'Fourth Coffee'
        Country     = 'US'
        AccountPassword = $accountPassword
    }


    New-AdUser @param
    Enable-AdAccount -Identity $samaccount
    Write-Verbose "Added $GivenName $Surname"
    }
```

This enables you to do the following:

```
JPS> Import-Csv '.\NewHire.csv'   |.\New-TeamMate.PS1 -verbose
VERBOSE: Added Mary Breve
VERBOSE: Added Sandeep Java
VERBOSE: Added Sarah Bean
```

Congratulations! You are well on your way to massive, no-drama productivity through the magic of PowerShell.

You could continually evolve this script with things like enabling the user principal in other systems like Exchange or a customer Human Resources application.

DISABLING USER'S ACCOUNT NOT ACTIVE IN 30 DAYS

Another common task is identifying users who haven't being logged on in more than 30 days and disabling them. First, you can use the Search-ADAccount cmdlet[3]

```
Search-ADAccount -AccountInactive -TimeSpan 30.00:00:00 -UsersOnly
```

This gives you a list of accounts that have not been logged on for more than 30 days. You can disable these accounts by using the Disable-ADAccount cmdlet. Fourth Coffee has a policy to disable inactive accounts every month. It implements this using the scheduling capabilities of AA and the following script:

```
Search-ADAccount -AccountInactive -TimeSpan 30.00:00:00 -UsersOnly |
    Disable-ADAccount
```

GROUP MANAGEMENT

You also could automate aspects of group management. If you need to add a user to a group, you can use PowerShell to do it. Following is a basic script that takes a username and group and adds the user into it. Although there are many different ways of doing this, and probably PowerShell now has new tools to do it in a single command, we're showing you this method to demonstrate a principle of taking a multistep task and turning it into a script:

```
param
(
    [string]$Useraccount,
    [string]$domaingroup
)
$user = Get-ADUser -Identity $useraccount
$group = Get-ADGroup -Identity $domaingroup
Add-ADGroupMember $group -Member $user
```

You can call this script AddGroupMembers.ps1 and use the following syntax to execute it:

```
.\AddGroupMembers.ps1 -UserAccount 'Joe Bloggs' -DomainGroup 'Domain Admins'
```

We have examined three areas for identity which we can take and build an automated solution to match the functionality of the manual process and deliver efficiency by reducing the amount of time it takes to perform the task. These tasks also could be ported to AA and wrapped with a self-service portal to provide more power to the end users and free up time for IT staff to perform more important tasks.

---

[3] By default, the Active Directory **LastLogonTimeStamp** attribute is correct, but it has a very slow update frequency (think weeks). It's not a real-time logon tracking mechanism. You can learn more details by reading the blog at blogs.technet.microsoft.com/askds/2009/04/15/the-lastlogontimestamp-attribute-what-it-was-designed-for-and-how-it-works/.

Security investments

Fourth Coffee used to buy a bunch of security products and hope that spending lots of money made them secure. The problem is that it didn't. Fourth Coffee now invests in its security people, giving them training and the mission to secure the company. The company leverages the built-in security capabilities of Windows 10, WS2016, and Azure—such as Shielded VMs, Device Guard, Credential Guard, Windows Defender, and Azure Security Center—to secure systems. Fourth Coffee also adopted a hunter mentality by actively baselining the signature of normal operations and looking for deviations that might indicate an attacker. Fourth Coffee's confidence in their security is now based in competence rather than hope.

REVIEWING LOGS ACROSS MULTIPLE COMPUTERS

A common task is trying to find out events across multiple computers to see if it is a common failure.

Say you want to look at the last 10 entries in the application log from a list of servers listed in a file named AllServers.txt. You can use the Invoke-Command and Get-Eventlog cmdlets as follows:

```
Invoke-Command -ComputerName (Cat AllServers.Txt) {
    Get-Eventlog -LogName Application -Newest 10 |
    Select MachineName, EventID, Source, Message
} |Format-Table
```

The output is displayed as follows

MachineName	EventID	Source	Message
sq101.fourthcoffee.com	4098	Group Policy Registry	The computer 'AllowKMSUpgrade'
sq101.fourthcoffee.com	1704	SceCli	Security policy in the Group po
sq101.fourthcoffee.com	916	ESENT	services (896,G,0) The beta fea
sq101.fourthcoffee.com	916	ESENT	svchost (4968,G,0) The beta fea
sq101.fourthcoffee.com	31	Microsoft-Windows-Spell-Checking	Failed to update 1 user custom
sq101.fourthcoffee.com	916	ESENT	SettingSyncHost (10220,G,0) The
sq101.fourthcoffee.com	916	ESENT	SettingSyncHost (10220,G,0) The
sq101.fourthcoffee.com	1001	Windows Error Reporting	Fault bucket 146962385495655736
sq101.fourthcoffee.com	16384	Software Protection Platform Service Successfully scheduled Software

sq101.fourthcoffee.com	1003	Software Protection Platform Service The Software Protection service	
dc01.fourthcoffee.com	15	SecurityCenter	Updated Windows Defender status
dc01.fourthcoffee.com	15	SecurityCenter	Updated Windows Defender status
dc01.fourthcoffee.com	916	ESENT	SettingSyncHost (10440,G,0) The
dc01.fourthcoffee.com	1001	Windows Error Reporting	Fault bucket 128049445031, type
dc01.fourthcoffee.com	1001	Windows Error Reporting	Fault bucket 128049445031, type
dc01.fourthcoffee.com	1001	Windows Error Reporting	Fault bucket 128049445031, type
dc01.fourthcoffee.com	1001	Windows Error Reporting	Fault bucket 128049445031, type
dc01.fourthcoffee.com	1001	Windows Error Reporting	Fault bucket 128049445031, type
dc01.fourthcoffee.com	1001	Windows Error Reporting	Fault bucket 128049445031, type

dc01.fourt

Get-EventLog is a good simple cmdlet, but it is better to invest in learning the Get-WinEvent cmdlet, which is more capable and much faster. The Event ID for a failed logon is 4625, but Get-EventLog does not allow you to specify that ID, so you would have to use the following:

```
Get-EventLog -LogName Security | where {$_.EventID -eq 4265}
```

Here is a fast and effective way to get the failed login events from all servers.

```
Invoke-Command -ComputerName (Cat AllServers.Txt) {
    Get-WinEvent -FilterHashTable @{LogName='security'; id=4625 }
}
```

PORT SCANNER

Often when you deploy systems you can have connectivity problems, or if you need to test your firewall rules to see whether a port responds, you need to simulate a connection. You can use PowerShell to implement a lightweight port scanner as follows:

```
param
(
    [string]$ComputerName,
    [String[]]$ports

)
```

```
$ErrorActionPreference='silentlycontinue'
Write-host 'Attempting to Connect...'
foreach($port in $ports)
{
    $test = Test-NetConnection -Port $port -ComputerName $ComputerName

    if($test.TcpTestSucceeded -eq $false)
    {
        Write-host "Connection to $ComputerName failed, Port $port is not listening"
        -ForegroundColor Red -BackgroundColor Black
    }
    else
    {
        write-host "Connection to $ComputerName Succeed, Port $port is listening"
        -ForegroundColor Green -BackgroundColor Black
    }
}
```

The syntax for using this for multiple ports to be scanned would be as follows:

```
.\New-BasicPortScanner.ps1 -ComputerName TestMachine -Port 80,53,1024
```

This is obviously a simple scanner, but it again highlights the potential tasks you can automate to become more efficient.

FIREWALL

Fourth Coffee uses Group Policy to turn off all its firewalls, but the company isn't trying to ensure the firewall is properly configured. Fourth Coffee needs a quick way to identify across multiple computers if a firewall rule has made it.

First, you should check whether the firewall is turned on; checking this on a remote machine involves using the invoke-command cmdlet and the Get-NetFirewallProfile cmdlet as follows:

```
Invoke-command -computername dc01 -scriptblock {Get-NetFirewallProfile}
```

The output for the domain profile is listed here:

```
Name                            : Domain
Enabled                         : True
DefaultInboundAction            : NotConfigured
DefaultOutboundAction           : NotConfigured
AllowInboundRules               : NotConfigured
AllowLocalFirewallRules         : NotConfigured
AllowLocalIPsecRules            : NotConfigured
AllowUserApps                   : NotConfigured
AllowUserPorts                  : NotConfigured
AllowUnicastResponseToMulticast : NotConfigured
NotifyOnListen                  : False
EnableStealthModeForIPsec       : NotConfigured
LogFileName                     : %systemroot%\system32\LogFiles\Firewall\pfirewall.log
```

```
LogMaxSizeKilobytes          : 4096
LogAllowed                   : False
LogBlocked                   : False
LogIgnored                   : NotConfigured
DisabledInterfaceAliases     : {NotConfigured}
PSComputerName               : dc01
```

Now that you know the firewall is enabled, you can check the rules and the ruleset, and you can filter on inbound-only rules using the following syntax:

```
Invoke-command -computername dc01 -scriptblock {Get-NetFirewallProfile `
-Name Domain |Get-NetFirewallRule |where {$_.Direction -eq 'Inbound'}}
```

This command lists all the rules and their state (allowed or denied). You can perform further checks or loop across all profiles to determine all the rule states.

AZURE—NETWORK SECURITY GROUPS

If you're working in Azure, you can generate new network security groups and rules and enforce traffic policies across an entire estate in a matter of minutes.

You use the New-AzureRMNetworkSecurityRuleConfig cmdlet to generate a new rule you want applied. In this example, we want to allow Port 22 for SSH:

```
$nsg = Get-AzureRmNetworkSecurityGroup -ResourceGroupName FourthCoffeeNSG `
-Name FrontEnd-Net

$rule1 = New-AzureRmNetworkSecurityRuleConfig -Name rdp-rule `
-NetworkSecurityGroup $nsg -Description 'Allow SSH' -Access Allow `
-Protocol Tcp -Direction Inbound `
-Priority 100 -SourceAddressPrefix Internet -SourcePortRange * `
-DestinationAddressPrefix * -DestinationPortRange 22


  Set-AzureRmNetworkSecurityGroup -NetworkSecurityGroup $nsg
```

We can loop this across multiple existing Network Security groups using PowerShell and enforce any new security boundaries.

FINDING WHICH PATCHES ARE DEPLOYED

Unpatched servers are the number-one cause of preventable security breaches. The day after the CEO of a public company was fired because of a security breach because of unpatched servers, Charlotte was called into the Fourth Coffee CEO's office. She walked out of that office with what she referred to as her "Salary Continuation Program." She had a clear mission to inventory every system in the enterprise and to ensure that they were patched within 60 days.

Charlotte's hair was on fire, and Eddie turned out to be a bucket of water. Moments after her meeting with the CEO, Charlotte held an emergency staff meeting to discuss how the team would get on top of this issue and find out where they were. Charlotte wanted everyone engaged on the problem and was growing irritated as she watched Eddie typing away on his laptop; she assumed he was writing an email. Minutes later, Eddie interrupted and brought the meeting to a halt by saying the single word, "DONE!".

While everyone else had been arguing about charters, timelines, and whether to bring in contractors, Eddie wrote the following script:

```
$allComputers = Get-ADComputer -Filter 'ObjectClass -neq "Computer"'
$patches = Get-CimInstance -ComputerName $allcomputers.Name -ClassName
Win32_QuickFixEngineering
$patches | Export-Csv .\Patches.csv
Invoke-Item .\Patches.csv
```

Eddie said, "I just ran a script to generate an Excel spreadsheet that shows every computer and every patch installed on those computers." When Joe asked how long the company had been able to do that, Eddie replied, "About 45 seconds. I just finished the script. This will give us quick answers, but if you give me a few more minutes, I'll write some helper scripts to generate reports as well."

Storage investments

Fourth Coffee used to use expensive Storage Area Networks (SANs or $ANs) using fiber channel. The problem was that the "gold plated" hardware was extremely expensive, and finding people that could support and debug fiber channel issues was a challenge. Fourth Coffee moved to Storage Spaces Direct, which uses high-volume/low-cost components and Ethernet. Now the company has great reliability and performance at a fraction of the cost, and it can easily hire people to support and diagnose issues.

CHECKING STORAGE POOL HEALTH ON REMOTE MACHINES

If you want to look at the health of storage pools that you've built on various machines, you can connect to the machine via a CIM session using the new-cimsession, and then you can use the Get-StoragePool cmdlet to use the CIM session you've created to retrieve the data from the remote machine.

```
$cimsession = new-cimsession -computername sql01
Get-StoragePool -cimsession $cimsession
```

The output of the command is shown here:

```
FriendlyName OperationalStatus HealthStatus IsPrimordial IsReadOnly PSComputerName
------------ ----------------- ------------ ------------ ---------- --------------
Primordial   OK                Healthy      True         False      sql01
sqldata      Read-only         Unknown      False        True       sql01
sqldata      Read-only         Unknown      False        True       sql01
Primordial   OK                Healthy      True         False      sql01
```

If you observe the output, you see the health status listed so you can determine what is healthy, what is unhealthy, and what is in an unknown status and requires further investigation.

You can create a script that loops across multiple machines and generates a report for all the storage pools so that you have one place to loop versus manually performing the task on each machine.

CREATING A FILE SHARE

To rapidly create files shares, you can use the New-SmbShare cmdlet, like so:

```
New-SmbShare -Name 'UserStore' -Path 'D:\UserStore'
-FullAccess 'FourthCoffee\Administrators', 'FourthCoffee\Domain Users', 'FourthCoffee\
Domain Admins'
```

You also can do this with remote machines by creating a CIM Session to a remote machine and executing the New-SmbShare cmdlet with the *-cimsession* parameter.

CREATING A VIRTUAL DISK

If Fourth Coffee implemented Storage Spaces Direct on their hosts and needed to create a new virtual disk for users to store data on, the company also could implement it rapidly in PowerShell. Using the New-VirtualDisk cmdlet as follows would create a 100 GB disk ready for use:

```
New-VirtualDisk -StoragePoolFriendlyName StoragePool01
-FriendlyName UserDataStore10 -Size 100GB -ProvisioningType Fixed
-ResiliencySettingName Simple
```

You could easily parameterize this or create code to enumerate the resources and check what is available in the pool before provisioning.

RESIZING A DISK

If you're running out of space on your storage virtual disks, you can use PowerShell to increase the amount of space available using the Resize-VirtualDisk cmdlet:

```
Resize-VirtualDisk -FriendlyName 'UserDataStore10' -Size (200GB)
```

Network investments

There are a variety of network automation investments that also could be achieved. In this section we discuss a few options.

CHANGE THE IP ADDRESS

A simple task like changing the IP address of a machine can take a minute or two on any machine. You can use the New-NetIPAddress cmdlet to change the IP address of a machine as part of a setup script. We show the basic usage of the New-NetIPAddress cmdlet here:

```
New-NetIPAddress -InterfaceAlias 'Wired Ethernet Connection'
-IPv4Address '172.18.0.100' -PrefixLength 24 -DefaultGateway 172.18.0.254
```

Then you can update the DNS servers the network interface card uses to the appropriate DNS servers using the Set-DnsClientServerAddress cmdlet like this:

```
Set-DnsClientServerAddress -InterfaceAlias 'Wired Ethernet Connection'
-ServerAddresses 172.18.0.1, 172.18.0.2
```

You also can perform this command using a CIMSession. For example, you can provision a machine on a DHCP network and then remotely connect to it and change it to a static IP address.

FLUSH DNS

Occasionally DNS on a machine doesn't flush its cache quickly enough, you and we need to force a flush of the cache to allow for proper name resolution. You can use the Clear-DnsClientCache cmdlet to clear the DNS cache locally or remotely.

For a local machine DNS cache, simply run the following from an elevated PowerShell:

```
Clear-DnsClientCache
```

For a remote machine, create a CIM session and then execute the following:

```
$cimsession = new-cimsession -computername dc01
Clear-DnsClientCache -CimSession $cimsession
```

A valid day-to-day use of this would be when you're working with Azure Site Recovery. As part of the recovery plan, you need to clear clients' DNS cache for them to properly resolve to the newly recovered servers in the disaster recovery site.

CAPTURE NETWORK TRACE

Capturing traffic on a system to analyze whether you are having problems like latency or disconnects in your application becomes a useful troubleshooting technique. PowerShell enables you to build a tool that you can use to capture network traffic data using the following steps:

1. Build a timestamp using the Get-Date cmdlet:

    ```
    $timestamp = Get-Date -f yyyy-MM-dd_HH-mm-ss
    ```

2. Create the capture session and give it a friendly name using the New-NetEventSession:

    ```
    New-NetEvenltSession -Name NetCapture
    -LocalFilePath d: emp\$env:computername-netcap-$timestamp.etl -MaxFileSize 512
    ```

3. Specify the type of capture provider you want to use. In this case, NetCapture using the Add-NetEventPacketCaptureProvider cmdlet:

    ```
    Add-NetEventPacketCaptureProvider -SessionName NetCapture
    ```

4. Start the capture using the Start-NetEventSession cmdlet:

    ```
    Start-NetEventSession -Name NetCapture
    ```

5. Stop the capture using the Stop-NetEventSession cmdlet:

```
Stop-NetEventSession -Name NetCapture
```

CIM Sessions can be used to perform this on remote computers.

Compute investments

Day to day, you need to do many tasks related to the compute aspects of an infrastructure. This could mean creating virtual machines or rebalancing virtual machine clusters to ensure proper distribution of resources.

VIRTUAL MACHINE DEPLOYMENT

A key to driving efficiency in an organization is the delivery of resources in a timely fashion. There are many examples across IT organizations of virtual machines being requested for applications, and it may take several weeks before they are deployed.

This is one process where an automated framework should be implemented with a self-service portal to minimize the IT resources involved in the overall deployment. This does not mean IT resources will allow any virtual machines to be deployed to their environment; rather that users will request a new virtual machine, and IT resources will be notified to approve or deny the request. If the request is approved, the virtual machine will be deployed based on the parameters; if the request is denied, a notification will be sent to the end user who submitted the request.

Figure 6-8 shows a flow chart of the process you could use for virtual machine provisioning.

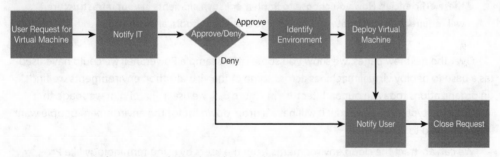

FIGURE 6-8 Process for automated virtual machine deployment

Figure 6-9 shows a sample architecture you could use to take the request in and perform the deployment task. You use on-premises and public cloud resources to achieve the solution and leverage the tooling that you have (such as ServiceNow, SharePoint, AA, and PowerShell).

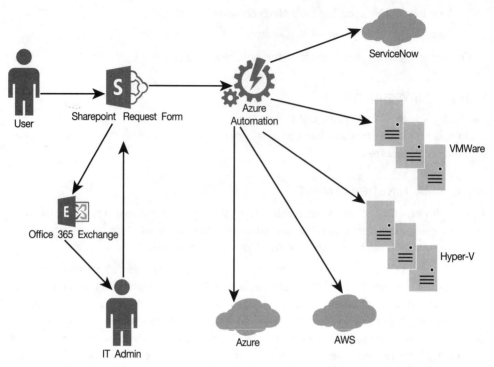

FIGURE 6-9 Sample architecture using private and public cloud technologies to deploy virtual machines across clouds

> **NOTE** Everything shown here is an example of how you might implement it or achieve these efficiencies. How you choose to implement such elements in your infrastructure will require the appropriate planning for your systems, tools, and processes.

Over the next few pages, we show you some of the sample PowerShell we could have used as a base to deploy virtual machines across some of the virtualization environments we find in organizations today. In our architecture in Figure 6-9, we use a SharePoint webpage that controls the type of data we get; it will have a drop-down list for the environment people want this deployed to.

We can abstract the cloud environments from the users by using terminology like Production, Test, Dev, and so on instead of Hyper-V, VMware, Azure, and AWS. Similarly, we can abstract all the information we require to make proper choices for deployment from the user and make those forms user friendly.

When it gets into AA, our control scripts parse out the data and call the relevant deployment script to ensure that it goes to the right environment. We can even get our control scripts to check environment capacity before deploying and make alternative decisions based on what the scripts discover.

DEPLOYING TO HYPER-V

Here is an example of a PowerShell command you could use to create a virtual machine in Hyper-V. This creates a hash table of the parameters that will be used to create the virtual machine:

```
$VMName = 'Server01'

$VM = @{
  Name = $VMName
  MemoryStartupBytes = 2147483648
  Generation = 2
  NewVHDPath = "C:\Virtual Machines\$VMName\$VMName.vhdx"
  NewVHDSizeBytes = 53687091200
  BootDevice = 'VHD'
  Path = "C:\Virtual Machines\$VMName"
  SwitchName = (Get-VMSwitch).Name[0]
}


New-VM @VM
```

We can wrap this with parameters to capture all the variables required and deploy the virtual machine.

Normally Hyper-V is managed using System Center Virtual Machine Manager, which also has PowerShell cmdlets to deploy a virtual machine. A sample script for that would be like this:

```
param
(

    [string]$vmmserver,
    [string]$templatename='WindowsServer2016Datacenter'
)


Get-VMMServer -ComputerName $VMMServer


$VMTemplate = $TemplateName
$VMHostGroup = Get-VMHostGroup -Name 'All Hosts'

$HostRatings = @(Get-VMHostRating -DiskSpaceGB 120 -Template $VMTemplate `
-VMHostGroup $VMHostGroup -VMName $VMName | where { $_.Rating -gt 0 })

 If($HostRatings.Count -eq "0")
 {
  throw "No hosts meet the requirements for the virtual machine"
 }
```

```
If ($HostRatings.Count -ne 0)
{

  $VMHost = $HostRatings[0].VMHost
  $VMPath = $HostRatings[0].VMHost.VMPaths[0]


  $VMJobGroup = [System.Guid]::NewGuid()

  Get-Template -VMMServer $VMMServer | where { $_.Name -eq $VMTemplate }


  New-VM -Template $VMTemplate -Name $VMName -Description "New VM" -VMHost $VMHost -Path
$VMPath -JobGroup $VMJobGroup -RunAsynchronously `
  -ComputerName "*" -JoinWorkgroup "WORKGROUP" -RunAsSystem -StopAction SaveVM
}
```

The deployment requires the VMM server name; in this example, we default it to the Windows Server 2016 Template, which has been prestaged in the VMM server. We could add parameters for the virtual machine name, join it to the domain, and even have postscript executions happen. VMM server has the host rating system, which we can use to help us determine the best host placement taking another job and automating using technology.

DEPLOYING TO VMWARE

VMware has the ability to deploy via PowerShell; it uses the PowerCLI client. It's similar to System Center Virtual Machine Manager; we can discover our hosts and, in VMware's case, the datastores and dynamically choose where the virtual machine should be deployed. The example script that follows shows a basic script you can use to rapidly deploy a Windows Server 2016 virtual machine into a VMware estate.

```
param
(
    [string]$vcenter,
    [string]$VMName,
    [string]$Password="Password123!"
)

$secpass = ConvertTo-SecureString -String $Password -AsPlainText -Force
$domaincreds = New-Object ` System.Management.Automation.PSCredential('FourthCoffee\
Adminisrator', $secpass)

Connect-VIServer -Server $vcenter
$VMHOST="VMHOST01"
$DATASTORE="SSDStore01"

New-OSCustomizationSpec -Name 'WindowsServer2016' -FullName $VMName
-OrgName 'FourthCoffee' -OSType Windows -ChangeSid
```

```
-AdminPassword $secpass -Domain 'FOURTHCOFFEE' -DomainCredentials $domaincreds `
-AutoLogonCount 1

$OSSpecs = Get-OSCustomizationSpec -Name 'WindowsServer2016'

$VMTemplate = Get-Template -Name 'Server2016Template'

New-VM -Name '$VMName' -Template $VMTemplate -OSCustomizationSpec $OSSpec `
-VMHost $VMHOST -Datastore $DataStore
```

DEPLOYING TO AZURE

There are multiple ways of deploying a virtual machine to Azure. Here are the three most common:

- The portal
- PowerShell/CLI
- ARM templates

You can automate virtual machine deployment with PowerShell/CLI or ARM templates. Sometimes you even can use a combination of both.

For the first example, we show a sample using PowerShell that could be used in AA to deploy a Windows Server Virtual machine.

In the first section, we ask for the parameters, and we introduce the more complex PowerShell features like mandatory parameters and the **ValidateNotNullOrEmpty()** method to ensure we don't leave a parameter that needs a value, empty. Then we move on to collect our credentials using the Azure Automation cmdlet Get-AutomationPSCredential. We then build the virtual machine configuration and pass that to the final New-AzureRMVM cmdlet.

```
param
(
[Parameter(Mandatory=$true)]
    [string]$VMname,
    [ValidateNotNullOrEmpty()]
    [string]$AzureRegion = "uswest2",
    [ValidateNotNullOrEmpty()]
    [string]$ImageName = "WindowsServer2016",
    [ValidateNotNullOrEmpty()]
    [string]$VMSize = "Standard_D1",
    [ValidateNotNullOrEmpty()]
    [string]$ResourceGroup

)

If ($ImageName -eq "WindowsServer2016")
{
    $PublisherName = "MicrosoftWindowsServer"
```

```
        $offer = "WindowsServer"
        $skus = "2016-Datacenter"
}


$cred = Get-AutomationPSCredential -Name "Azure"
$vm = New-AzureRmVMConfig -VMName $VMName -VMSize $VMSize

$vm = Set-AzureRmVMOperatingSystem `
    -VM $vm `
    -Windows `
    -ComputerName $VMName `
    -Credential $cred `
    -ProvisionVMAgent -EnableAutoUpdate

$vm = Set-AzureRmVMSourceImage `
    -VM $vm `
    -PublisherName $PublisherName `
    -Offer $Offer `
    -Skus $skus `
    -Version latest

$vm = Set-AzureRmVMOSDisk `
    -VM $vm `
    -Name "$VMNAme_OSDisk" `
    -DiskSizeInGB 128 `
    -CreateOption FromImage `
    -Caching ReadWrite

 $vm = Add-AzureRmVMNetworkInterface -VM $vm -Id $nic.Id


New-AzureRmVM -ResourceGroupName $resourcegroup -Location $AzureRegion -VM $vm
```

ARM templates are slightly different, however. They're defined in a JSON file. This file describes the infrastructure to be deployed. It also includes taking parameters, defining usable variables, and providing outputs. This is infrastructure as code, and when we start to adopt concepts like DevOps into Fourth Coffee's IT organization, this will be a cornerstone of driving consistency and efficiency throughout the company's environments.

The following is a sample ARM template for deploying a Windows Virtual Machine:

```
{
  "$schema": "https://schema.management.azure.com/schemas/2015-01-01/deploymentTemplate.json#",
  "contentVersion": "1.0.0.0",
  "parameters": {
    "adminUsername": { "type": "string" },
    "adminPassword": { "type": "securestring" }
  },
```

```
"variables": {
  "vnetID": "[resourceId('Microsoft.Network/virtualNetworks','myVNet')]",
  "subnetRef": "[concat(variables('vnetID'),'/subnets/mySubnet')]",
},
"resources": [
  {
    "apiVersion": "2016-03-30",
    "type": "Microsoft.Network/publicIPAddresses",
    "name": "myPublicIPAddress",
    "location": "[resourceGroup().location]",
    "properties": {
      "publicIPAllocationMethod": "Dynamic",
      "dnsSettings": {
        "domainNameLabel": "myresourcegroupdns1"
      }
    }
  },
  {
    "apiVersion": "2016-03-30",
    "type": "Microsoft.Network/virtualNetworks",
    "name": "myVNet",
    "location": "[resourceGroup().location]",
    "properties": {
      "addressSpace": { "addressPrefixes": [ "10.0.0.0/16" ] },
      "subnets": [
        {
          "name": "mySubnet",
          "properties": { "addressPrefix": "10.0.0.0/24" }
        }
      ]
    }
  },
  {
    "apiVersion": "2016-03-30",
    "type": "Microsoft.Network/networkInterfaces",
    "name": "myNic",
    "location": "[resourceGroup().location]",
    "dependsOn": [
      "[resourceId('Microsoft.Network/publicIPAddresses/', 'myPublicIPAddress')]",
      "[resourceId('Microsoft.Network/virtualNetworks/', 'myVNet')]"
    ],
    "properties": {
      "ipConfigurations": [
        {
          "name": "ipconfig1",
          "properties": {
            "privateIPAllocationMethod": "Dynamic",
```

```json
                "publicIPAddress": { "id": "[resourceId('Microsoft.Network/publicIPAddresses',
'myPublicIPAddress')]" },
                "subnet": { "id": "[variables('subnetRef')]" }
              }
            }
          ]
        }
      },
      {
        "apiVersion": "2016-04-30-preview",
        "type": "Microsoft.Compute/virtualMachines",
        "name": "myVM",
        "location": "[resourceGroup().location]",
        "dependsOn": [
          "[resourceId('Microsoft.Network/networkInterfaces/', 'myNic')]"
        ],
        "properties": {
          "hardwareProfile": { "vmSize": "Standard_DS1" },
          "osProfile": {
            "computerName": "myVM",
            "adminUsername": "[parameters('adminUsername')]",
            "adminPassword": "[parameters('adminPassword')]"
          },
          "storageProfile": {
            "imageReference": {
              "publisher": "MicrosoftWindowsServer",
              "offer": "WindowsServer",
              "sku": "2012-R2-Datacenter",
              "version": "latest"
            },
            "osDisk": {
              "name": "myManagedOSDisk",
              "caching": "ReadWrite",
              "createOption": "FromImage"
            }
          },
          "networkProfile": {
            "networkInterfaces": [
              {
                "id": "[resourceId('Microsoft.Network/networkInterfaces','myNic')]"
              }
            ]
          }
        }
      }
    ]
}
```

We can use CLI, PowerShell, REST API, or Portal to deploy this template.

When considering automation in Azure, ARM Templates is the preferred choice. Even if you use AA as the controlling engine, you can store your templates in a public repository and have AA call to the public repository during runbook execution and execute the template.

DEPLOYING TO AWS

If you want to deploy to AWS, you can use PowerShell to achieve this. The following is a base script that will deploy an AWS virtual machine. In the first section, we ask for the parameters, and we use the more complex PowerShell features like mandatory parameters and the **ValidateNotNullOrEmpty()** method. We proceed to build the credentials to connect to AWS, and the Get-AutomationPSCredential cmdlet is Azure Automation–specific, allowing us to store the credential and retrieve it securely when our script executes. Then we retrieve the image and build the virtual machine.

```
param (
    [Parameter(Mandatory=$true)]
    [string]$VMname,
    [ValidateNotNullOrEmpty()]
    [string]$AWSRegion = "us-west-2",
    [ValidateNotNullOrEmpty()]
    [string]$EC2ImageName = "WINDOWS_2012R2_BASE",
    [ValidateNotNullOrEmpty()]
    [string]$MinCount = 1,
    [ValidateNotNullOrEmpty()]
    [string]$MaxCount = 1,
    [ValidateNotNullOrEmpty()]
    [string]$InstanceType = "t2.micro"
    )


$AwsCred = Get-AutomationPSCredential -Name "AwsCred"
$AwsAccessKeyId = $AwsCred.UserName
$AwsSecretKey = $AwsCred.GetNetworkCredential().Password



Set-AWSCredentials -AccessKey $AwsAccessKeyId -SecretKey $AwsSecretKey -StoreAs AWSProfile
Set-DefaultAWSRegion -Region $AWSRegion



$ami = Get-EC2ImageByName $EC2ImageName -ProfileName AWSProfile -ErrorAction Stop



Write-host "Creating new AWS Instance..."
$NewVM = New-EC2Instance `
    -ImageId $ami.ImageId `
```

```
    -MinCount $MinCount `
    -MaxCount $MaxCount `
    -InstanceType $InstanceType `
    -ProfileName AWSProfile `
    -ErrorAction Stop
 $InstanceID = $NewVM.Instances.InstanceID
 $NewVM


Write-host "Applying new VM Name...."
New-EC2Tag -Resource $InstanceID -Tag @( @{ Key = "Name" ; Value = $VMname}) -ProfileName
AWSProfile
Write-host ("Successfully created AWS VM: " + $VMname)
```

Because this is a public cloud, we don't have to worry about capacity issues, but we do have to worry about cost! That is why in the SharePoint workflow we have approval steps, or in the control scripts we probe the ticket in ServiceNow to see that it has been approved.

CONTAINERS

Although deploying virtual machines in an automated fashion definitely leads to greater efficiency for the datacenter, another transformation could take place to push Fourth Coffee to the next level.

In the next set of examples, we slightly move away from PowerShell to take a look at infrastructure as code with Dockerfiles. A Dockerfile describes the environment you want to deploy, including adding files to the container and executing or installing anything required to run the application. Here's an example:

```
FROM microsoft/windowsservercore
ADD ApacheInstall.ps1 /windows/temp/ApacheInstall.ps1
ADD VCRedistInstall.ps1 /windows/temp/VCRedistInstall.ps1
RUN powershell.exe -executionpolicy bypass c:\windows emp\ApacheInstall.ps1
RUN powershell.exe -executionpolicy bypass c:\windows emp\VCRedistInstall.ps1
WORKDIR /Apache24/bin
CMD /Apache24/bin/httpd.exe -w
```

In our example, we use the windowsservercore base image for our container, copy two scripts for deploying Apache webserver and Visual C redistributable, run these scripts to install the software, and then start Apache.

The ApacheInstall.ps1 file would look as follows:

```
Invoke-WebRequest -Method Get `
-Uri http://www.apachelounge.com/download/VC14/binaries/httpd-2.4.25-win64-VC14.zip
-OutFile c:\apache.zip

Expand-Archive -Path c:\apache.zip -DestinationPath c:\
Remove-Item c:\apache.zip -Force
```

As you can see, we're downloading the file from the public Apache source and extracting it.

Every time we deploy this container, it's provisioned in this exact manner—pulling our base image, downloading the components required, installing them, and then launching the Apache web server.

If we scale out the container instances, the exact same procedure would occur. Of course, we could commit our changes to the container and have our custom "base" image to launch each and every time.

Then why use Dockerfiles? Why not just build our own application into a custom image and deploy the custom image each time? Well, this is exactly like the process of a virtual machine deployment for an application. Someone has to deploy the app and commit the image each time. With the Dockerfile, we can write out the steps to deploy the image (or add a PowerShell script!) and allow it to deploy it.

Think of it in terms of DevOps. More importantly, what if Fourth Coffee chooses to implement a CI/CD pipeline?

The development team needs an environment where they can deploy and test their application. If we are close to capacity on the virtualization platforms they have implemented, requesting additional resources to try something new will be a difficult ask. Given that a container footprint is considerably less, we could use that technology to give them an environment easily. What's more, if they use a cloud-based container service like Azure Container Service and then deploy to Docker on premises, it won't matter because they will describe their environment through Dockerfiles or Docker Compose files.

Following is a sample Docker Compose file that references a folder where the web Dockerfile exists and the db Dockerfile exists, comprising the "application":

```
version: '2.1'
services:
 web:
  build: ./web
  ports:
  - "80:80"
  depends_on:
  - db
  tty:
    true
 db:
  build: ./db
  expose:
  - "1433"
  tty:
    true
networks:
 default:
  external:
   name: "nat"
```

The development team and the operations team work on building a small container host environment and begin the process of describing the applications and operating systems that will run their software in a Dockerfile to tie all parts of an application (that is, the database and the front end) together. They will describe them in a Docker Compose file that will reference the Dockerfiles.

These Docker Compose files can be "played" against any Docker container deployment and will build out the service. The development team can verify its functionality, while operations can determine how to monitor it. Best of all, once all the verification is done, the same process applies to moving between the development, test, and production environments.

When the development team releases a new update based on feedback and monitoring data, the Docker Compose file gets updated to point to the new application, and a redeploy happens.

In a DevOps pipeline scenario, the development team would integrate the creation of the Docker Compose files and deployment into the entire process so that when they commit code, it gets validated under automated tests (which may involve deploying to a container). Then it's deployed into the test environments and, if it passes another set of tests, finally moves into the production environment. All this happens without IT operations being directly involved. The operations team would have been involved from the start of planning and working out this process, however.

Remember also that this process can be done across cloud environments. For example, the dev and test environments might be on premises, and the production environment might be in the cloud. The number of scripts we need to support multiple environments for deploying a virtual machine is considerably less than the number we need for containers.

For CI/CD, Figure 6-10 shows a flow of how we would build a pipeline with Visual Studio team services.

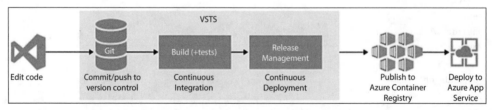

FIGURE 6-10 Visual Studio team services integration with containers for CI/CD

The code is written and committed to a source control repository. The automation build and test begin to ensure code functionality. Once it is ready and has passed the tests, it moves on to release management, which pushes the image to the container registry and then can invoke a deployment process with the latest software.

This helps bring a modern IT environment closer to Fourth Coffee. When they choose to implement a mobile ordering system, the container element will allow for great efficiency and agility for all teams.

Over the course of this chapter, we have talked about the areas Fourth Coffee will need to invest in to deliver on datacenter efficiency. There are millions of examples available on the internet for almost any scenario you can think of. A lot of the technical samples work today; however, like all things in IT, they need to be updated over time as the technology changes. If Fourth Coffee applies the life cycle principals we've discussed, then updates will happen naturally to enable the company to eat the elephant and deliver on the promises of a modern IT infrastructure.

The mobile ordering system

What does this all mean for Fourth Coffee and their drive to digital transformation via their mobile ordering system? Charlotte knew that to deliver such a system effectively she first needed to free up budget, time, and resources. She accomplished that by doing the following things:

- **Using Software as a Service (SaaS) whenever possible:** She had to spend money to make this happen, but the expense got the company on the latest technology; ensured that they were always secure, patched, and up to date; and freed people's time.

- **Using Azure whenever possible:** By using Azure, Fourth Coffee was able to close a datacenter and eliminate a set of servers and software (such as backup systems, management servers, and so on) that were not contributing to customer value. Once again, the company moved to use the latest technology, which ensured that they were always secure, patched, up to date, and people had more time to address other issues.

- **Using Windows Server 2016:** The dramatic efficiencies made possible by WS2016 infrastructure as well as the increased security and automation allowed Fourth Coffee to eliminate its expensive SAN and VMware components.

- **Investing in the technical and cultural training of the staff:** Expectations and job responsibilities were changing, and Charlotte gave her staff motivation, time, and resources to make those changes.

Design choices

During the inception phase of introducing a mobile ordering experience, Fourth Coffee identified some design choices that would modernize the IT experience and deliver the desired efficiency from datacenter transformation. Here we discuss some of those choices to highlight how they affected the design and how the things led to great efficiency in the datacenter.

Identity in a mobile app world

One of the first aspects of adopting a mobile experience must involve handling identity. For example, when a user signs up for the Fourth Coffee mobile experience, is an Active Directory account created or is an identity table built in the database with authentication protocols to support them? Choosing how you handle customers' identity and what information you store relating to them will also affects what governance requirements need to be implemented. And those decisions affect the choice of vendors and technology to ensure they can meet the needs for Fourth Coffee to be covered!

For authentication, Fourth Coffee wanted to move away from Kerberos- or NTLM-based protocols to adopt something like Security Assertion Markup Language (SAML) for authentication and authorization in a mobile app world. One option was to use Microsoft Accounts or Facebook to provide and authenticate the user into the mobile order experience. This solution would simplify the coding practices because Fourth Coffee would adopt an open standard and not have to build custom identity providers and authentication systems.

As customers sign up, they can select from the identity providers (Microsoft, Facebook, Google, and so on) that Fourth Coffee enabled, and data passes between the mobile order application and the identity provider. Fourth Coffee asks to retrieve relevant information about the user from the identity provider, so it can store it in the database; however, no security information (passwords or multifactor authentication codes) are stored because they're maintained by the identity provider. The information that Fourth Coffee stores is used to present the end users' experience and to allow the company to tag additional behavioral data in the future.

Security

Security is a complex topic. How do we stop attacks on Fourth Coffee's systems while maintaining a positive working experience for the employees and a usable consumer experience? Part of the evolution to modern operating systems and application stacks is to help address that very need and minimize the exposure footprint.

Security considerations were also a mitigating factor for choosing a cloud-based deployment for the Fourth Coffee mobile ordering experience. The cloud provides access to platforms, tools, and techniques that are built in or readily available. On premises, the same types of platforms and tools take time, money, and considerable effort to maintain and operate.

Fourth Coffee exposed the application to handle the mobile ordering experience via the application gateway technology in Azure. With the Web Application Firewall enabled, attacks like SQL injection are mitigated out of the box without the Fourth Coffee team having to touch any code.

Other factors, like governance and how it's implemented, play an important part in the design. For example, if Fourth Coffee stores credit card information, they need to implement PCI-DSS. Azure has PCI-DSS certification for the platform, which means Fourth Coffee just needs to implement the controls as part of the application. And if Fourth Coffee uses some of the Azure PaaS services, they might need to only check a box to enable the feature.

For operations, Fourth Coffee leveraged tools like Log Analytics and Azure Security Center to quickly identify threats and correlate activities across the entire IT infrastructure, no matter the location.

Monitoring

Modernizing provides a huge step forward to identify problems in the application or infrastructure that could lead to a negative effect on the user experience.

For example, by using Application Insights, Fourth Coffee can get real-time data from inside the application on how quickly a method is executing or the exact failure of a stack call. Using this data, Fourth Coffee also can collect trace information for the developers to use to determine and resolve the problem.

We also can use Azure Monitor to gain deeper insight into the workings of Azure PaaS services, our container host infrastructure, our network connections, and practically any source we can extract or push data from. Similar to the developer experience with Application Insights, we can track and correlate problems rapidly and resolve them.

Payment processing

Modernizing the payment processing environment provides greater agility and minimizes dependencies on older technology. Fourth Coffee won't need to have connectivity back to the corporate network to talk to the old payment processing server.

In most cases, the improvement could be a few lines of code to reflect the call to the payment processor. The goal is to simplify the code and build a robust application while meeting the needs of the customer.

Also, when Fourth Coffee moves to a modern payment processor, the company technically doesn't need to store credit card data. Instead, it can store value amounts once the processor has billed the customer through the system. This can simplify the governance requirements.

The architecture

Figure 6-11 shows a sample architecture Fourth Coffee could use to handle two elements at once: updating the POS system and introducing the mobile ordering experience.

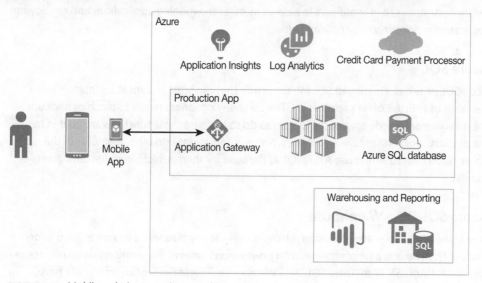

FIGURE 6-11 Mobile ordering experience architecture

Fourth Coffee chose to combine the update of the POS system with the introduction of the mobile ordering experience; the company updated and ported to the code to execute in containers. The team also built an application front end, which is hosted in a container, and updated the database structure and code to support Azure SQL.

The efficiencies

The efficiencies are ten-fold, but the following sections describe how Fourth Coffee has driven efficiencies and modernized the infrastructure and application.

Use of containers

Containers drive a large amount of efficiency within an IT organization. First, with the declarative infrastructure as code (IaC) approach, Fourth Coffee knows what it's getting from a deployment perspective every single time the team deploys, no matter the infrastructure destination. The deployment process is simplified because the team can describe what is desired in the deployment. Because Fourth Coffee standardized on the docker container format, they also have the benefit of being able to deploy it to any infrastructure—private or public or managed—so they're truly cloud agnostic. Given that containers are immutable and in general stateless or in a state, which has been externalized, they can also be considered as a shell that can be recreated at a moment's notice. The consequence is that Fourth Coffee doesn't have to perform a backup of every container running because they will just redeploy and connect to the state store. Scaling to meet performance demand is also simplified because Fourth Coffee has already defined the desired state of the container in the IaC configuration; that way, increasing the number of containers to serve the application is simple and takes seconds versus minutes. Monitoring also becomes simpler as we adopt two simple practices: utilizing the orchestrator used in containers to help us monitor the running applications and employing application monitoring like Application Insights.

Azure SQL

AzureSQL provides a managed SQL infrastructure that can scale and meet the performance demands of Fourth Coffee's application. The company no longer needs to patch or back up the database or provide any special tooling to do so because those functions are built in to the product, which saves time and money. Native integrations into other elements of the Azure cloud data suite also use AzureSQL as the base for them, which simplifies data access or transfer.

Azure SQL Data Warehouse

One of the hard things about looking retrospectively at any business is having to keep information. This requires a lot of storage. With on-premises sytems, the solution was usually some sort of SAN storage. With Azure SQL Data Warehouse, Fourth Coffee can technically have unlimited data storage with native integration to Azure SQL, which reduces the load of data transfer. Fourth Coffee also can integrate natively into PowerBI for generating reports easily, and the company has access to multiple tools for data analytics and machine learning. Reducing specialized tooling, complex integration, and management of these services drives much more efficiency than having to manually build and maintain all these services and gain the appropriate skills to maintain production-grade infrastructures.

Application Gateway

No matter how good the application developer might be, infrastructure safeguards are always needed. The application gateway reduces the need for specialized knowledge and hardware to achieve application high availability and throughput. It also prevents a range of attacks which might have been missed in a code security scan.

Payment Processor

Using a cloud payment processor inherently drives efficiency because we don't need to maintain a specialized payment infrastructure and can potentially reduce the governance required. It usually takes just a few lines of code to redirect to a process that simplifies the code base. Also, cloud payment processors adopt newer payment technologies and provide them through their "interfaces," which again uses small code fragments for developers.

Final thoughts

We've discussed a lot of different concepts in this chapter. The key take-away is that at every step, you can make an assessment about where you stand today across the pillars of people, process, and technology and invest in each as required. The examples we've provided are simple and intended to begin stirring your mind about what you need to change for your organization.

Technologies will change between the time of writing and when you read this because of the rapid advances being made in the cloud. Processes and the skills required to deliver datacenter efficiency will also need to change. Embrace the rapid and ever-changing nature of cloud but do so at a pace that your organization can connect with. Otherwise, all the efficiencies that come with delivering datacenter efficiency will never be realized.

Chapter 7

Supporting innovation

Innovation means many things to many people. To some innovation is an impossible challenge; to others innovation is so deep-rooted into their DNA that they are considered mad scientists! In transforming datacenters and driving toward the efficiencies of the promises of the cloud, you have no choice but to innovate. In this chapter, we discuss what it means for an organization to support practices, patterns, and behaviors to support innovation and engrain it into their cultural and technological DNA.

Breaking paradigms

Fourth Coffee has a lot of problems—as most enterprises do. The problems range across culture and technology. For Fourth Coffee to be successful, things need to change. Often in the past, when the company wanted to adopt new technology, the "tenured" team would grunt and frown. They liked the existing toolset, and their excuse for not changing was that the status quo "worked.". However, when the mandate came down that change would be required, they had no choice but to begin evaluating other toolsets to help them achieve their goal of moving to the cloud and transforming the business to grow and compete at a larger scale.

In many respects there were ironic aspects to the business. Baristas would often experiment to develop new products and come up with twists on originals that became favorites of customers. Managers would play with rosters to ensure the best coverage for staffing and design daily deals to entice regular customers to spend more and new customers to come into the stores. Employees wrote witty comments on chalk boards to engage customers by drawing their notice and encouraging them to comment.

When change started to get to the upper echelons of the business, the scope of innovation began to be shaped like an hour glass, with a thin center and wide ends. Executive management and the lower tiers of the business (where employees connected with the customer) were coming up with bright ideas to change the business, but the middle part of the business almost killed out innovation because they demanded predictability.

For many years now IT has been tasked with running the systems that keep the business operating—from ERP systems to rosters systems and beyond. When these systems went offline, for the most part it meant that money wasn't being generated, which is always bad for business. It's not a secret that production systems need to stay online for long periods, but this situation introduces a slew of problems with keeping operating systems up to date with the latest patches or providing new functionality in an application. For example, not patching an operating system can lead to other devastating consequences for business, like a security breach and customer information leaks.

No matter the scenario that we use for our approach, the situation requires things to change. While it is true that we need to break the paradigm on what a business operates (that is, the technology stack), it will be a higher priority to introduce new paradigms to allow IT to operate differently (that is, new processes, staff education, budget for new tech, and so on).

It's crucial to understand that the primary focus of change is to make the IT environment more lean and agile. However, change to the IT environment may lead to other wide-sweeping changes. In this chapter, we specifically discuss that people changes may be a requirement.

During many moments of revolution, people are often the last blocker to change. During times of change and innovation (that is, the revolution), we endeavor for minimal staff attrition, but unfortunately there are times when some people can't adapt to the changes being implemented or simply don't want to. Sadly in these cases, we have to make the difficult decision to make personnel changes, but not before we give the individuals every opportunity possible to help them realize the necessity and benefits of the changes that will occur. Realistically, if all else fails, it is essential to take the next steps in datacenter and digital transformation, which can include change to the people in an organization.

If the organization is demanding innovation to attract and retain customers, then all the IT paradigms (at very least) that Fourth Coffee has in place require change. At the very least the company requires a life cycle to be attached to all IT paradigms in place and furthermore an agreement with all divisions in Fourth Coffee that they will adopt continuous evolution in everything that they do. The responsibility lands with IT to quantify what must happen to meet those ever-evolving needs and adjust accordingly to the new demands.

Finally, as you approach paradigm changes, be cognizant of the time it will take for the changes to happen. Although executive management may be looking for an aggressive timeline, the reality of change and embedding a new culture, operating model, and technology will have burn-in periods. It's important to recognize and address the disconnects between old and new and keep focus on why the new paradigms are critical to the businesses success.

Theory of digital transformation

Digital transformation harbors a culture and ecosystem of supporting innovation. It helps us to begin to understand a variety of aspects of the business we are in. Did you ever ask yourself the simple question, "Do you *really* know your customer?" Many people would answer, "Of course! We know Joe Bloggs comes into coffee shop X and orders the same drink every single day at 8:00 a.m. with a sausage and cheese egg bagel. Joe always says hello and thanks and leaves a $2 tip."

Now we want challenge you: Who knows this customer? Is it you, the person in IT/executive management, or is it the counter staff in the coffee shop? How do you in IT or in executive management know who Joe is and what his habits are? Do you get the information sent by the shop staff about Joe? How can you distinguish Joe's order from the hundreds of other orders you process in a single store in a single day (or scale it up to hundreds or thousands of stores)?

Joe is important, no doubt about it. But you don't *know* Joe. In fact, Joe is a creature of convenience, and he knows that getting a black coffee and the bagel with sausage and cheese will take three minutes to receive from the point of order. He knows that anything else will get in a queue because the baristas in the shop take a bit more time to craft the specialty drinks for the customers.

If you take a step back and understand that you don't know your customers as well as you could, and that the data that drives behavioral patterns needs to be collected in a variety of ever-changing ways, you begin to understand the basis of the theory of digital transformation.

The theory of digital transformation says that an organization will be successful by understanding its customers, being data-driven, and using best-of-breed and perfectly aligned technologies to support the previous systems. If we examine where Fourth Coffee is today, do we think this is possible? Do we think Fourth Coffee understands all its customers or a few customers? Do they have all the data that makes up behavioral decisions? Are they able to collect the data they need without being intrusive?

Chances are, Fourth Coffee is not able to capture this data outside of the telephone method, in which information passes from one person to another along a chain instead of going directly from point A to point B. This needs to change so that Fourth Coffee can realize its next stages of success! For example, a starting point may be to understand customer sentiment. Fourth Coffee decides to implement a four-button pedestal panel at the exit of the stores. This pedestal has four emoji faces—from happy to angry. Customers optionally press whatever emoji represents their store experience. This allows the company to collect data about performance in a store in general sweeps. For example, if the customers are greeted correctly, have short queues, and get their order efficiently and correctly then they press a happy face. If the customers have to wait or there is a mistake, then the response slides toward the other end of the continuum.

This emoji rating system is a very simple measurement, but without being intrusive. Fourth Coffee is beginning to understand the customers based on data. This allows the company to begin examining and making changes. The next steps could be anything from quality staff training to implementing a digital ordering system.

For example, Fourth Coffee could move to an app to extract more data from the customers about preferences and demographics, and then the company could observe order behavior. Fourth Coffee could even measure time from arrival in the store to the exit based on location data! This type of data enables the company to make even more decisions; for example, they may notice a lot of customers dropping in get black coffee before heading to the subway, which provides an opportunity to set up a pop-up stand with just black coffee outside the subway.

These are simple examples, but they demonstrate the principles of using data to drive an organization's behavior. The data enables you to understand what risks you can take to ensure you can meet current customers' needs and retain them while also attracting new business.

As we mentioned earlier in this chapter, evolving change is the approach you should take to business. You must be prepared to change based on the data you have and put in place agile systems operationally and technologically to support a potential ever-moving compass point!

Establishing the new norm

While technology has a very important part in establishing a new normal for an organization, the culture is what will carry it through. Many books have been written about being an effective team and explaining the modern management skills for successful teams. Changing the culture is imperative to supporting innovation.

This book is not a leadership book, but it is important to discuss the following four elements, which will help establish a new norm.

Data-driven change

This is straightforward. Every decision made in an organization requires data to back it up. The purpose of why the change is required and ultimately what the change will entail is correlated back to the data that's been captured. Obviously, there is a requirement that you capture the correct data and evolve the captured data over each iteration.

Respectful disagreements

Being able to listen, acknowledge, and respectfully disagree with your colleagues about the direction a change is bringing is paramount. When you raise concerns about a direction and the proposer of the change can't provide supporting data to counter your concerns, then the culture of the organization has a lot to work out. If you are the challenger to an idea, you must offer the same respect back to the proposer, and you must supply data that demonstrates the change isn't sound. If you do not have sufficient data to back up your vantage point, then you must back off until you have the information to back the challenge up.

Where two sets of equally tangible data exist, someone will have to agree to try a new way (for now, at least). This is where respect come into play. All ideas may have equal merit, but if the investment to change for a path is smaller and the ROI is tangible in a shorter timeframe for a particular path, enacting the change may well be the correct choice.

Openness to change

Being open to change takes an incredible amount of effort and goes hand in hand with respectful disagreements. This is also the area where people feel most isolated. The culture can change quickly, but people may operate in the old traditional models and be unwilling to adjust. Similarly, IT might not want to change its systems because the team knows the existing systems work, they're familiar with them, and they can predict how the systems will operate. Both situations pose challenges to changing rapidly that you must deal with in a respectful, supportive manner.

There will be lots of potential areas of change that you genuinely feel open to, but it is a fundamental commitment that needs to be made by the organization and its people to adopt the correct behaviors to allow change to take effect. The behaviors that you encounter after the change occurs will dictate if the people were truly open to change in the first place. If you know that they are not open to change, challenge why they're not respectful and supportive. In most cases, there is a root cause of not being open to change, and often you can solve it easily. For example, in a case of digital transformation, people were afraid of losing their jobs because the changes moving to the cloud meant fewer "physical" systems to manage. Consequently, the people resisted the change and made the process difficult. When the path was laid out on how they are going to be trained to support the new modalities and what their roles in the evolution were going to look like, the people either fully opened to change or left the company because they realized they wanted something else out of their careers.

Accountability

Accountability is tricky. People need to be respectful both in agreements and disagreements. They need to feel comfortable challenging ideas—"asking the stupid question."

However, if people aren't accountable for their actions and the delivery of projects that they take on then the environment will not be able to transform to support the innovations that need to happen to make a business successful. Holding everyone accountable and owning that accountability is very tough.

You must understand life gets in the way. You must empathize about challenges that stopped something from being delivered and support people to help them achieve their goals. This culture of accountability will foster innovation and better collaboration within an organization.

Making plans, taking risks, and embracing success and failure

When approaching all the changes that may need to happen, both organizationally and technologically, there are four clear steps. These steps essentially are in their own life cycle, as shown in Figure 7-1.

FIGURE 7-1 Life cycle of making plans, taking risk, embracing success and failure.

For every end goal you want to achieve, you can use these steps to help attain them. You will make plans based on where you currently are and where you want to go. These plans could address the technology that needs to change, the operational processes that need to evolve, and the people who need to be trained.

Some of the plan may involve taking calculated risks that are backed up by the data you have used to help formulate the plan. You also need to take larger risks if you're trying to forge into areas that are new terrain, which means you have no information to gather as to whether it could be a success.

The final two steps—Embrace Success and Embrace Failure—are truly important. Success is amazing and gives us great feelings and a great bottom line.

You may feel that because you're successful in one area you could be successful in every area and begin to take unprecedented risks that jeopardize the entire business. You also may stagnate and begin to believe that the manner in which you have been successful will take you to other areas of success. Unfortunately, nothing could be further from the truth.

Success is important, and from it you can take plenty of feedback into the process of making plans and quantifying the next set of risks, but you also need to embrace failure and the knowledge you can gain from it.

Embracing failure is probably more important than embracing success. Using the culture values in digital transformation to allow everyone to embrace failure and learn from it provides the foundation of long-term success.

Even if the current plan seems successful, having an open feedback process and an accountable team helps organizations identify the microfailures that occurred in a successful project. Addressing these microfailures and understanding how they affect plans leads to exponential success in each iteration because the cultural foundation has been built to evolve constantly into something better through each iteration.

Supporting innovation: Waterfall to agile bringing Fourth Coffee alive

In the previous sections of this chapter we have discussed in light detail the cultural changes that may be required to allow for Fourth Coffee to innovate on every level of the organization. In this section and for the rest of the chapter we explore the technology concepts that can be implemented to support innovation.

We need to be clear from the beginning that there will be resistance to change. Change will take time, not everything will work smoothly on day one, and there will be countless challenges to be documented. If the culture we previously described is instilled in and supported by the people of the organization on all levels, then the changes that occur technologically will provide a far better IT organization to support the needs of the Fourth Coffee organization, no matter which path they choose to move forward on and what innovation they want to bring to their customers.

Waterfall to agile: Introducing DevOps

First, let's take some time to review Figure 7-2, which depicts a traditional waterfall development model.

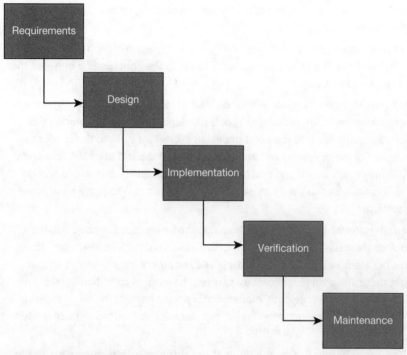

FIGURE 7-2   Waterfall development model.

What is interesting with the waterfall model is that it represents the traditional monolithic software design process in which a release could take anywhere from one to three years. The requirements of what the application needs to do are gathered, a design is architected from the requirements, and the software is built from the design. The design then is validated against the original specifications before being released and maintained. The maintenance phase includes bug fixes and updates to the original core application. Generally, you would never revisit the fundamental requirements and design of the application; changes would generally be a new screen or field to add functionality that may be required as the business evolves. If the market dramatically changed, the changes you invested time in could absolutely lead to wasted time and effort as the requirements gathering would have to start from scratch!

Microsoft used to use this process, and the company would release major versions of its software (Microsoft Windows) about every three years. Although Microsoft delivered innovation in each generation of Microsoft Windows or any other project, the cycle is simply too slow for today's needs and for an agile business.

The waterfall model also adapts well to how evolving IT infrastructure technology happens in many organizations even today. Generally, when companies buy hardware, for example, they do it every three to five years depending on the depreciation period they've assigned. This piece of hardware usually got the latest available operating system at the time of purchase, and that same operating system would be on it until the day the hardware expired. (This is generalization, of course, but it's still an important statement.) Occasionally the operating system would be upgraded to a newer version, but often the latest operating system doesn't operate efficiently on older hardware.

Virtualization helped solve some of this problem by efficiently using older hardware and allowing virtual machines to run on top, but you're still left with the tight binding between the application and its operating system.

Today we often see that when a vendor announces end of life for an operating system, there can be chaos in organizations to upgrade away from the defunct system. Often during this time, rash decisions are made, even to the point of paying exorbitant sums to the vendor to maintain some support of the operating system that's coming to the end of its life. Today, you still can walk into some organizations and find NT 4.0 or Windows 2003 running production line of business applications because the companies have not been able to move away from those operating systems.

Another issue with waterfall development is the amount of investment needed into the overall process before there is a tangible return or deliverable. This model doesn't care about market downturns or cash flow in a business. Waterfall development has a plan and an end goal, and it will get there. If a change is necessary to meet challenging conditions, you simply have to write off the investments previously made or incorporate parts of the original design into a Frankenstein type of software monster (as in, "the piece fits and it does some of the functionality and we already paid for it, so use it!").

In Fourth Coffee, the applications are monolithic N-tier software architectures with legacy data storage platforms under the waterfall principals. To introduce new features and support for the innovation executive management wants to bring to the consumers, the developers must write new front ends and new data stores and complicated data sync mechanisms. They also must do a large amount of clean-up jobs and manual validation to keep the system performant.

This leads to challenges because the development team can take on one or two projects at best, and it takes up to a year to deliver a project. No one is happy in this situation. Additionally, the infrastructure team must plan for capacity, purchase new hardware and software, and purchase new management tools to support the infrastructure and application. Fourth Coffee also must introduce new layers of security to meet any compliance regulations that will occur. The company also must train staff, potentially hire temporary consultants, and, with luck, eventually deliver the project to completion.

I can tell you from experience this is at least a six-month timeline for the infrastructure team. Once you make a decision, you're locked in. Even if you've made a wrong decision or the decision is outside of your control and someone purchases the "cheapest option," the problems will eventually cascade to failure on epic proportions.

Given both the development and infrastructure teams have long timeframes for project delivery, how is it possible to meet the needs of a changing business and deliver a platform to support innovation for the customer experience and obtain the growth and success that Fourth Coffee want to achieve? Simply put, the company needs to support innovation in its environment, and it requires change.

DevOps for all: Supporting innovation

It's a widely known fact that significant change is required to transition from a traditional waterfall-style model to a more agile model. Earlier we discussed culture changes, and in previous chapters we discussed the organizational changes that may be required. In this section, we talk about the technology changes and dip into the DevOps philosophy a little deeper. Figure 7-3 shows the DevOps life cycle.

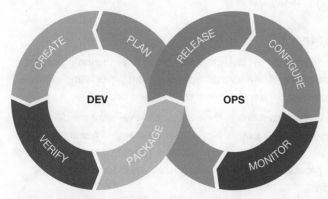

FIGURE 7-3   DevOps life cycle.

See how this life cycle is similar to Make Plans, Take Risks, Embrace Success, and Embrace Failure. The concepts don't change, and as we previously mentioned it requires as much cultural change as it does technology change. One of the first aspects that you need to examine is where you stand today in relation to adopting a DevOps culture and toolset.

For example, Fourth Coffee has application developers who write the software and build it to a deployable package. The package is transferred to a build share, which is used later in the process. The developers use source control, but different teams use other source control systems and don't share code often.

The IT infrastructure team deploy servers manually; whether the servers are physical or virtual, someone clicks through all the prompts to enter the required information. Someone watches the deployment, performs post-deployment steps, and involves the application team to deploy the application.

The application team involves the database team to create a new database for them, and then the application team installs the software and hands control back to the monitoring team. The monitoring team doesn't monitor the application; they monitor the host for CPU, memory, and disk performance.

This process takes time and is probably one of the most important changes an IT organization can tackle. Embedding a DevOps culture here is important for the success of the business.

Let's break the process down further into how we might evolve each of the teams and the technologies that they could use to transition to agile methodologies and embrace a DevOps culture. We're discussing individual teams, but this should be taken into the context of breaking down traditional barriers and coming together as an overall cloud team.

Development, infrastructure, application, database, and security teams should begin to work together and provide seamless experiences from development to production. Think of it as King Arthur, Camelot, and the Round Table; everyone has an equal position and a voice to influence the DevOps processes and culture. Also remember that while we're talking about specific scenarios under the context of a specific team, the specific scenario will influence all teams. We endeavor to call the specific scenarios for the specific team out during wider discussions, so broader teams have the appropriate context.

Evolving the development team

When approaching the development team, the goal is to adopt more agile technologies and methodologies to increase frequency and efficiency in the development process and improve consistency across multiple environments of development, staging, and production.

Previously, development cycles lasted from one to three years. Now we want the development to turn new features around in six-week sprints. Notice that we mention *features* and not *a feature*. For the six-week sprint, we want multiple streams of work proceeding. This brings agility to how the application will grow and ultimately operate. It allows the application to adapt to the business needs rapidly.

Of course, this requires reorganization of the development teams to meet the new way of developing. In the next sections, we discuss the required changes.

CENTRALIZED SOURCE CONTROL: CONSOLIDATING THE CODING EFFORTS

The first thing is to allow the teams to better capitalize on any potential work other teams are doing, especially if you begin to evolve to microservices later. You must implement a centralized source control. This could be any source control system but understand that whatever you choose should provide native integration into your end-to-end toolchain.

For example, if you use Visual Studio Team Services (VSTS) for build and release, what source control systems can you use to natively integrate with it? Similarly, if you use Jenkins for your build and release pipelines, what source control systems natively integrate with Jenkins?

Common source control environments (such as VSTS, GitHub, and GitLab) are usually hosted in the cloud. You also will find that on-premises deployments are available for some source control systems.

> **NOTE** If you don't already know, VSTS can generate repositories that can emulate a Git repository.

Figure 7-4 shows a sample of a VSTS build pipeline and which source control systems it can natively integrate with.

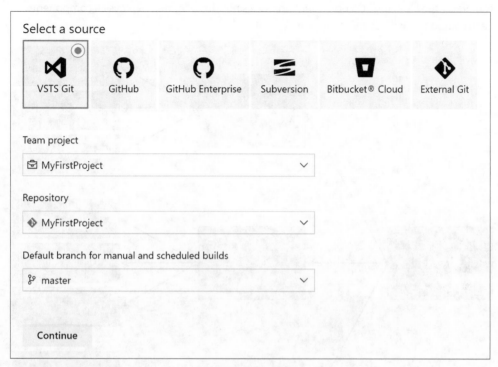

FIGURE 7-4 Source control integration with a VSTS build pipeline.

We strongly encourage you to adopt a cloud version of a source control environment. Once you evolve your software and adopt more DevOps principals, like Continuous Integrate and Continuous Deployment (CI/CD), you may look at the cloud being a target for deployment. Cloud systems often provide native integration into the public clouds.

MICROSERVICES

Monolithic applications don't allow the easy adoption of Agile methodologies. In fact, as we write this we would very boldly say that it is almost impossible to achieve Agile with a monolithic application.

The purpose of breaking an application into microservices is to allow you to independently update segments of an application without affecting the overall application. It also removes the requirement for a full recompile and redeployment of the application. It dramatically reduces "broken" deployments; even if you have a broken "microservice," only that area of the application is affected. It also addresses other factors, like scaling the necessary parts of a system as and when needed rather than having to scale the entire monolithic app.

Microservices should be approached very carefully, though. The application needs to be well thought out and broken down.

Figure 7-5 shows Fourth Coffee's point-of-sale (POS) application and the subcomponents that make up the application. From a monolithic standpoint, although the entire application is represented here, the POS box would signify a single installer that deploys all components. Each component is "hidden" from view.

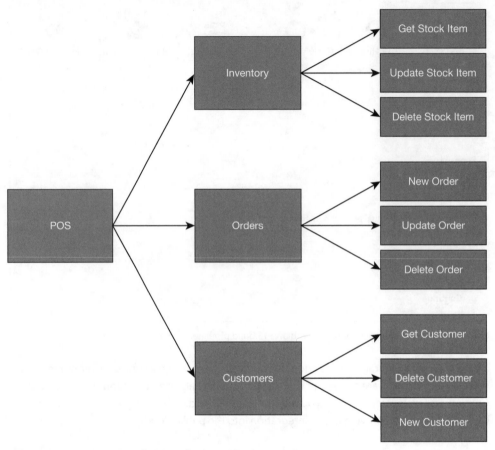

FIGURE 7-5 Representation of POS application with subcomponents.

Using the subdomain pattern in microservices, you can create "domains" that represent the inventory, orders, and customers. In fact, you could create domains to represent the get stock item, update stock item, and delete stock item. Each domain would have a single responsibility and could be exposed as an API. For example, if you're creating a new order, you would use the get customer API to retrieve details for existing customers and use the get stock item to determine whether what they're trying to order is in stock.

You can bolt on new services independently and grow the application seamlessly with rich features and functionality. You can scale each domain independently as required to deal with the different pressures a system might come under.

Refactoring to microservices is nothing short of complicated, and it takes time. However, if you think about the end goal in terms of the cloud, you could essentially run these microservices on serverless compute clouds and have almost no underlying infrastructure to run the application.

CONTAINERIZATION

Containerization provides a quick win for any organization that wants to start a transformation journey. It allows teams to reduce hardware dependencies, increase independence from platforms, and begin the modernization journey regardless of the cloud the organization has deployed to. It also provides a platform to begin segmenting an application into a microservices-like architecture.

Let's say the POS application was a web application and that you already have the inventory, order, and customer integrated into a single web application. This web application could be executed from within a container running IIS without almost no modification.

Containers allows the development team to increase its agility and maintain consistency when it produces a production-quality release and moves it between the development, staging, and production environments. Containers also allow the code that will be used to provision the container to be integrated into the CI/CD pipeline, which reduces the deployment tasks that the infrastructure and application teams will need to do in the future.

When you consider the cloud, containers shine, if you start with an on-premises container deployment and run your systems there. You can build your application on top of standard container images, so no matter which cloud you choose if the application can execute in a container then you can run your application in that cloud.

Here is an example of a Dockerfile that builds an image using the source code for our application.

```
# escape=`
    FROM microsoft/aspnet:3.5-windowsservercore-10.0.14393.1715
    SHELL ["powershell", "-Command", "$ErrorActionPreference = 'Stop'; $ProgressPreference
= 'SilentlyContinue';"]

    RUN Remove-Website 'Default Web Site';

    # Set up website: Jobs
    RUN New-Item -Path 'C:\inetpub\wwwroot\POS' -Type Directory -Force;

    RUN New-Website -Name 'POS' -PhysicalPath 'C:\inetpub\wwwroot\POS' -Port 80 -Applica-
tionPool '.NET v2.0' -Force;

    EXPOSE 80
```

```
COPY ["possite", "/inetpub/wwwroot/pos"]

RUN $path='C:\inetpub\wwwroot\pos'; `
    $acl = Get-Acl $path; `
    $newOwner = [System.Security.Principal.NTAccount]('BUILTIN\IIS_IUSRS'); `
    $acl.SetOwner($newOwner); `
    dir -r $path | Set-Acl -aclobject  $acl
```

The developers essentially will produce this file and bind it together with the source control and CI/CD pipeline, as shown in Figure 7-6. We also could push the image to an image registry and call it for deployment, but given that we want to integrate, automate, and simplify tasks, using it in a CI/CD pipeline is more effective.

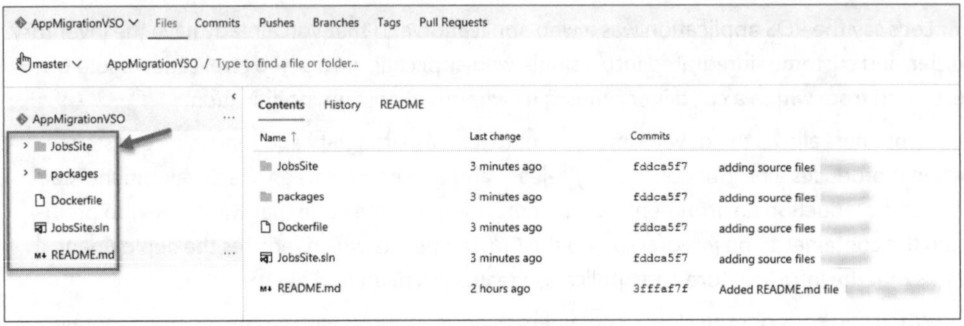

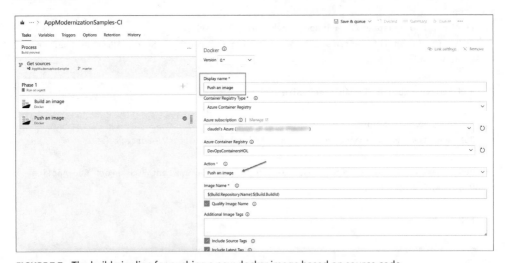

FIGURE 7-6   Dockerfile integrated with the source code for the app.

Using this, we can create a build task that will ensure that when the developers create or update with features or functionality then a new container will be automatically built and the image will be stored in the registry. Figure 7-7 shows the build steps we use in the pipeline to achieve this.

FIGURE 7-7   The build pipeline for pushing a new docker image based on source code.

In the release pipeline you can determine the environment which the deployment goes to initially and then integrate testing into the CI/CD pipeline to ensure that the application is functional before moving between the development, staging, and production environments.

VSTS and Jenkins have multiple targets that they can deploy to, including cloud environments. This simplifies a few different elements of life for the different teams and between containers and segmenting into microservices starts to give us the agility we need to transform our application to suit the needs of the business.

APPLICATION TELEMETRY

Application telemetry to developers provides exceptionally deep insights into how their application is performing. Remember when we discussed data-driven behavior? Well, this is it for developers. Developing application telemetry hooks can be a difficult job, but with modern tooling it becomes a simple task. Application telemetry gives perspectives on how the application is performing and if the user experience is good.

For example, application telemetry can give insights on the user logging into the POS of a sales system and how quickly the pages load and the data is retrieved. This then feeds back to the developer, who can modify the code to increase performance and reduce any potential latency a cashier might experience during normal operation.

Figure 7-8 shows a sample live stream dashboard from Application Insights, which both application developers and operations teams can use to determine how an application is performing.

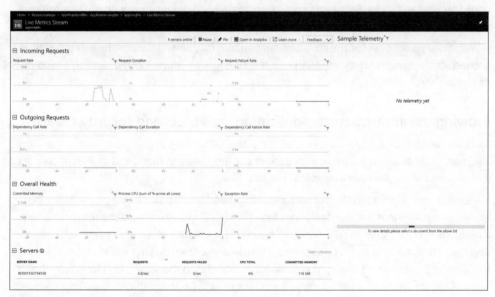

FIGURE 7-8   Live stream dashboard with Application Insights.

Another interesting thing about using modern tooling like Application Insights is that this data sometimes can be retrieved with no code changes. In the sample we show in Figure 7-8, we took the source code of a .NET 2.0 web app and redeployed it to the Azure App Service and enabled Application Insights Telemetry.

In seconds we began obtaining useful data, which all teams can use to make data-driven decisions. For traditional infrastructure teams, we can now integrate this dashboard into Log Analytics and have a single pane of glass for monitoring our IT environment.

CONTINUOUS INTEGRATION AND DEPLOYMENT

We have alluded to this in some of the other sections so far, but our goal with CI/CD is to auto-mate the testing and deployment of source code, including the testing to ensure functionality from an end-to-end perspective. This is to reduce the need for human interference, but we're trying to obtain a consistent standardized approach that gives us predictability.

CI/CD reduces the time for employees (both developers and operations staff) to bring an application to life in any environment. At the start of this chapter, we mentioned that it could take weeks, if not months, for Fourth Coffee to get a single application environment up and running. With an end-to-end CI/CD process, the deployment time could quite literally go down to minutes or hours with automated tested included.

In some organizations we see multiple pipelines and integration between them being created. For example, the infrastructure team may still require tight control over the virtual machines that get deployed, the security team may require security controls constructed in a particular way, and so on. Each team could technically build the pipeline with the controls that they need, and the developer team and application team can hook into those pipelines.

Whatever you choose for the environment you build, CI/CD will support further innovation and reduce the complexity of adopting new technologies so Fourth Coffee can stay ahead of its competitors.

Evolving the infrastructure, application, database, and security teams

Next, we have a look at the infrastructure, application, database, and security teams. Tradition-ally, most of these teams have had very distinct barriers between them, and as with all barriers it causes problems when work needs to be done.

For example, when a problem occurs, diagnosing and troubleshooting a problem has led to several outages that went on far longer than they should have because the response when a problem is handed over to an individual team is, "Not our problem." The infrastructure team says the virtual machine is running correctly, the database team doesn't see issues in its logs, the security teams haven't changed anything that would stop the application from working, and the application team hasn't deployed any new releases that would cause the application to break.

The following sections provide frameworks to start building trust between the teams so that the visibility that a DevOps team requires can be provided, and hopefully issues like the example won't occur.

ADOPTING AUTOMATION

If you're stuck doing mundane tasks, then there is no time for innovation. Automating every repeatable task will initially be time-consuming. However, you'll be building reusable tools that other teams and projects also can use.

We discussed at the start of this chapter that Fourth Coffee still manually deploys its virtual machines among a variety of day-to-day operations and administrative tasks. If we take the virtual machine example, we can explore many topics surrounding it that will highlight how we can take a task that's often complex and has multiple levels of items that need to be done and automate them to reduce the time and errors that have a tendency to happen during these tasks.

Usually the first step in anything we do from an application or infrastructure perspective is deploy a virtual machine. That's a simple enough premise, but when you begin to think about it, you start thinking of questions like the following:

- What's the operating system?

- What software needs to go on it?

- Do we need encryption on the machine?

Each question drives a subsequent layer of questions. For example, if the operating system is Windows, does it need to be domain joined? Software becomes complicated because you must address dependencies. The point of adopting automation is to try to make lives easier and to ensure consistency. This can only be done through standardization of your environment. If you standardize, you can ask a distinct set of questions to which you can obtain predictable answers and subsequently wrap them in automation.

Here's a quick example of a virtual machine deployment with PowerShell. This is transportable between any environment that will allow execution of PowerShell and can form the basis of a script:

```
New-AzureRmVm `
    -ResourceGroupName "myResourceGroupVM" `
    -Name "myVM2" `
    -Location "EastUS" `
    -VirtualNetworkName "myVnet" `
    -SubnetName "mySubnet" `
    -SecurityGroupName "myNetworkSecurityGroup" `
    -PublicIpAddressName "myPublicIpAddress2" `
    -ImageName "MicrosoftWindowsServer:WindowsServer:2016-Datacenter-with-
Containers:latest" `
    -Credential $cred `
    -AsJob
```

In this circumstance, this script deploys a Windows Server 2016 Datacenter virtual machine running containers. The virtual machine is deployed into the resource group myResourceGroupVM and has a name of myVM2. There are several other options that are statically assigned to ensure the virtual machine gets deployed to the right place with the right options.

Let's take a quick tangent. One very common premise in automation is the idea of tool making. Tools like a hammer can be reused constantly for the same job of hammering a nail. In automation, we want to take our single-line PowerShell and wrap them so that they become tools. In our example case, we can introduce parameters and conditional logic that will deploy a virtual machine. To be more specific, say we introduce a parameter called OS and have conditional logic that essentially detects the word *Linux* or *Windows*. If we have Linux as the OS then we change what credentials we collect, and we also change the ImageName to a supported Linux Image; if we had Windows, we could have additional logic to determine which version of Windows we wanted.

This single-line PowerShell has now become reusable like a tool! We can use this in many ways, either manually triggered or externally triggered via some automation environment. Figure 7-9 shows a sample of a user submitting a form via a web portal that requests virtual machine details with fields that are predefined to the parameters of the script.

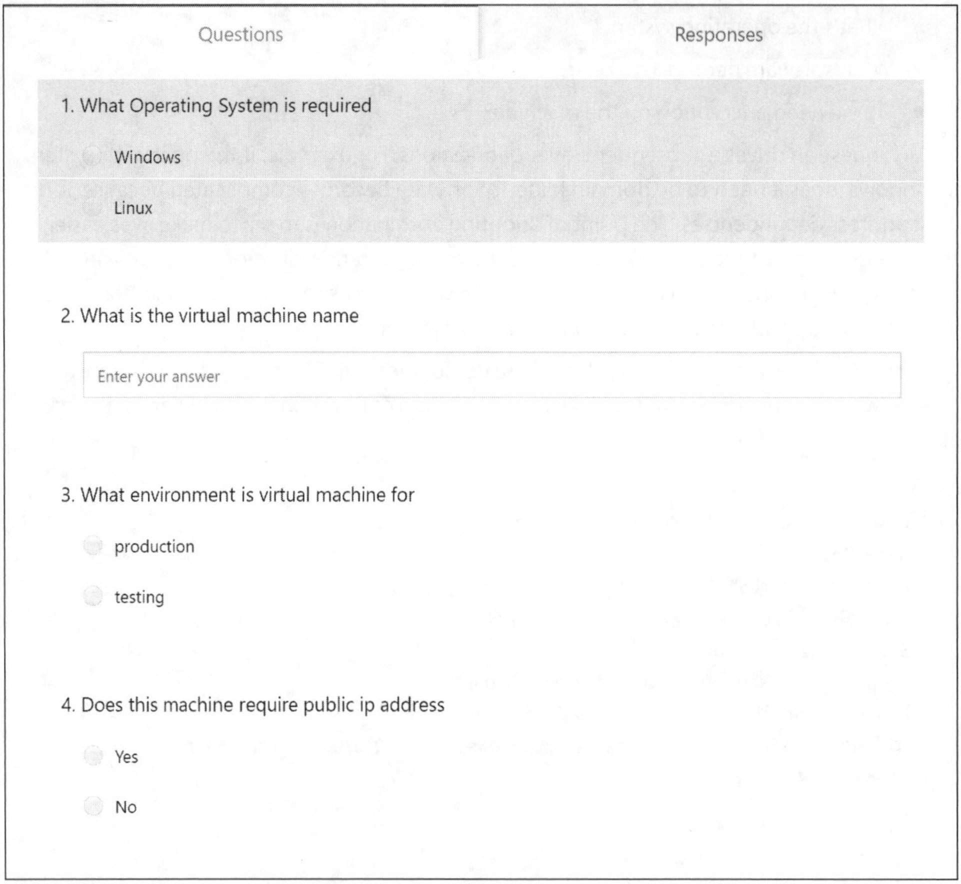

Questions	Responses

1. What Operating System is required

   Windows

   Linux

2. What is the virtual machine name

   Enter your answer

3. What environment is virtual machine for

   production

   testing

4. Does this machine require public ip address

   Yes

   No

FIGURE 7-9 Sample Microsoft form questions for virtual machine deployment.

Each question is aligned with a parameter. For example, the first question is about the OS parameter. Question two addresses the vmname parameter. Question three is about the environment parameter, but it also can map with conditional logic to the region and resource group. Question four asks if it requires a public IP address, which in turn could trigger a workflow to the security team to ensure the virtual machine has the applied standards for being "publicly exposed."

When the response is submitted, it triggers a Microsoft Flow workflow. Figure 7-10 shows the flow that's triggered on submission. As you can see from the figure, it gets triggered from submission and then parses the request details. The responses to the "questions" get placed into a format—in this case JSON—which map to the parameters for the webhook to process when it gets invoked.

FIGURE 7-10 Microsoft Flow workflow.

Azure Automation allows the creation of Runbooks (essentially a PowerShell script in tool format) and gives the option to create a webhook. The webhook allows the invocation of the runbook via an Http POST call to the exposed URI. This URI allows for the mapping of a JSON payload to the parameters, which we can deserialize in our runbook to process the virtual machine deployment.

With this approach, we have essentially removed human interference with the task of provisioning a virtual machine. The end users (if we allow them) or the IT team can use this form, make it more complex, or hook in other systems to build upon this basic framework of deploying a virtual machine.

We can enforce standards in coding to ensure that the tools that are created to support the environment meet a certain standard before code gets injected into a source control repository.

> **NOTE** For more information relating to PowerShell Coding standards review the following link: github.com/PowerShell/PowerShell/blob/master/docs/dev-process/coding-guidelines.md.

We could leverage a combination of tools to ensure that when a user checks code into a repository that it goes through a validation procedure for best practices and a unit test framework to ensure functionality requirements are met before the code is allowed out into the IT organization. This process could also include code signing, so that when the code passes the tests it also will get signed and pushed out to a runbook or share so the wider teams can use it. This also requires configuration of the server environment to allow only execution of signed code.

Microsoft has published a PowerShell Script Analyzer located at github.com/PowerShell/PSScriptAnalyzer.

The PowerShell Script Analyzer uses the best practices to scan your code through static analysis. It generates an actionable output for the code creator to act against. Microsoft has also published a unit test framework called Pester, which you can use and integrate into a CI/CD pipeline. You can find Pester at github.com/pester/Pester.

Everything we previously mentioned works in any situation—for example, if we manually have a share where the code gets executed or if we use an orchestration tool like Azure Automation. Azure automation becomes the endpoint where the final validated and tested code gets published as a runbook. The runbooks can be called from external systems or execution from Azure automation itself.

DESIRED STATE DEPLOYMENT

In the previous section, we gave a simple example of a virtual machine deployment and discussed only the operating system level of the deployment. Deploying a virtual machine is more complex than that. In 99.9% of cases, you usually must do something else with the virtual machine, like join it to the domain, configure it based on the organization standards or install some software as a variety of examples. This often is the most complex and time-consuming task when deploying a virtual machine.

Let's examine for a minute what additional steps you would normally take after a virtual machine is deployed. At the very least, you would install antivirus protection and any other application dependencies, such as .NET framework or IIS. You can install these things via PowerShell one liners. For example, you can add IIS to a server with all its dependencies like this:

```
Add-WindowsFeature -Name Web-Server -IncludeAllSubFeature -IncludeManagementTools
```

Similarly, you can install antivirus protection with PowerShell by invoking an MSI using the following:

```
Start-Process msiexec.exe -ArgumentList "/L* C:\setup.log /qn /I c:\client.msi"
```

Although it's great that you can use something like PowerShell to install software, it proves difficult to handle errors or reboots when combining multiple tasks. Another aspect that's difficult to work with is configuration drift, which can cause havoc in an enterprise, especially if the software being installed is dependent on specific versions. While working on small deployments, you can easily manage this and quickly verify the software versions on a system. However, when dealing with large amounts of servers, it becomes an unmanageable task.

Let's take a simple example. We've deployed a Windows virtual machine and now want to join it to the domain. We can execute a PowerShell script using a command like the following:

```
Add-Computer -ComputerName "Server01" -LocalCredential "Server01\Administrator" -Domain-
Name "fourthcoffee.com" -Credential fourthcoffee\Administrator -Restart -Force
```

The machine would domain join and require a reboot. The reboot would stop the script from continuing, and we would have to build in the logic to process it from the next step. This isn't an easy task to do, and in general it doesn't scale well.

Utilizing PowerShell DSC, you can define a configuration and apply it to a virtual machine. DSC will handle reboots, checking existing states and handling errors. If you have additional tasks post–domain join, like enabling dependencies for applications to be installed, you also can specify the dependency chain. You can use PowerShell DSC across environments and even tie into your Automation tool.

Here is an example using PowerShell DSC to domain join a Windows virtual machine:

```
Configuration RenameJoinComputer {
    param (
    [Parameter(Mandatory=$true)][string]$Domain,
        [Parameter(Mandatory=$true)][PSCredential]$DomainCred
    )

    Import-DscResource -ModuleName xComputerManagement
    Node "localhost"
    {
        xComputer ChangeDomain
        {
            DomainName = $Domain
            Credential = $DomainCred
        }
    }
}
```

When applied, this will join the virtual machine to a domain and reboot. The DSC code block handles all the logic related to determining if it is already part of a domain and if it should in fact join the domain. You can use this simple configuration manually, with automated deployments and in multi-cloud environments with zero changes. You need apply the configuration, and the machine will apply the state you have defined in the configuration. For example, if the machine gets removed from the domain, the desired state is out of sync, and the machine will begin the process of reapplying the configuration to the machine to ensure it returns to its goal state.

Imagine having large banks of web servers that need to be managed, and all of them have the exact same configuration. Now imagine having to make a change and going through each server one by one. Or you could define a new configuration and apply it to the server. The new configuration might define a new package to install, but you write the configuration and apply it to the server bank, and the machines will begin to transition to the new desired state.

Of course, we've given you simple examples. The power of PowerShell DSC is vast not only in its functionality but also because it's now multi-platform and operates across Linux and Windows.

> **NOTE** For more information on PowerShell DSC see the following link:
>
> https://docs.microsoft.com/en-us/powershell/dsc/quickstart.

INFRASTRUCTURE PIPELINES

A common practice today is the use of what is called an infrastructure pipeline. In on-premises systems, when an application developer wanted a machine of any type they had to request one from the infrastructure team. The infrastructure team managed all the resources and ensured that they had the capacity to run the application and to challenge any ridiculous requests. Once the infrastructure team had validated the developer's request, the team would deploy the virtual machine and pass the deployment information back to the application developer, who would log on and complete the task.

In the cloud this can still happen, but speed and agility play a bigger part. One of the staples of the cloud is that you are supposed to be able to access virtually unlimited resources rapidly. To achieve this, application developers want to use CI/CD processes so that they don't have to wait for the infrastructure team to play its part. Given that all clouds have a programmatical way of deploying the services, infrastructure teams should, for the most part, never be involved.

However, the traditional role of infrastructure teams ensured the uptime of production systems by enforcing standards. They obviously need to play a key part in making sure the systems being deployed in the cloud follow the same level of scrutiny as they did on premises. In this situation, the infrastructure teams are developing infrastructure pipelines where they build the CI/CD process to deploy virtual machines/services into the respective cloud in the structured way required by the enterprise. They expose their pipeline to the developers, who can leverage this functionality and build their application on top of this.

TELEMETRY: AN INSIGHT INTO YOUR APPLICATION AND INFRASTRUCTURE

Earlier we talked briefly about application insights, but you also must think about the surrounding ecosystem in an IT environment. If you're building larger and larger systems with more complex moving parts, the last thing you need is to have disparate systems like you had traditionally. For example, the network team would have one system, the application team would have another, the infrastructure team would have one, and the security team would have another!

When a problem occurs, who owns it? Where do you begin to diagnose and resolve the issue? Although it's possible to have disparate systems and have a team that comes together to work on the problem, often that's not the case, and outages are extended due to lack of visibility into areas outside your domain of responsibility.

To support innovation, these barriers need to be broken down. Data from all systems needs to be aggregated centrally, so that event correlation can occur, and you can dive right into the root of the problem. Visibility is equal among all parties so that the right team can engage and resolve and there is a clear definition of problem ownership.

Microsoft provides many tools under the Azure Monitor brand that can give the visibility required to achieve innovative support for a modern-day enterprise. You can gain insights into every aspect of the IT life cycle of a server, application, user, and so on and visualize the information for easy interpretation. You also can use event-based triggers to perform further diagnostics, remediation, or escalation.

SECURITY: PROTECT YOUR ENVIRONMENT

No matter the environment, innovating on security will benefit the organization. The key here is to ensure that the tooling that you use is kept up to date and can assist not only in the forensic analysis of security events but also strives to mitigate any events from occurring.

Modern enterprises have a firm grasp over their on-premises IT security (or at least they think they do), but when it comes to cloud environments, and more specifically PaaS environments, they struggle. They aren't fully aware of all best practices that can be implemented. Or if a PaaS service can't route traffic on the secure infrastructure, they lose the feeling of comfort they had previously.

Microsoft Azure Security Center (which we discussed in Chapter 2) is a tool that can work across environments and detect events that may cause harm to your environment. Figure 7-11 shows a sample Microsoft Azure Security Center dashboard

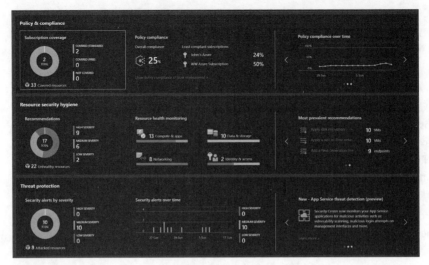

FIGURE 7-11   Sample Microsoft Azure Security Center dashboard.

From the dashboard, you can see areas to focus on. When you drill down as shown in Figure 7-12, you see the description of the problem, the affected machines, and links to recommendations. In some cases, an action button is available, so you can perform a remediation task straight away.

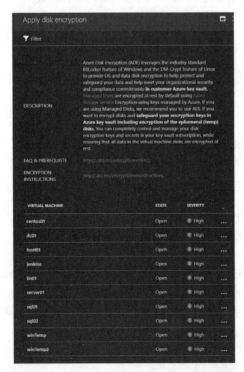

FIGURE 7-12   Sample issues drilldown to missing encryption.

Figure 7-11 and Figure 7-12 show all Azure-based machines and PaaS services, but Security Center also works across environments no matter their location. It generates rich telemetry about security events in your environment. Given that it aggregates the data in Log Analytics, you could build custom event queries and tag Automation runbooks to alerts that are generated.

Figure 7-13 shows a sample query that detects failed logon events for the Administrator account. The query runs against all the aggregated data from all the servers. Let's say a systems administrator deploys a virtual machine to Azure, assigns it a public IP address, and exposes port 3389 for ease of access because they only needed it for an hour or so. But then the administrator gets distracted and leaves the system in place. The virtual machine sits on a corporately connected virtual network.

With the query we have in place for the example, we can determine that if we get a failed logon attempt and the source IP address is not in our corporate IP range then we should create a rule in our network security group to block traffic from that unauthorized IP range or block it altogether and then subsequently notify the security team of a potential breach. All these tasks can be automated based on this single query and the aggregated data we have collected in Log Analytics.

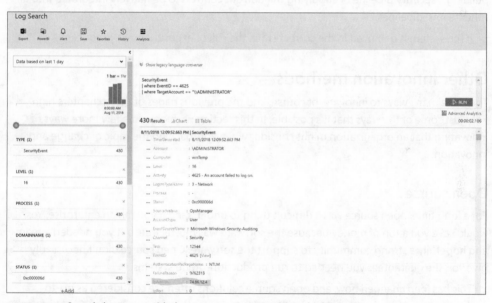

FIGURE 7-13 Sample log query with the non-corporate IP address highlighted.

This is just a scratch on the potential innovation you can have for security for a modern enterprise.

BRINGING IT TOGETHER FOR THE TEAMS

At the start of this section, we said what about the infrastructure, application, database, and security teams. Knowing the framework provides a wealth of possibilities for them to operate together and provide production-grade services while gaining visibility into the environment they need for supporting it moving forward.

The infrastructure, application, and database teams can adopt high levels of automation to deploy their services and connect them to the monitoring platform. Each team can have its own set of dashboards for visibility into what is important but also search on the aggregated data to determine where a problem may exist.

Security teams can have a wider presence and mandate policy for systems that get deployed. Centralized logging of activity data as well as granular RBAC controls can ensure they can maintain a secure cloud environment.

The infrastructure team builds the virtual machine pipelines. The database team supplies PowerShell DSC scripts for the SQL builds or adopts SQL Managed Instances or SQL Azure. The application team leverages the pipeline built by the infrastructure team and has develop their own application pipeline for deployment. The security team once again influences all of this by building a security pipeline or supplying the upfront controls to be natively integrated into all other teams' pipelines.

If the system is deployed in the correct state, the risk of exposure greatly reduces.

Other innovation methods

There are many ways to innovate, of course, and the previous pages of these chapters high-light just some of the ways that it's possible. In this section we highlight a few more ways of innovating that an organization might consider when approaching the topic of change and innovation.

Open source

For a long time, open source was a difficult thing to understand if you ran an enterprise. Yes, it would save you a ton of money because the software was mostly free, but you needed a team and hopefully a strong community to support the software. Open source didn't necessarily give you the guarantees you needed to run production-grade systems.

This has long changed now, and open source solutions often are considered as go-to options for an enterprise. The source code and binaries for the system are often free, but you can get paid professional support if you run into issues.

Open source enables you to contribute to the source code or customize it for your needs. Apache Web Server, RabbitMQ, and Hadoop are examples of just a few open source software that are in enterprises running their productions systems at scale.

Fourth Coffee could adopt some of these platforms for rapid development, tailor the software to its precise needs, and give back to the community with the optimizations they implement.

Fourth Coffee also could combine open source and commercial software for an approach that's the best of both worlds. Modern enterprises should be looking at the best tools for the job and the tools that are widely supported across environments. This allows for incredible innovation when designing applications to support any venture an enterprise wants to take on.

Crowdsourcing

In any given enterprise, there are plenty of talented people looking for a chance to improve and contribute to the overall running of the IT environment. Crowdsourcing gives these talented people a chance to express interest in different areas or contribute to wider programs they might not necessarily get a chance to work on normally.

If Fourth Coffee wants to move to the modern enterprise and support innovative applications, crowdsourcing this is a quick way to allow people to be part of that transition and contribute to the transformation.

For example, Fourth Coffee wants to create PowerShell scripts that can perform basic day-to-day tasks, like pruning a database or looking for users who haven't logged on in for six months. Then they could set the task for the crowdsourcing to create a script to perform these tasks and get multiple people to contribute. Team members other than the traditional Active Directory administrators might have the time up front to build a base script so that the Active Directory administrators gain some time to further develop and contribute to the script.

There are multiple examples of ways crowdsourcing could be used, but the premise of crowdsourcing can drive large amounts of innovation rapidly for an enterprise.

Smart data

If Fourth Coffee goes through the process of aggregating the data not only from a systems management perspective but also operational data and customer data then the company can use this data to make more intelligent decisions about the direction of the organization and where investment should happen. There are several technologies that support this innovation in data.

IoT

Internet of Things (IoT) would enable Fourth Coffee to have all its coffee shops connected and streaming data. In another chapter, we used an example of having a connected coffee machine that would send telemetry about the machine's performance, the last service time, and various other aspects, such as how full the coffee hopper is. All this data can be analyzed and used to understand how busy the shop is. If the machine is generating a lot of data, it can be an indication that the store is making lots of coffee, and if a machine is being used a lot, it may need to be serviced often. Knowing that the machine needs to be serviced often might lead Fourth Coffee to negotiate better terms for a service contract on the coffee machine.

Fourth Coffee could combine this type of data with customer sentiment data. The customer could vote anonymously with a happy face or a sad face about the quality of the drink they received at the time of purchase. The team can look at this data and the event data on how "busy" the coffee machine was to determine if it was a busy period or if the machine had not been cleaned to try to correlate why the drink the customer purchased was of not sufficient quality.

MACHINE LEARNING

Machine learning can be applied to all the data that is collected and provide predictive trends from that data. This essentially means we can plan to a large degree of predictability on types of events occurring.

Going back to our IOT data from the coffee machines, Fourth Coffee could apply machine learning techniques to determine the failure of a machine or correlate events between keeping the hopper half empty versus full. They also could compare customer sentiment with a good drink versus the performance of the machine and adjust how coffee might be made in other stores.

CHAT BOTS

Another innovation is a chat bot service. This simple automated response engine can be trained to answer a large number of common questions. Answers would be developed based on the customer data that's been collected.

For example, if a user has an app and wants to know what specials are in the local store, the user could ask a chat bot and receive a response. Or if the customer needs to know the opening hours of a store in New York because the person is traveling there, then the chat bot can provide the answer.

The chat bot also could provide a more personal experience and interact with the customers to better understand their needs and feed this data back to Fourth Coffee executives to help them understand what the customers need or want.

Index

Numbers

I

Plug into learning at

MicrosoftPressStore.com

The Microsoft Press Store by Pearson offers:

- Free U.S. shipping

- Buy an eBook, get three formats – Includes PDF, EPUB, and MOBI to use with your computer, tablet, and mobile devices

- Print & eBook Best Value Packs

- eBook Deal of the Week – Save up to 50% on featured title

- Newsletter – Be the first to hear about new releases, announcements, special offers, and more

- Register your book – Find companion files, errata, and product updates, plus receive a special coupon* to save on your next purchase

Discounts are applied to the list price of a product. Some products are not eligible to receive additional discounts, so your discount code may not be applied to all items in your cart. Discount codes cannot be applied to products that are already discounted, such as eBook Deal of the Week, eBooks that are part of a book + eBook pack, and products with special discounts applied as part of a promotional offering. Only one coupon can be used per order.

 Pearson

Hear about it first.

Since 1984, Microsoft Press has helped IT professionals, developers, and home office users advance their technical skills and knowledge with books and learning resources.

Sign up today to deliver exclusive offers directly to your inbox.

- New products and announcements

- Free sample chapters

- Special promotions and discounts

- ... and more!

MicrosoftPressStore.com/newsletters

 Pearson